ESTIMATION RISK
AND
OPTIMAL PORTFOLIO CHOICE

STUDIES IN BAYESIAN ECONOMETRICS

Editors
ARNOLD ZELLNER
JOSEPH B. KADANE

Volume 3

NORTH-HOLLAND PUBLISHING COMPANY – AMSTERDAM • NEW YORK • OXFORD

ESTIMATION RISK AND OPTIMAL PORTFOLIO CHOICE

Vijay S. BAWA
Bell Laboratories
Murray Hill, New Jersey
and
Graduate School of Business Administration
New York University, New York

Stephen J. BROWN
Bell Laboratories
Murray Hill, New Jersey

Roger W. KLEIN
Bell Laboratories
Murray Hill, New Jersey

N·H
P C

1979

NORTH-HOLLAND PUBLISHING COMPANY – AMSTERDAM • NEW YORK • OXFORD

ISBN: 0 444 85344 8

Publishers:
NORTH-HOLLAND PUBLISHING COMPANY
AMSTERDAM • NEW YORK • OXFORD

Sole distributors for the U.S.A. and Canada:
ELSEVIER NORTH-HOLLAND, INC.
52 VANDERBILT AVENUE
NEW YORK, N.Y. 10017

Library of Congress Cataloging in Publication Data

Bawa, Vijay S
Estimation risk and optimal portfolio choice.

(Studies in Bayesian econometrics ; v. 3)
Includes bibliographical references and indexes.
1. Investments. 2. Capital market. 3. Risk.
4. Bayesian statistical decision theory. I. Brown, Stephen J., joint author. II. Klein, Roger W., joint author. III. Title. IV. Series.
HG4539.B37 332.6'7 79-15577
ISBN 0-444-85344-8

PRINTED IN THE NETHERLANDS

INTRODUCTION TO THE SERIES

Research on Bayesian methodology and applications of it has progressed remarkably* and thus it is appropriate to institute a series on Bayesian econometrics and statistics. The series will include monographs reporting significant research on the theory and application of Bayesian analysis in econometrics and statistics. The theoretical research to be reported in the series will focus on Bayesian inference and decision procedures that are relevant for analyzing scientific and applied problems while the applied research will involve applications of Bayesian analysis to solve specific private and public policy and decision problems. This blend of Bayesian theory and application in the series will help to promote interaction between theorists and applied workers that is thought to be valuable in promoting progress in both theoretical and applied research.

The Editors hope that the series will become an international forum for reporting improved solutions to general and specific scientific and applied problems that arise in econometrics and statistics.

The Editors

* See e.g., S.E. Fienberg and A. Zellner (eds.), Studies in Bayesian Econometrics and Statistics in Honor of Leonard J. Savage, North-Holland Publishing Company, 1975

PREFACE

Portfolio theory, which is central to the theory of financial economics assumes that the multivariate distribution of asset returns is completely known to the investor. In the pioneering work of Markowitz (1952) it was recognized that this particular assumption might present a problem in the practical application of the theory. This concern has motivated a considerable literature that seeks to minimize the impact of estimation risk induced by the deviation of estimates of the distribution of asset returns from the true distribution. Yet rarely has this literature adopted the suggestion of Markowitz that a decision theoretic Bayesian approach would resolve the problem, an approach that would integrate econometric considerations into the problem of economic decision under uncertainty. This book analyses the implications of this Bayesian approach for optimal portfolio choice and related questions of capital market equilibrium.

Portfolio theory is important not only for its own sake and for its normative implications, but also for its role as a canonical representation of the problem of optimal choice under uncertainty. This book introduces the question of estimation risk in this general context of optimal choice under uncertainty and addresses, in detail, its implications for portfolio theory. As indicated in Chapter 1, different chapters will address the direction and the magnitude of its effect, the consequences of different specifications of prior information, and the effect of estimation risk upon capital market equilibrium conditions. These results are summarized in the final chapter.

By bringing these theoretical and empirical results together on a unified basis, we hope to illustrate more clearly the central result that estimation risk 'makes a difference'. Rather than ignore or seek to minimize the effects of estimation risk by suppressing potentially relevant information, it is possible to take this factor into account directly. It is our hope that the methodology and techniques illustrated in the context of the portfolio choice problem will stimulate further research into estimation risk in the context of the more general class of problems involving choice under uncertainty.

The research, of which this book represents a culmination, began as independent work of Bawa and Klein at Bell Laboratories and Brown at the University of Chicago. The doctoral dissertation of Brown (1976) would not have been possible without the support and encouragement given by Professors Nicholas Gonedes, Arnold Zellner and Robert Hamada who supervised this work. The initial research of the other two authors published as Klein and Bawa (1976) owed much to stimulating discussions with several colleagues at Bell Laboratories. Our subsequent research in this area has benefited from comments received at NBER-NSF Bayesian Inference in Econometrics seminars, other professional society meetings, and at Financial and Econometrics seminars at several universities. We have also benefited from comments on earlier drafts of several chapters that were used by one of us (V.S.B.) while teaching a Finance Theory and Markets doctoral seminar at the Graduate School of Business Administration, New York University. We thank Professors Christopher Barry and Robert Winkler for providing us with several of their working papers and their help in preparing the extensive bibliography provided at the end of this book. They together with Professor Ronald Masulis provided us with many helpful comments on earlier drafts of the manuscript.

We wish to express our gratitude to Professor Arnold Zellner for encouraging us to write this book and for assisting us through the various stages of production. Professors Zellner and Joseph Kadane, coeditors of the North-Holland series in which this book appears, provided us with extensive comments and discussion that substantially improved the presentation of the material, allowed us to resolve ambiguities and make numerous corrections. We are of course solely responsible for any remaining errors.

This book would not exist but for the outstanding research environment provided by Bell Laboratories. We wish to thank Elizabeth E. Bailey, Warren A. Cornell, Gerald R. Faulhaber and V. Michael Wolontis for their support during the early stages of the research. We wish to thank also Robert C. Prim and Edward E. Zajac for their support and encouragement while the book was being completed. We are deeply indebted to the Word Processing Center at Bell Laboratories at Murray Hill and its supervisor Nanette E. Stortz for meeting what to us seemed impossible time constraints. However, our especial thanks are due to Diane DeVico who not only typed successive drafts of the sometimes illegible manuscript swiftly and superlatively but also (miraculous to us not initiated into such mysteries) managed to have the UNIX™ system phototypeset the entire book, the quality of which is evident on this and successive pages.

To Sonia, V.S.B.
Catherine, S.J.B.
Elaine, Becca and Ben. R.W.K.

TABLE OF CONTENTS

CHAPTER 1

ESTIMATION RISK: AN INTRODUCTION

1. Introductory Remarks

Models of portfolio choice under uncertainty have been the subject of innumerable research efforts in financial economics. These models have been studied for both their normative and positive implications. Indeed, the theoretical and empirical work on this topic has had a greater effect on the general area of financial economics than work on any other single topic.

One of the troubling features of work in this area has been that in theoretical models, it is unrealistically assumed that the joint probability distribution of the returns on individual assets is completely known. That is, the theoretical analysis assumes that the parameters that characterize this probability distribution have known values. In subsequent practical applications this is often not the case. It is common practice to estimate these parameter values and to substitute the estimates into theoretically derived decision rules that hold where the parameters have known values. Standard errors of the estimators are not taken into account, but rather the estimates are treated as if they were the true parameter values. Consequently, by separating the econometric from the theoretical economic analysis, an important source of the uncertainty facing economic agents -- namely that arising from the unknown probability distribution of security returns -- is ignored. Throughout this book, we will refer to this distributional uncertainty as estimation risk. The implications of ignoring this source of uncertainty for an individual's optimal portfolio choice and for characterizing capital market equilibrium have not been previously thoroughly explored. These issues are important because what is optimal in the absence of parameter uncertainty (estimation risk), need not be optimal or even approximately optimal in the presence of such uncertainty.

This study analyzes optimal portfolio choice in the presence of estimation risk. We use a Bayesian framework in which estimation risk can be explicitly considered. Optimal portfolio choice is obtained in the von Neumann-Morgenstern-Savage paradigm by using what is termed the predictive distribution of returns. This predictive distribution , which properly reflects the effect of estimation risk, depends upon the assumed functional form of the model as well as the prior and sample (data) information that relates to the values of the different parameters that enter the model. In this Bayesian framework, we explore in depth the important implications of estimation risk for optimal portfolios as well as for the characterization of capital market equilibrium. Furthermore,since the portfolio problem may be viewed as a canonical representation of the general economic problem of choice under uncertainty, this book is relevant to the study of many other "real-world" economic decision problems.

In Section 2 of this chapter, we make precise the notion of estimation risk. We also identify several "real-world" problems, including the portfolio choice problem, for which estimation risk is present and needs to be explicitly accounted. In Section 3, we define and justify the Bayesian method for taking estimation risk into account. This method applies not only to the problems identified in Section 2, but also to decision-making under uncertainty in its full generality. In Section 4, we outline the remainder of this book.

2. The Definition and Scope Of Estimation Risk

For decision-making under uncertainty, it is well known that under the commonly accepted von Neumann-Morgenstern (1944) paradigm, a decision-maker chooses an alternative that maximizes the expected utility of the return resulting from that decision. The utility function is defined uniquely, up to a positive linear transformation, by the decision-maker's preferences. Formally, let $\mathbf{D}$ denote the vector of decision variables and let $\tilde{\mathbf{y}}$ denote a vector of random variables associated with the decision problem. For example, $\tilde{\mathbf{y}}$ might be a vector of future security returns and $\mathbf{D}$ a vector of the proportions of wealth invested in the securities. The joint probability density function for $\tilde{\mathbf{y}}$ is denoted by $f(\mathbf{y}|\boldsymbol{\theta})$, where $\boldsymbol{\theta}$ is a parameter vector that characterizes this distribution. We let $\tilde{R}(\tilde{\mathbf{y}}, \mathbf{D})$ denote the random return resulting from the decision, $\mathbf{D}$. Finally, let $U(\tilde{R})$ denote the decision maker's utility function, which is defined over the random return $\tilde{R}$. Then, if the value of $\boldsymbol{\theta}$ is known, the decision-maker chooses from among the feasible set of choices that $\mathbf{D}$ which maximizes expected utility:

$$E_{\tilde{\mathbf{y}}|\boldsymbol{\theta}}(U) \equiv \int_{\mathbf{y}} U[R(\mathbf{y}, \mathbf{D})] f(\mathbf{y}|\boldsymbol{\theta})\, d\mathbf{y}. \tag{1}$$

By estimation risk, we mean formally that f is not completely known. This includes the situation in which the functional form of f is unknown, a nonparametric case that will be discussed in detail in Chapter 2. It also includes the more common case in which the functional form of f is presumed known, but the value of the parameter vector $\boldsymbol{\theta}$ (of finite dimension) is unknown. For example, if f belongs to the family of multivariate normal distributions, then $\boldsymbol{\theta}$ consists of the elements in a mean vector and a variance-covariance matrix. For purposes of the following discussion, we restrict ourselves to this parametric case in which the functional form of f is known, but the value of $\boldsymbol{\theta}$ is unknown.

To indicate the scope of estimation risk, we now consider three illustrative problems involving decision under uncertainty:

Portfolio Selection. For the portfolio selection problem as noted above, the decision maker chooses the proportional amount ($\mathbf{D}$) of initial wealth to invest among the available securities that represent the investment alternatives. The vector of security returns, $\tilde{\mathbf{y}}$, is random with joint probability density function $f(\mathbf{y}|\boldsymbol{\theta})$. The (random) portfolio return for the portfolio represented by $\mathbf{D}$ is given by $\tilde{R}(\tilde{\mathbf{y}}, \mathbf{D}) = \mathbf{D}'\tilde{\mathbf{y}}$. This decision problem is solved by choosing a portfolio that maximizes the expected utility given in (1). The notation on the left-hand-side of (1) indicates that expected utility and consequently the optimal portfolio depend on $\boldsymbol{\theta}$.

If $\boldsymbol{\theta}$'s value were known, the decision-maker could now proceed to maximize the expected utility of portfolio returns. However, the value of $\boldsymbol{\theta}$ is seldom if ever known. We might assume that the joint distribution of security returns, f, is multivariate normal with unknown mean vector $\boldsymbol{\mu}$ and variance-covariance matrix $\boldsymbol{\Sigma}$. In the notation of (1), $\boldsymbol{\theta}$ would be a parameter vector consisting of the elements of $\boldsymbol{\mu}$ and $\boldsymbol{\Sigma}$. If we are to take estimation risk into account, the decision-maker must not only recognize that security returns are random and (ex-ante) unknown, but also that the probability distribution of security returns is itself uncertain.

Profit Maximizing Monopolist. For this problem, assume that the firm (decision-maker) wants to choose its price, D so as to maximize expected profit, where the demand for its product, $\tilde{y}$, is random. For purposes of illustration, let the price elasticity of demand, $\partial \ln y / \partial \ln D$, be constant, and let $\tilde{\mathbf{y}}$ be given by:

$$\tilde{y} = D^e \exp(\tilde{u}), \tag{2}$$

where e is the price elasticity of demand with unknown value and $\tilde{u}$ is a normal, zero mean error term. Let total cost be $c\tilde{y}$, where c is a known constant. Then, in the notation of (1), profit is given as:

$$\tilde{R}(\tilde{y},D) = D^e(D-c)\exp(\tilde{u}). \tag{3}$$

If the price elasticity were known, then it is a simple matter to find the expected profit maximizing price $[D = ce/(e+1)]$. However, if the large volume of econometric studies is any indication, there is no justification in assuming that the value of the price elasticity, e, is known. Therefore, estimation risk is present and needs to be considered explicitly to obtain that value of D which maximizes expected profits.

Prediction. For purposes of governmental policy, assume that one wants to predict the future value of energy demand. Energy demand, $\tilde{y}$, is a random variable with distribution $f(y|\boldsymbol{\theta})$. Here, it is useful to interpret $\boldsymbol{\theta}$ as a collection of parameters and "exogenous" variables that influence $\tilde{y}$. Then, denoting $\hat{y}$ (*i.e.*, D) as a predictor and $L(y,\hat{y})$ as a loss function, the decision problem is to choose $\hat{y}$ to minimize expected loss:

$$E_{\tilde{y}|\boldsymbol{\theta}}(L) \equiv \int_y L(y,\hat{y}) f(y|\boldsymbol{\theta})\, dy. \tag{4}$$

Here, (4) is in the form of (1) with the utility function replaced by a loss function and the maximum operator by the minimum (this loss function may be viewed as equivalent to the negative of a utility function). Again, if the distribution of the random variable in which we are interested, $\tilde{y}$, were known, then we could make a prediction by minimizing the expected loss in (4).[1] However, in practice there will be uncertainty regarding the distribution of $\tilde{y}$. The values of the parameters and/or exogenous variables ($\boldsymbol{\theta}$) of this distribution are seldom known. For example, the distribution of $\tilde{y}$ will depend on other variables whose future values are also unknown. In the case of energy demand, such demand might depend on unknown future Gross National Product. As in earlier examples, estimation risk is present and must be taken into account.

The above examples illustrate that estimation risk is indeed a feature of many diverse problems of decision-making under uncertainty. Few, if any, 'real-world' decision problems can be characterized by a known probability distribution for the variable(s) of interest. Thus, one needs to develop decision rules that explicitly account for estimation risk.

3. Incorporating Estimation Risk Directly Into The Decision Problem: The Use of The Predictive Distribution

Returning to the expected utility formulation in (1), recall that expected utility depends (in part) on the probability distribution $f(y|\boldsymbol{\theta})$ of the random variables $\tilde{\mathbf{y}}$. If the parameters, $\boldsymbol{\theta}$, of this distribution have unknown values, then the expected utility in (1) depends on these unknown values. Accordingly, the optimization problem cannot be solved until one takes account of these parameters with unknown values.

Before we discuss and justify the Bayesian method that takes account of estimation risk, it is useful to formalize the commonly employed method that ignores such risk. Under this method, one replaces the unknown value of the parameter vector $\boldsymbol{\theta}$ by a point estimate, $\hat{\boldsymbol{\theta}}$. The decision maker would then choose that decision $\mathbf{D}$ that maximizes:

$$\underset{\mathbf{y}|\hat{\boldsymbol{\theta}}=\boldsymbol{\theta}}{E}(U) = \int_{\mathbf{y}} U[R(\mathbf{y},\mathbf{D})]f(\mathbf{y}|\hat{\boldsymbol{\theta}})\,d\mathbf{y} \tag{5}$$

It is important to recognize that in treating parameter estimates as if they were the true values of the parameters, this method ignores estimation risk. For convenience, we refer to this method as the Parameter Certainty Equivalent (CE) method.[2] To take estimation risk into account, now consider the Bayes method.

1. With minor notational changes, we will illustrate in Chapter 2 that the discussion of estimation risk for the loss function in (4) also extends to target-control problems.

2. There is another method referred to in the literature as a certainty equivalent. In some formulations, $f(\tilde{\mathbf{y}}|\boldsymbol{\theta})$ is known, and the objective is to remove all uncertainty regarding $\tilde{\mathbf{y}}$. Here, we would replace the random variable $\tilde{\mathbf{y}}$ by a non-stochastic value, $\mathbf{y}^*$, and proceed to maximize utility: $U[R(\mathbf{y}^*,\mathbf{D})]$ [e.g., Simon (1956)]. In contrast, instead of removing all uncertainty regarding $\tilde{\mathbf{y}}$, we might eliminate (not necessarily with justification) only the distributional uncertainty. It is this latter type of certainty equivalent in which we are interested. To avoid ambiguity, Klein et al. (1978) refer to this method as the Estimated Conditional Method, because it involves estimating

Rather than replacing $f(\mathbf{y}|\boldsymbol{\theta})$ by $f(\mathbf{y}|\hat{\boldsymbol{\theta}})$, this method recognizes that a distribution for the random variable of interest, $\tilde{\mathbf{y}}$, should be conditioned only on known information. Consequently, this method does not incorrectly condition on $\boldsymbol{\theta} = \hat{\boldsymbol{\theta}}$ as in the CE method. Surely, except for large (whatever that means) data samples, we are not entitled to regard $\boldsymbol{\theta} = \hat{\boldsymbol{\theta}}$ as known information. The known information consists in part of but is not limited to the sample data. We might, for example, have a random sample of observations drawn from $f(\mathbf{y}|\boldsymbol{\theta})$. However, an important source of information consists of information that we might have prior to taking any observations on $f(\mathbf{y}|\boldsymbol{\theta})$. If, for example, $\boldsymbol{\theta} = \theta$ is a marginal propensity to consume, then we might believe that $0 < \theta < 1$. Such information is termed prior information.

These two types of information can be combined and summarized into what is termed the posterior distribution of $\boldsymbol{\theta}$. Recognizing that $f(\mathbf{y}|\boldsymbol{\theta})$ is a distribution conditioned on $\boldsymbol{\theta}$, we can now derive the desired distribution unconditioned on $\boldsymbol{\theta}$, a distribution formally termed the predictive distribution:

$$g(\mathbf{y}) \equiv \underset{\boldsymbol{\theta}}{E}[f(\mathbf{y}|\boldsymbol{\theta})] = \int_{\boldsymbol{\theta}} f(\mathbf{y}|\boldsymbol{\theta})\, p(\boldsymbol{\theta}|\mathbf{I})\, d\boldsymbol{\theta} \tag{6}$$

In (6), the expectation is taken with respect to the posterior distribution for $\boldsymbol{\theta}$, $p(\boldsymbol{\theta}|\mathbf{I})$, where $\mathbf{I}$ represents the set of prior and sample information. Employing this unconditional distribution (unconditioned on $\boldsymbol{\theta}$, but conditioned on sample and prior information, $\mathbf{I}$), in the Bayes method decision $\mathbf{D}$ is chosen to maximize:[3]

$$E_{\tilde{\mathbf{y}}}(U) \equiv \int_{\mathbf{y}} U[R(\mathbf{y}, \mathbf{D})]\, g(\mathbf{y})\, d\mathbf{y}. \tag{7}$$

The Bayes procedure outlined above has several justifications. First, and foremost, it is derivable under a set of reasonable axioms which have been expounded by von Neumann-Morgenstern and Savage (1944, 1954). It is beyond the scope of this book to discuss the details of these axioms. Interested readers may benefit from a thorough reading of Pratt et al. (1964), wherein an elegant but relatively straightforward and very satisfactory exposition of these axioms and their consequences is provided.[4] In contrast, the Parameter Certainty Equivalent (CE) method has no axiomatic foundation. At best, this method is justified asymptotically when there is no estimation risk.

As a second justification, it seems reasonable that one needs in general an entire distribution to characterize uncertainty. The Bayes method processes information in terms of an entire distribution for $\boldsymbol{\theta}$ via the predictive distribution [see (6)]. In contrast, the CE method processes information on $\boldsymbol{\theta}$ by a single summary measure -- the point estimate $\hat{\boldsymbol{\theta}}$. Interestingly enough, $\hat{\boldsymbol{\theta}}$ is in many applications the posterior mean of $\boldsymbol{\theta}$. Not surprisingly, to characterize uncertainty, it will seldom be adequate to know just the mean of the posterior distribution --- the entire distribution is needed. By employing the posterior distribution for $\boldsymbol{\theta}$ rather than a single summary measure, $\hat{\boldsymbol{\theta}}$, the Bayes method takes estimation risk or uncertainty into

---

the conditional distribution: $f(\mathbf{y}|\boldsymbol{\theta})$. Here, we refer to this method as the Parameter Certainty Equivalent (CE) method.

3. A discussion related to this distinction between estimation and the use of the predictive distribution can be found in de Finetti (1974) Chapter 3, where "prediction" refers to estimation and "prev-

account much more adequately. The following examples illustrate this point and shows how the predictive distribution is derived.

The Predictive Distribution and Estimation Risk: Choice Between Risky Securities. Consider an investor who chooses to invest in one and only one of two securities with random returns $\tilde{R}_i$, $i = 1, 2$. Assume for simplicity that $\tilde{R}_i$ is normally distributed with unknown mean μ_i and common known variance σ^2. The data consists of a random sample of T_i observations on each return. The prior information is assumed to be negligible.

To represent little prior information we use the diffuse prior distribution[5]

$$p_o(\mu_i) \; \alpha \; c \qquad -\infty < \mu_i < \infty \tag{8}$$

Where "α" denotes proportionality and c is a constant. It is well known [Zellner (1971) p. 20] that conditional on a sample of size T_i the posterior distribution for the mean μ_i, $p(\mu_i|\mathbf{R}_i, \sigma^2)$, is itself normal with mean $\bar{R}_i$, the sample mean, and variance σ^2/T_i. Then the predictive distribution, which is given as in Equation (6) by

$$g(R_i) = \int f[R_i|\mu_i, \sigma^2] p[\mu_i|\mathbf{R}_i, \sigma^2] d\mu_i, \tag{9}$$

is easily shown to be normal with mean $\bar{R}_i$ and variance $(1+1/T_i)\sigma^2$ [Zellner (1971), p. 29-30].[6]

Having shown how the predictive distribution is derived, we can now see how estimation risk enters into the decision problem. If we simply estimated the mean of the distribution of $\tilde{R}_i$ by $\bar{R}_i$ (the maximum likelihood estimate) and ignored estimation risk, then we would act as if the distribution of $\tilde{R}_i$ were normal:

$$\tilde{R}_i \underset{CE}{\sim} N(\bar{R}_i, \sigma^2). \tag{10}$$

If both securities have the same estimated mean, then this CE method would not distinguish among the two securities. However, suppose that the estimate of μ_1 is based on 10 observations while the estimate of μ_2 is based on 100 observations. Intuitively, any risk averse investor should prefer the second security as it has a more precisely estimated mean. Yet, unless estimation risk is taken into account, the decision maker will be indifferent between the two (exclusive) choices.

Now consider the Bayes approach in which we make decisions using the

---

ision" to the use of the predictive distribution.

4. Pratt et al. (1964) explain these axioms and their implications for the existence of prior distributions, the derivation of posterior distributions, and the justification for expected utility maximization. In regard to the latter, the use of the predictive distribution is implicitly justified.

5. For a discussion of such distributions see Zellner (1971) p. 41-53.

6. This result can be demonstrated alternatively as follows. Write

$$\tilde{R}_i = \mu_i + \tilde{\epsilon}_i,$$

where $\tilde{\epsilon}_i$ is normal with mean zero and variance σ^2. Then the result follows directly with μ_i and predictive distribution of $\tilde{R}_i$. From the discussion following Equation (9), the predictive distribution of $\tilde{R}_i$ is:

$$\tilde{R}_i \underset{P}{\sim} N(\bar{R}_i, (1+1/T_i)\sigma^2. \tag{11}$$

Intuitively, with $T_1 = 10$ and $T_2 = 100$ observations, security one will, as it should, be termed the riskier alternative. Furthermore, it is clear from the variance of $\tilde{R}_i$ in (11) that the predictive distribution distribution of $\tilde{R}_i$ incorporates two types of uncertainty or risk. The first variance component, σ^2, reflects the basic or inherent randomness of $\tilde{R}_i$. The second component, σ^2/T_i reflects the estimation risk due to incomplete knowledge of the mean, μ_i, in the return distribution. Indeed, from a classical perspective, σ^2/T_i is the variance of the estimator for μ_i.

The Predictive Distribution and Estimation Risk: Two Asset Portfolio Problem. In this example, consider an investor who chooses the proportion D of his wealth to invest in a single risky asset yielding return $\tilde{R}$ where the alternative is to invest the wealth in the form of a riskless security yielding a known rate of return R_f. For the purposes of this example, $\tilde{R}$ could represent the return on a market fund of securities and R_f the return on a fund of government obligations. As before, we shall assume for simplicity that $\tilde{R}$ is normally distributed with mean μ_i having an unknown value and variance with known value σ^2. There are T observations on $\tilde{R}$, and as before the prior information is assumed negligible.

The rate of return, $\tilde{R}_D$, on this portfolio of securities is given as:

$$\tilde{R}_D = (1-D)R_f + D\tilde{R}, \tag{12}$$

which conditional on μ is distributed as normal with mean $(1-D)R_f + D\mu$ and variance $D^2\sigma^2$. The analysis of the previous example can be used to establish that the predictive distribution of $\tilde{R}_D$ is also normal with mean $(1-D)R_f + D\bar{R}$ and variance $D^2(1+1/T)\sigma^2$. Here, as in the previous example, $\bar{R}$ is the sample mean. The investor who used a CE rule, and thereby ignored estimation risk, would assert that the distribution were normal with mean $(1-D)R_f + D\bar{R}$ and variance $D^2\sigma^2$. For any given portfolio allocation, D, estimation risk increases variance by a factor of $(1+1/T)$ for the same mean. For a general class of risk-averse utility functions, this fact establishes the intuitive result that estimation risk leads the investor to reduce his investment in the risky security [Klein and Bawa (1976), Theorem 2].

This analysis can be extended in an obvious way to consider diffuse and informative conjugate priors for σ. The only complication that arises here is that the predictive distribution of $\tilde{R}_D$ is Student-t [e.g., Brown (1979)]. The analysis can be further extended to consider many risky securities [Klein and Bawa (1976)] without affecting the central result that estimation risk will lead the investor to adopt a more conservative investment strategy.

$\bar{\epsilon}_i$ considered independent and normal.

These examples illustrate how the use of the predictive distribution accounts for the uncertainty induced by estimation risk. However, they do not give any indication of the performance one could expect from repeated use of the Bayes method in the decision context.

As a third justification, the Bayesian method has what might be termed a minimum average risk or maximum average value justification. Letting s denote the sample data, define

$$V(\mathbf{D}|\boldsymbol{\theta}) = E_{\mathbf{s}|\boldsymbol{\theta}}\left\{E_{\mathbf{y}|(\mathbf{s},\boldsymbol{\theta})}\left[U[R(\mathbf{y}, \mathbf{D}(\mathbf{s}))]\right]\right\} \tag{13}$$

as the value of the decision **D** (conditioned on $\boldsymbol{\theta}$ and s). The inner expectation simply denotes expected utility as defined in (1), where the decision **D** is permitted to depend on the sample data, s. The outer expectation is taken over the sample s (conditioned on $\boldsymbol{\theta}$). This function, which is the negative of the statistical risk function used to compare estimators in the econometric literature, could typically be calculated (actually closely approximated) in a Monte Carlo setting. For a given data set (and $\boldsymbol{\theta}$), one would evaluate a decision by calculating its expected utility. Then, to avoid an evaluation that would depend on the peculiarities of a single data set, one might (as is done in Monte Carlo experiments) draw a large number of data sets. In each case, the expected utility of the data dependent decision would be calculated. To summarize the performance of a decision in a Monte Carlo experiment, one would now take the average of these expected utilities. In this manner, one would closely approximate the value function in (13).

The Bayes decision can now be justified in terms of the properties of its value function. One can show that the Bayes decision has the desirable property of maximizing the average value, where the average is taken over the prior distribution. Following Lindley (1972), if we assume that average value exists, and letting $\mathbf{D}^* \equiv arg \max_D$ (average value) be the value of D that maximizes average value:

$$\begin{aligned}\mathbf{D}^* &= arg \max_{\mathbf{D}} \int_{\boldsymbol{\theta}} V(\mathbf{D}|\boldsymbol{\theta}) p_o(\boldsymbol{\theta}) d\boldsymbol{\theta} \\ &= arg \max_{\mathbf{D}} \int_{\boldsymbol{\theta}}\int_{\mathbf{s}}\int_{\mathbf{y}} U(\mathbf{y}, \mathbf{D}(\mathbf{s})) f(\mathbf{y}|\boldsymbol{\theta}) f(\mathbf{s}|\boldsymbol{\theta}) p_o(\boldsymbol{\theta}) d\mathbf{y} d\mathbf{s} d\boldsymbol{\theta} \\ &= arg \max_{\mathbf{D}} \int_{\boldsymbol{\theta}}\int_{\mathbf{s}}\int_{\mathbf{y}} U(\mathbf{y}, \mathbf{D}(\mathbf{s})] f(\mathbf{y}|\boldsymbol{\theta}) f(\mathbf{s}) p(\boldsymbol{\theta}|\mathbf{s}) d\mathbf{y} d\mathbf{s} d\boldsymbol{\theta},\end{aligned} \tag{14}$$

where p_o is the prior, $f(\mathbf{s}|\boldsymbol{\theta})$ is the joint distribution of the data (given $\boldsymbol{\theta}$), $f(\mathbf{s})$ is the unconditional distribution of s, and $p(\boldsymbol{\theta}|\mathbf{s})$ is the posterior distribution. The last expression in (14) follows from Bayes Theorem. Assuming that the multiple integral in (14) converges, we can interchange the order of integration to find that

$$\begin{aligned}\mathbf{D}^* &= arg \max_{\mathbf{D}} \int_{\mathbf{s}} f(\mathbf{s}) \int_{\mathbf{y}} U[R(\mathbf{y}, \mathbf{D}(\mathbf{s}))] \int_{\boldsymbol{\theta}} f(\mathbf{y}|\boldsymbol{\theta}) p(\boldsymbol{\theta}|\mathbf{s})\, d\boldsymbol{\theta}\, d\mathbf{y}\, d\mathbf{s} \\ &= arg \max_{\mathbf{D}} \int_{\mathbf{s}} f(\mathbf{s}) \int_{\mathbf{y}} U[R(\mathbf{y}, \mathbf{D}(\mathbf{s}))] g(\mathbf{y})\, d\mathbf{y}\, d\mathbf{s} \\ &= \int_{\mathbf{s}} f(\mathbf{s}) \left\{ arg \max_{\mathbf{D}} \int_{\mathbf{y}} U[R(\mathbf{y}, \mathbf{D}(\mathbf{s}))] g(\mathbf{y})\, d\mathbf{y} \right\} d\mathbf{s}.\end{aligned} \tag{15}$$

Clearly, the latter expression yields the optimal (Bayes) decision under the predictive distribution, g, which is identical to the average value maximizing decision $\mathbf{D}^*$.

Since the Bayes decision, $\mathbf{D}^*$, can be interpreted as having the highest average value, there is no other decision whose value function is higher everywhere (i.e., for all $\boldsymbol{\theta}$) than $\mathbf{D}^*$. There may, and typically will, be some decision whose value exceeds $\mathbf{D}^*$ somewhere in the parameter space.[7] In this case, it seems reasonable to weight each decision's value function at each point in the parameter space according to where we believe the true parameter lies. Then, we might compute average value as a summary measure of a decision's performance. Employing the prior distribution as the weighting function, the Bayes decision maximizes this summary performance measure.[8]

From the above discussions, it follows that the predictive distribution plays a central role in decision making under uncertainty. Its use can be justified formally from a set of basic axioms. In addition, this distribution reflects estimation risk and results, as described above, in a desirable average value (loss) maximizing (minimizing) decision. In the remainder of this book, emphasis will be placed on employing the predictive distribution of security returns to analyze the portfolio choice problem. In so doing, we will theoretically and empirically examine the consequences of estimation risk. It should be re-emphasized that while we will focus primarily on the portfolio choice problem, the analysis employed is applicable to a very wide range of decision problems, including problems of economic optimization (single and multiple period), forecasting, and estimation.

4. Outline: Estimation Risk and Optimal Portfolio Choice

We begin our analysis of estimation risk in Chapter 2 with a selective review of the non-portfolio literature on estimation risk and optimal choice under uncertainty. The first sections of this chapter examine many diverse applications in which estimation risk is appropriately taken into account. This review will provide guidance for incorporating estimation risk, and will show the pervasiveness and importance of this distributional uncertainty. The papers that we have selected to

7. For example, arbitrarily set $\boldsymbol{\theta} = \boldsymbol{\theta}_o$, where $\boldsymbol{\theta}_o$ is any particular value of $\boldsymbol{\theta}$. The decision maker would now make a decision, $\mathbf{D}_o$, conditioned on $\boldsymbol{\theta} = \boldsymbol{\theta}_o : D_o = D(\theta_o)$. There is no decision whose value always exceeds that of D_o, because at $\theta = \theta_o$, D_o has the highest value. This method of making a decision by arbitrarily selecting a value of $\boldsymbol{\theta}$ is clearly absurd. However, this example does lead one to expect value functions to cross in general.

8. In the portfolio context, Brown (1977, 1978) compares the Bayes rule with the CE method. For the wide range of parameter values considered, the value function for the Bayes rule was always above that for the CE method.

review deal with a number of specific applications. Our selection procedure involves no value judgments. The few papers that we have included are primarily intended to highlight certain issues that pervasively arise in the consideration of estimation risk. An extensive research bibliography on this subject is provided at the end of the book. It is also important, and is the objective of the remainder of Chapter 2, to provide general guidance as to when estimation risk should be taken into account. In a very general setting, we will examine this issue in both non-parametric and parametric contexts.

In Chapter 3, we turn to the portfolio choice problem. We survey a wide range of papers that provide an indication of the importance of estimation risk for the portfolio choice problem. This review provides substantial motivation for a detailed analysis of estimation risk in the portfolio choice problem undertaken in this book.

This chapter also discusses the sources of prior information that underlie a predictive distribution of security returns. In discussing sources of prior information, this chapter discusses information not only on the parameters of the security return distribution, but also information on the parametric form of the distribution (e.g., normal, log-normal, Student-*t*, etc.).

The remaining chapters focus on specific theoretical and empirical issues pertaining to the portfolio choice problem. Chapters 4 and 5 examine the qualitative effects of estimation risk on optimal portfolio choice. Chapter 4 examines estimation risk when the joint distribution of security returns is multivariate normal, the case most frequently considered in the financial economics literature. Cases of both 'non-informative' and informative prior information are considered. In all cases, the optimal choice is examined and shown to be very different from that obtained in the absence of, or by ignoring, estimation risk. Chapter 5 provides assumptions under which a risk-averse investor will invest more in the riskless asset as a measure of prior and/or sample information decreases. In addition, this chapter provides plausible assumptions under which it is asymptotically optimal for an investor to limit diversification to a security subset. Typically, this result would not be obtained in the absence of estimation risk, yet is supported by what one actually observes in practice.

Chapter 6 examines the observable implications of estimation risk for capital market equilibrium. It is assumed that individuals have the same prior beliefs and access to the same set of data. Then, although estimation risk can greatly affect an individual's optimal choice, the implied capital market equilibrium, with estimation risk, is observationally equivalent to that implied by a model in which investors ignore estimation risk (by treating parameter estimates as the true parameter values).

Chapter 7 analyzes portfolio choice and market equilibrium when the probability distribution of returns is itself completely unknown (a nonparametric context). Simple conditions are provided under which one can use the empirical distribution and obtain a reasonable approximation to optimal portfolio choice and a capital asset pricing model in the two parameter (mean, lower partial moment) framework. The results of this chapter also relate to the traditional mean-variance and mean-scale parameter framework commonly used in the finance literature.

Chapters 8 and 9 emphasize some empirical aspects of estimation risk as it relates to portfolio choice. Chapter 8 investigates the consequences of estimation risk for portfolio choice and provides numerical measures of the impact of estimation risk given by the statistical risk function. In a repeated sampling framework, the Bayes rule, which incorporates estimation risk, is compared with the Parameter Certainty Equivalent (CE) rule, which ignores this risk. Across the range of parameter values considered, the Bayes rule dominates the CE rule, often substantially. Moreover, even when the distribution of security returns is misspecified, this result is shown to still hold. Chapter 9 examines estimation risk where returns are generated by the so-called 'index' model of Sharpe. This model yields a parsimonious representation of the process generating security returns and has received considerable attention in the finance literature. Allowing for estimation risk in this context, this chapter shows that portfolio choice is obtained by the use of a three parameter rule rather than the two parameter rule used when estimation risk is ignored. This rule is illustrated with New York Stock Exchange returns data for the period January 1961 through January 1968. Chapter 10 concludes this study with a brief summary of our results.

CHAPTER 2

ESTIMATION RISK AND OPTIMAL CHOICE UNDER UNCERTAINTY: A SELECTIVE REVIEW

1. Introduction

The material surveyed in this chapter is intended neither to be an exhaustive survey nor necessarily a representative sample of the literature on estimation risk and optimal choice under uncertainty. By analyzing several diverse applications, this selective survey examines various aspects of estimation risk that repeatedly occur throughout the literature. It is also our intent to illustrate how estimation risk should be accounted for by using the predictive distribution and to show why it is important to do so.

This chapter focuses on non-portfolio applications that deal appropriately with estimation risk. In Sections 2 and 3, we will distinguish single from multiperiod optimization problems, because there are issues of experimental design and learning that are present in the latter but not in the former. In all of these applications, the decision maker's utility (or loss) function depends on a variable whose predictive distribution reflects the underlying estimation risk. Accordingly it is important in a very general context to examine the manner in which estimation risk affects this predictive distribution. Section 4 examines this issue in both nonparametric and parametric contexts. Section 5 provides a brief summary of the material surveyed in this chapter.

2. Single Period Optimization Problems

The material surveyed in this section examines four single period optimization problems. These applications will illustrate several of the important aspects of estimation risk.[1]

It should be noted that in these and in all other applications that correct for estimation risk, estimation risk is taken into account by recognizing the ultimate objective of the decision-maker. In practice, parameters with unknown values will characterize any decision problem under uncertainty. One common approach to this problem is to incorrectly treat the estimation of these parameters as the objective of the decision-maker.

Thus, using estimates that have "desirable" statistical properties, one could proceed to "solve" the decision problem by treating the parameter estimates as the true parameters. However, there is no justification (except possibly asymptotically) in assuming that the parameter estimators have zero standard errors, that is the

1. In addition to the papers reviewed here, see also, for example, Barry and Wildt (1977), Brainard (1967), and Fisher (1962).

estimates are identical to the true parameter values. Accordingly, decisions made in this manner will not be optimal, because they fail to account for estimation risk. By recognizing that the objective of the decision maker is not to estimate unknown parameters (e.g. parameters of a demand function), but rather to optimize some objective (e.g., expected profits), estimation risk can be properly taken into account. We now turn to several applications that properly take estimation risk into account.

Real Estate Assessment Problem.

In studying housing assessment, Varian (1975) emphasizes the importance of recognizing the ultimate objective of the decision-maker. Here, the decision-maker is an assessor whose decision is to estimate the value of a house. Varian assumes, as is often done in practice, that the actual value, $\tilde{y}$, depends linearly on a set of housing characteristics, **X**:

$$\tilde{y} = \mathbf{X}\boldsymbol{\beta} + \tilde{u}, \tag{1}$$

where $\boldsymbol{\beta}$ is an unknown coefficient vector and $\tilde{u}$ is the error term. The data for this problem consist of T observations on (1), where the errors are i.i.d. normal with mean zero and variance σ^2. With these data, and a prior for $(\boldsymbol{\beta}, \sigma^2)$, the assessor must choose the assessment, $\hat{y}^*$, to minimize expected loss. This expectation is taken over the predictive distribution of $\tilde{y}$.

With the commonly employed quadratic loss function

$$L = (\hat{y} - y)^2, \tag{2}$$

the optimal predictor is the mean of the predictive distribution, $\bar{y}$. Assuming, as Varian does, that the prior is diffuse:

$$p_o(\boldsymbol{\beta}, \sigma) \propto 1/\sigma, \; -\infty\boldsymbol{\iota} < \boldsymbol{\beta} < \infty\boldsymbol{\iota}, \; 0 < \sigma < \infty, \tag{3}$$

where $\boldsymbol{\iota}$ denotes a vector of ones, then $\bar{y}$ is given as

$$\bar{y} = \mathbf{Z}\hat{\boldsymbol{\beta}}. \tag{4}$$

In (4), **Z** is a vector of housing characteristics for the given house in question, and $\hat{\boldsymbol{\beta}}$ is the Ordinary Least-Squares (OLS) estimate of $\boldsymbol{\beta}$:

$$\hat{\boldsymbol{\beta}} = (\mathbf{X}'\mathbf{X})^{-1}\mathbf{X}'\mathbf{y}, \tag{5}$$

where **X** is a $T \times K$ matrix of T observations on K characteristics of houses in the data sample, and y is a corresponding $T \times 1$ vector of observations on the selling prices of houses.

The OLS predictor in (4) is widely employed because of its "desirable" statistical properties. For the model in (1), this predictor, $\bar{y}$, is the minimum variance unbiased predictor. With the diffuse prior in (3) and a quadratic loss function, $\bar{y}$ is also the minimum expected loss predictor. However, the ultimate objective of the assessor's office is not to provide predictors with the above "desirable" statistical properties. The objective is to provide an assessment that will be employed to set property taxes. Recognizing this objective, Varian argues that the quadratic loss function, which underlies the mean predictor, $\bar{y}$, is not appropriate.

When a house is under-assessed, the assessor's office loses an amount proportional to the under assessment in tax revenue. However, if the house is over-assessed, the home owner can petition to have the issue resolved in court. In this case, for the area in California that was examined, the assessor's office incurs court costs even if it wins the case. Accordingly, Varian argues that one might expect the losses to increase at more than a linear rate for large over-assessments. Therefore, given the purpose of the assessment, the unbiased predictor $\bar{y}$, which results in part from the quadratic loss function in (2), is not optimal.

In view of the above discussion, rather than the symmetric quadratic loss function, Varian employs the following asymmetric loss function:

$$L(\hat{y},y) = 1/a \exp[a(\hat{y}-y)] - (\hat{y}-y) - 1/a, \ a > 0. \tag{6}$$

This loss function is desirable first because it exhibits the asymmetry discussed above. As Varian notes, the loss is approximately exponential for large over-assessments and linear for large under-assessments. Second, as is clear from Figure 2.1, the asymmetry of this function depends on a; for small values of a, it is approximately symmetric.[2] Third, this loss function has the desirable property that it has a minimum of zero at $\hat{y} = y$. Finally, with this loss function, it is possible to analytically compute the expected loss under a normal distribution.

With the diffuse prior in (3) and the likelihood implicit in (1), the predictive distribution for $\tilde{y}$ is a Student-t distribution. Employing the normal approximation to the Student-t distribution and the loss function in (6), Varian shows that the optimal assessment is given as:

$$\hat{y}^* = \mathbf{Z}\hat{\boldsymbol{\beta}} - a\sigma_p^2, \tag{7}$$

where σ_p^2 is the variance of the predictive distribution. Because of the asymmetry in the loss function (greater losses for large over-assessments than for under-assessments), the assessment is biased downwards. The bias, $a\sigma_p^2$, depends on the degree of the asymmetry, a, and on the degree of uncertainty regarding $\tilde{y}$ (as measured by the predictive variance, σ_p^2).

To evaluate the importance of taking the decision maker's final objective into account, Varian compares expected losses for the two decisions, $\bar{y}$ [the predictor in (4) with the "desirable" statistical properties discussed above] and $\hat{y}^*$ [the predictor in (7) that is optimal from the viewpoint of the assessor's office]. These expectations were computed with the loss function in (6), with $a = .0025$. The reasonableness of this parameter value is asserted, though not justified in Varian's study. The loss function for this parameter value is shown in Figure 2.1. The results for sample sizes $T = 125$ and $T = 168$ are shown in Table 2.1.[3]

2. This figure was reproduced from Figure 1 in Varian (1975).

3. This table shows results reported by Varian (1975).

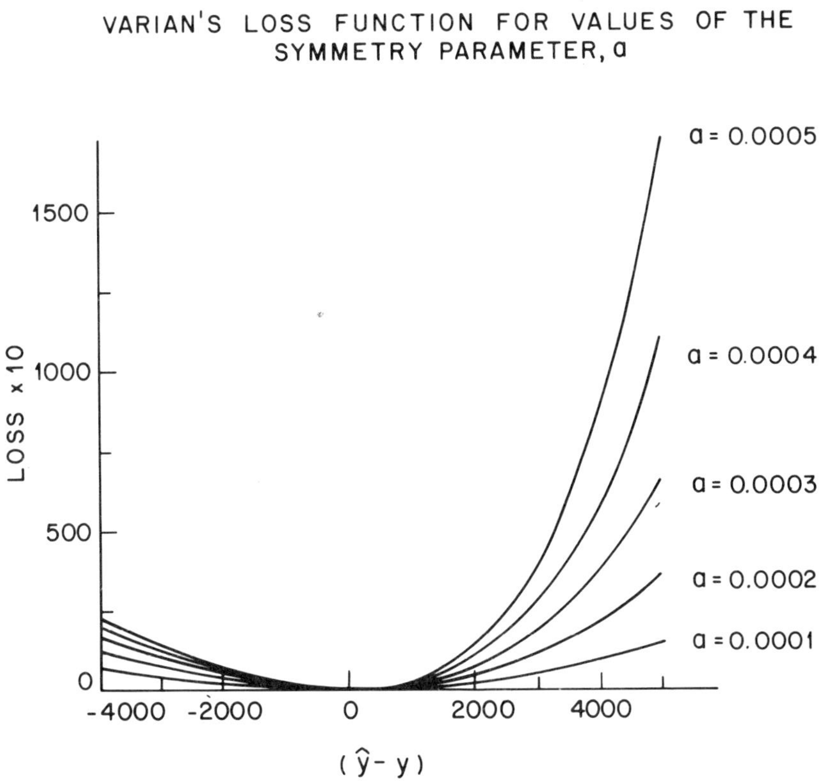
VARIAN'S LOSS FUNCTION FOR VALUES OF THE SYMMETRY PARAMETER, a
LOSS x 10
1500
1000
500
0
-4000
-2000
0
2000
4000
(ŷ - y)
a = 0.0005
a = 0.0004
a = 0.0003
a = 0.0002
a = 0.0001

Figure 2.1

Expected Loss Comparison
Optimal ($\hat{y}^*$) and OLS ($\bar{y}$) Predictors

Sample Size	Expected Loss	
	$\hat{y}^*$	$\bar{y}$
$T = 125$	790.0	999.0
$T = 168$	718.0	901.0

Table 2.1

From this table, it is at once evident that there can be a substantial gain to taking the final objective of the decision-maker into account. By employing the optimal decision $\hat{y}^*$ rather than the commonly employed predictor $\hat{y}$, expected loss is reduced by more than 20 percent for both sample sizes. It is also evident from this table that, as expected, more information ($T = 168$ rather than $T = 125$) results in a decrease in expected loss.

Price Setting Monopolist's Problem.

To further emphasize the importance of the decision maker's final objective and to examine the impact of varying degrees of estimation risk, consider a decision problem reported in Klein et al. (1978). Here, the decision problem is that confronting a price-setting monopolist facing the uncertain demand:

$$\tilde{Q} = \gamma \cdot P^e \exp(\tilde{u}), \tag{8}$$

where γ and e are parameters and $\tilde{Q}$, P, and $\tilde{u}$ are variables that denote respectively quantity, price, and a random error. The error, $\tilde{u}$, is normally distributed with mean zero and variance σ^2. To complete this characterization, Klein et al. assume that the monopolist has the cost function:

$$C(Q) = cQ. \tag{9}$$

To simplify the discussion, it is assumed that the price elasticity of demand, e, is the only unknown parameter for the monopolist. The values of the parameters γ in (8) and c in (9) are both set equal to 1.0. Then, from (8) and (9), profits are given by

$$\pi(P) = (P-1)P^e \exp(u). \tag{10}$$

Accordingly, expected profits, conditioned on e,[4] are proportional to:

4. In (11), let the price set by any decision method depend on the sample of data, s: $P = P(s)$.

$$V(P;e) = (P-1)P^e. \tag{11}$$

If the monopolist ignores estimation risk, then he replaces the elasticity e in (11) by an estimate, $\hat{e}$, and maximizes $V(P;\hat{e})$. The resulting optimal price under the parameter certainty equivalent (CE) method is given by:

$$\bar{P} \equiv arg\left\{\max_{P} V(P;\hat{e})\right\} = \hat{e}/(\hat{e}+1). \tag{12}$$

If the monopolist takes estimation risk into account, then he must choose P to maximize the expected value of $V(P;e)$, where the expectation is taken over the posterior distribution for e. The optimal price is then given by:

$$P^* = arg\left\{\max_{P} E_e[V(P;e)]\right\}. \tag{13}$$

To calculate and compare the solutions in (12) and (13), Klein et al. assume that the prior for e is uniform on the interval $[-4.0, -1.1]$. The upper limit is less than -1.0, because profits become infinite as e approaches -1.0 from below. The lower limit is arbitrary, though a decrease in the lower limit would not significantly affect the domain of $\bar{P}$ in (12).

The data for this application consist of T observations on the demand equation, where the error term is i.i.d. normal with mean zero and variance σ^2. Employing these data, the estimate of e, $\hat{e}$, was the constrained maximum likelihood estimate, where $\hat{e}$ was restricted to the interval $[-4.0, -1.1]$. Accordingly, the information employed by Bayesian and non-Bayesian decision makers is very similar. As a result, this comparison emphasizes the manner in which information is processed to reflect estimation risk, rather than differences in information.

To illustrate the impact of estimation risk, it is useful to generate data reflecting varying degrees of estimation risk. Klein et al. measure estimation risk by the standard error of the unconstrained maximum likelihood estimate for e, SEE. From the demand function in (8) with $\gamma = 1.0$, σ^2 the disturbance variance, and $t = 1,\ldots,T$ observations:

$$SEE \equiv \sigma^2/\sum_{t=1}^{T}(LnP_t)^2. \tag{14}$$

This measure provides a convenient summary of the degree of estimation risk. It increases with the disturbance variance, decreases with the sample size, and does not depend on the value of e.[5]

Then, the expectation of the function in (11), with the expectation taken over the data conditioned on e, is, in the terminology of Chapter 1, the value function for the pricing decision.

5. This measure overstates the actual standard error for the constrained maximum likelihood estimate. Both measures reflect the degree of estimation risk, as reflected in the sample size and the disturbance variance. The advantage to SEE as a convenient description of estimation risk is that it does not depend on the value of e.

The first set of results illustrates the effect of estimation risk by analyzing

$$\Delta V(e) \equiv [V(P^*;e) - V(\bar{P};e)]/V(\bar{P};e), \tag{15}$$

the percentage difference in conditional expected profits for the two decision solutions. Figure 2.2 below shows $\Delta V(e)$ as a function of e for high and low degrees of estimation risk, SEE [see equation (14) and footnote 5].[6] When SEE = .23, a low degree of estimation risk,[7] the Bayes solution, P^*, results in at most a 3.3 percent reduction in expected loss (at $e = 1.4$) over the CE solution, $\bar{P}$. The unambiguous region of dominance for P^* over $\bar{P}$ is for e in the interval [1.3, 1.7]. When estimation risk increases to SEE = 1.02, a high but not unrealistic degree of estimation risk[8] the advantage of incorporating estimation risk increases substantially. Now, P^* offers a 23.2 percent maximal reduction in expected loss (at $e = 1.9$) over $\bar{P}$. Moreover, the dominance region for P^* is the wider interval [1.3, 3.1]. The pattern in these results, though not depicted in Figure 2.2, continues for other values of SEE.[9] Therefore, it is clear that the dominance region for the Bayes' solution and the extent of dominance depend on the degree of estimation risk.

From Figure 2.2, it is also clear that the Bayes solution is dominated near the boundaries of the prior domain. This finding is not surprising, because e was estimated by constrained maximum likelihood. The actual standard error (overstated by SEE) decreases as e approaches -1.1 or -4.0. Consequently, and as expected, the (CE) solution, which is based on e's estimate, does the best in the region where e is most precisely estimated.

This study also reports the average (over e) of $\Delta V(e)$ (i.e., for each value of SEE, the area under each of the types of curves in Figure 2.2). Figure 2.3 below, which reproduces these results, shows the average percentage change in expected profits for various degrees of estimation risk (SEE).[10] From this figure, the monopolist could earn an additional 7.5 percent on average by taking estimation uncertainty into account. As in the Varian study, the final objective must not be ignored. The objective of the monopolist is not to estimate the price elasticity of demand, but to maximize expected profits. By recognizing the real objective and accounting for estimation risk, the gain to the monopolist can be considerable.

---

6. Figure 2.2 is constructed from Table 1 in Klein et al. (1978).

7. The ratio of $|e|$ to SEE, to be interpreted as a downward biased "t-ratio", lies between 5.2 and 17.4.

8. For this case, $|e|$/SEE, a downward biased "t-ratio", lies between 1.1 and 3.9.

9. See Tables 1 and 2 of Klein et al. (1978).

10. This figure is taken from Figure 2 of Klein et al. (1978). As Klein et al. note, one could calculate the change in average expected profits rather than the average change in expected profits. Under the former measure, the advantage to P^* is even larger than for the measure reported in Figure 2.3.

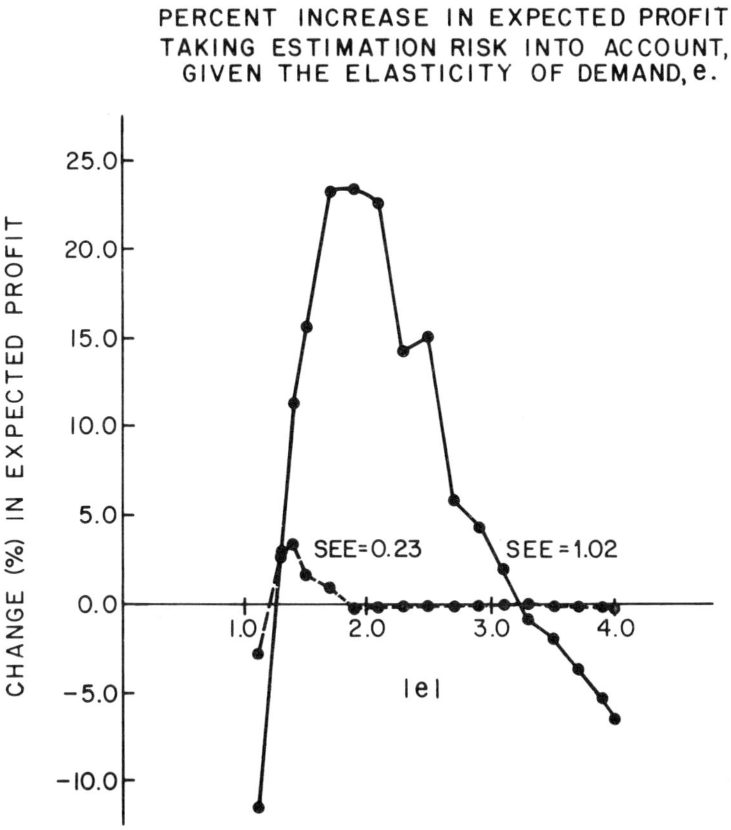

PERCENT INCREASE IN EXPECTED PROFIT
TAKING ESTIMATION RISK INTO ACCOUNT,
GIVEN THE ELASTICITY OF DEMAND, e.
CHANGE (%) IN EXPECTED PROFIT
25.0
20.0
15.0
10.0
5.0
0.0
-5.0
-10.0
SEE=0.23
SEE=1.02
1.0
2.0
3.0
4.0
|e|

Figure 2.2

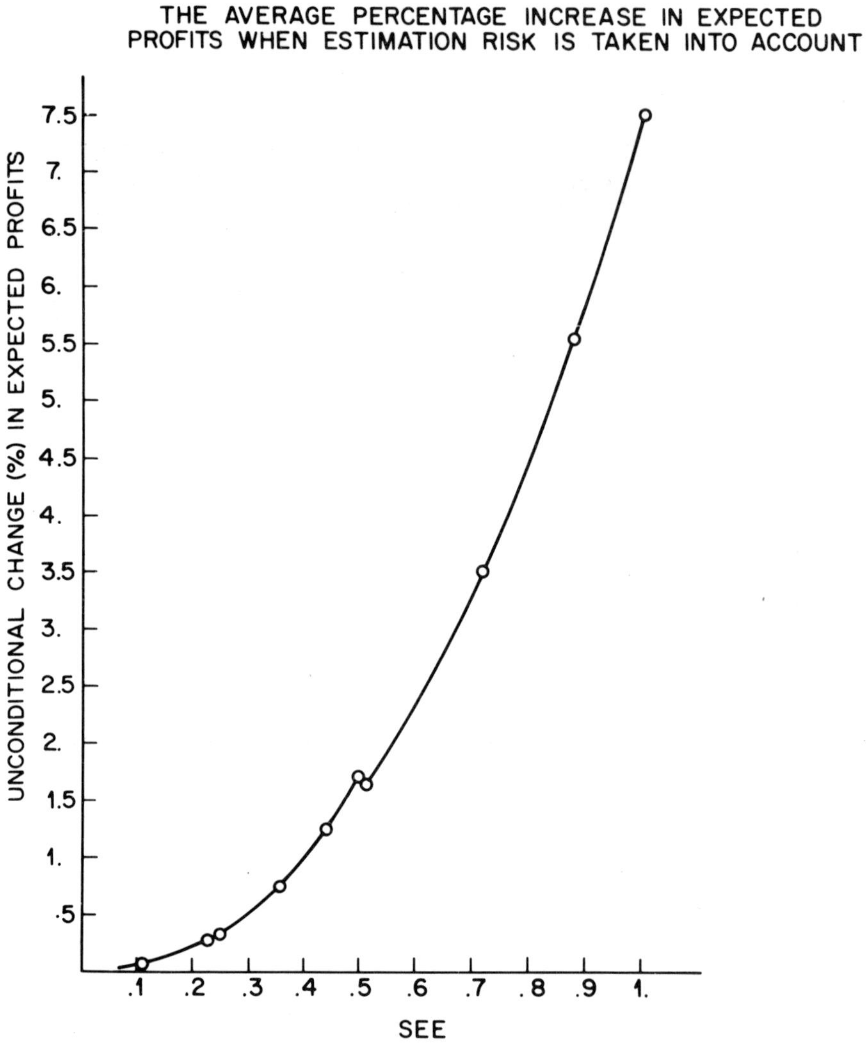
THE AVERAGE PERCENTAGE INCREASE IN EXPECTED PROFITS WHEN ESTIMATION RISK IS TAKEN INTO ACCOUNT
UNCONDITIONAL CHANGE (%) IN EXPECTED PROFITS
7.5
7.
6.5
6.
5.5
5.
4.5
4.
3.5
3.
2.5
2.
1.5
1.
.5
.1
.2
.3
.4
.5
.6
.7
.8
.9
1.
SEE

Figure 2.3

Target Control Problem.

In the above review, estimation risk was important in a particular formulation. Accordingly, it would seem important to examine the impact of estimation risk for a variety of utility (or loss) structures. Zellner and Geisel (1968) examine this sensitivity issue in the context of a target control problem. They assume that T observations are generated from the model:

$$\tilde{y}_t = X_t\,\beta + \tilde{u}_t,\ t = 1,...,T, \tag{16}$$

where $\tilde{y}$ and X are the endogenous and exogenous variables respectively, β is an unknown parameter, and $\tilde{u}_t$ is an i.i.d. normal error term with mean zero and unknown variance σ^2. With $\tilde{z} \equiv \tilde{y}_{T+1}$, denote the loss function as $L(\tilde{z}, a)$, where a is the known target value that we want to achieve. Then, with $w \equiv X_{T+1}$ as the control, the objective is to choose w to minimize expected loss

To calculate expected loss, the expectation is taken over the predictive distribution for $\tilde{z}$. To derive this distribution, Zellner and Geisel employ the diffuse prior:

$$P(\beta, \sigma)\ \alpha\ 1/\sigma,\ -\infty < \beta < \infty;\ 0 < \sigma < \infty. \tag{17}$$

Then, with the likelihood function implicit in (16), the predictive distribution is the Student-t:

$$f(z)\ \alpha\ [v+g(z-w\hat{\beta})^2]^{-(v+1)/2}, \tag{18}$$

where

$$g = [S^2(1+w^2/\Sigma X_i^2)]^{-1}, \tag{19}$$

$$S^2 = \sum_{i=1}^{T} (y_i-\hat{\beta}X_i)^2/v,$$

$$\hat{\beta} = \sum_{i=1}^{T} X_i y_i/\Sigma X_i^2,$$

and

$$v = T - 1.$$

For various loss functions, Zellner and Geisel now compare the parameter certainty equivalent (CE) solution with the Bayes solution. Beginning with the quadratic loss

$$L = (\tilde{z}-a)^2, \tag{20}$$

the CE and Bayes solutions, $\bar{w}$ and w^* respectively, are:

$$\bar{w} = a/\hat{\beta} \tag{21}$$

and

$$w^* = (a/\hat{\beta})(1+\tau^2), \quad 1/\tau^2 = \hat{\beta}^2 \sum_{i=1}^{T} X_i^2/[\nu S^2/(\nu-2)].$$

In comparing these solutions, note first that as a result of estimation risk, $|w^*| < |\bar{w}|$. In other words, this additional uncertainty has resulted in a more conservative setting of the control variable. Furthermore the extent to which $|w^*| < |\bar{w}|$ depends on the (relative) degree of estimation uncertainty as measured by τ^2 (essentially the reciprocal of a squared t-ratio).

For the loss function in (20), Zellner and Geisel also report the difference in expected loss for these control settings:

$$E[L\,|\,w=\bar{w}] - E[L\,|\,w=w^*] = a^2\tau^4/(\tau^2+1). \tag{22}$$

As must be the case, this difference is non-negative. Furthermore, from (22), this difference is an increasing function of the degree of estimation risk and of the squared target value (i.e., a^2). Intuitively, the greater the degree of estimation risk or the greater the target (in absolute magnitude), the more important it is to take estimation risk into account.

To deal with an important robustness question, Zellner and Geisel also compare these solutions for a variety of symmetric loss functions of the form:

$$L(\tilde{z},a) = |\tilde{z}-a|^{\alpha}, \quad \alpha = .5,\ 1,\ 2,\ 4. \tag{23}$$

Since analytical comparisons were not possible, they numerically compared expected losses for a given set of data generated from the model in (14) and for fixed values of a and α. These data were generated from fifteen observations with $\beta = 2.0$, $\sigma^2 = 9.0$, and values of X independently drawn from a normal distribution with mean zero and variance .64.

Let w^* be the optimal control under quadratic loss, $\bar{w}$ the CE setting under quadratic loss, and $w^*(\alpha)$ the optimal control setting for each loss function in (23). Then, with the data generated as described above and the loss function in (22) Zellner and Geisel calculated the ratios:

$$E[L\,|\,w=w^*]/E[L\,|\,w=w^*(\alpha)] \tag{24}$$

and

$$E[L\,|\,w=\bar{w}]/E[L\,|\,w=w^*(\alpha)].$$

The purpose of these calculations is to examine and compare the robustness of decision methods when the loss function is incorrectly specified as the commonly employed quadratic. For various target values of a and loss function parameter values of α, these results are reported in Table 2.2.[11]

Relative Expected Loss:

$E[L\,|\,w=\bar{w}]/E[L\,|\,w=w^*(\alpha)],\ E[L\,|\,w=w^*]/E[L\,|\,w=w^*(\alpha)]$

Target:a	Loss Function: $\lvert\tilde{Z}-a\rvert^{\alpha}$ $\alpha = .5$	$\alpha = 1.0$	$\alpha = 2.0$	$\alpha = 4.0$
a = 3				
$w=\bar{w}$	1.0168	1.0351	1.0769	1.1891
$w=w^*$	1.0002	1.0002	1.0000	1.0041
a = 4				
$w=\bar{w}$	1.0246	1.0518	1.1150	1.2928
$w=w^*$	1.0004	1.0004	1.0000	1.0073
a = 5				
$w=\bar{w}$	1.0314	1.0662	1.1489	1.3918
$w=w^*$	1.0007	1.0006	1.0000	1.0109

Table 2.2

From this table, it is first evident that when the loss function is not misspecified and is in fact the quadratic (α=2), there is a significant gain of 7-15 percent in taking estimation risk into account. As Zellner and Geisel note, the relative performance of $\bar{w}$ depends on the value of the target, *a*. The control setting will be an increasing function of the target. As can be seen from the predictive distribution in (18)-(19), a larger control will result in a higher predictive variance (more estimation risk). Since the CE solution ignores estimation risk, it is intuitive that this method performs poorly when *a* is large.

Turning to the cases in which loss is misspecified, from Table 2.2, the CE method, $\bar{w}$ is not very robust. Depending on the values of *a* and α, this method results in a 1.7-39.2 percent increase in expected loss over the optimal method, $w^*(\alpha)$. As is intuitive, this relative loss is an increasing function of *a* and α. As discussed above, for larger *a* there will be a larger degree of estimation risk that is being ignored. As α increases, the penalty to ignoring such risk will increase.

Finally, from Table 2.2, the optimal Bayes method under quadratic loss, w^*, is remarkably robust. At most, with a = 5 and α = 4, there is an additional 1.1 percent loss to employing the misspecified loss function. For other values of *a* and α, this additional loss is much smaller. Therefore, for the symmetric loss functions considered,the Bayes method under quadratic loss is very robust and significantly outperforms the parameter certainty equivalent method.

Zellner and Geisel also examine the robustness issue for a class of asymmetric loss functions. In this case, however, there are no conclusions that one can draw when the misspecified quadratic loss function is employed. Neither the Bayes nor the CE method under quadratic loss performed very well.

From the above study, there can be a significant gain to taking estimation risk into account when the loss function is specified correctly. Even when the loss function is misspecified as a quadratic, there is still a large gain to incorporating estimation risk as long as the true loss function is symmetric. However, as is clear here and as previously noted in Varian's (1975) study, when the loss function is not symmetric, then the quadratic approximation may not perform well.

Control Problem with Multiple Controls.

In the context of a single equation regression model, Zellner and Geisel examine the effect of estimation risk in a control problem with a single target. Bowman and Laporte (1972) examine a somewhat more general control problem where the underlying model is a linear system of recursive equations. With a single policy instrument, the objective is to minimize expected loss, where the loss depends on multiple targets. Although they consider this problem in a very general setting, we will report here several of their findings for a specific application.

In a specialized version, their loss function is given as:

$$L = w_I(I-a_I)^2 + w_U(U-a_U)^2, \tag{25}$$

where I and U respectively denote the inflation and unemployment rates with corresponding targets a_I and a_U both set equal to zero. The parameters w_I and w_U are the weights associated with these two objectives. The data for this problem were generated from two versions of the Saint Louis Model (Bowman and Laporte (1972; p. 431)). Model I (MI) is characterized by a higher degree of estimation uncertainty in the unemployment equation (higher standard errors) than Model II (MII). Employing a diffuse prior specification, Bowman and Laporte compare the parameter certainty equivalent (CE) to the Bayes solution for various weights in the loss function. This comparison illustrates the determinants of the extent to which expected loss can be reduced by incorporating estimation risk. However, for the purpose of controlling unemployment and inflation, the loss function in (25) is questionable.[12]

Table 2.3 below reports several of the findings of this study, where the unemployment weight, W_u, is normalized to unity.[13] From this table, as expected,the certainty equivalent method has a smaller relative expected loss in MII relative to MI. Intuitively, this result follows because there is a lower degree of estimation risk in MII than in MI. Second, with respect to the inflation weight, w_I, it is clear

11. This table is taken from Tables II(a) and II(b) in Zellner and Geisel (1968; p. 276).

12. One difficulty with this loss function is that it is symmetric. As in Varian's (1975) study, an asymmetric loss function would seem more appropriate. Bowman and Laporte state that they resolve this difficulty by constraining the loss function. They argue that in so doing, to keep loss constant on any level, an increase in the inflation rate must be accompanied by a decrease in unemployment. Although this tradeoff is reasonable, it would seem preferable to postulate and justify an asymmetric loss function in the first place. Moreover, the problem is not only that the symmetric loss function imposes the same penalty for overshooting as for undershooting a target. Rather, it is unclear why there is any penalty for undershooting, a target in this context. This was not considered by Bowman and Laporte.

Comparison of Expected Losses
for the C.E. and Bayes' Solutions

Inflation Weight	Ratio of Expected Losses: C.E./Bayes
$w_I = 0.0$	MI:52.060 MII: 1.126
$w_I = 0.5$	MI: 1.001 MII: 1.067

Table 2.3

that the certainty equivalent solution has the highest relative expected loss (52.060) in MI when $w_I = 0$. Intuitively, this loss structure places the most weight on the target whose associated variable (unemployment) has the highest degree of uncertainty. In other words, not only is the degree of estimation uncertainty high, but the sensitivity to estimation uncertainty (with $w_I = 0$) is also high.[14]

In all of these single period decision applications, we have first seen that the problem of estimating unknown parameters should not be separated from the ultimate decision problem. Indeed, it is precisely this separation that typically results in estimation risk being ignored. Secondly, the impact of estimation risk is greatest when the degree of and sensitivity to estimation risk is high. In the next section, we will continue to explore these issues in multiperiod optimization problems. Here, we will find an important learning effect that plays a crucial role in determining the impact of estimation risk

3. Multiperiod Optimization Problems

In this section, we will survey two papers that examine the impact of estimation risk in a multiperiod context. The material surveyed in this section is not intended to show theoretically how to solve general multiple period problems. Chow (1973) and (1976) has provided such theoretical guidance. Our objective in this section is

13. These results were taken from Table II of Bowman and Laporte (1972, p. 433.).

14. The sensitivity to estimation risk is important not only in the Bowman and Laporte application, but also in other contexts. Klein (1978) compared the Bayes' with several certainty equivalent solutions, where the decision was to estimate the independent variables coefficient, β, in a regression model with first order serial correlation in the errors. Here, the certainty equivalent estimates of β, $\hat{\beta}$, were based on estimates, $\hat{\rho}$, of the serial correlation coefficient ρ, i.e., $\hat{\beta} = \beta(\hat{\rho})$. To characterize the sensitivity of estimation risk for ρ, two models were considered. In Model I, the independent variable was exogenous, while in Model II it was a lagged endogenous variable. Since it is in some sense more crucial to account for autocorrelation in Model II than in Model I, the sensitivity to estimation risk is greatest in Model II. As in the Bowman and Laporte study, the certainty equivalent solutions performed the worst (in terms of average mean-squared error) when the

to illustrate several of the effects of estimation risk that persist in multiperiod optimization problems as well.[15]

Regression - Control Problem

Prescott (1972) analytically and numerically examines the impact of estimation risk in a regression-control setting. The model is given by:

$$\tilde{y}_t = \beta x_t + \tilde{u}_t \,, \tag{26}$$

where $t = 1,\ldots,T$, β is a parameter, whose value is unknown, x_t is the control, and $\tilde{u}_t$, is an i.i.d. normal error term with mean zero and known variance σ^2. Prescott assumes that the prior distribution for β at $t = 1$ is normal with mean m_1 and precision (the reciprocal of the variance) h_1. Consequently, with the model in (26), the prior is updated over time such that at time t, the revised prior is normal with mean and precision parameters given respectively as:

$$m_t = (m_{t-1}h_{t-1}+x_{t-1}y_{t-1})/h_t \tag{27}$$

and

$$h_t = h_{t-1} + x_{t-1}^2$$

Prescott also assumes that the control, x_t, is constrained such that $x_t \leqslant K \cdot h_t$, where K is a finite. To complete the description of this decision problem, the loss function is the additively separable quadratic loss function:

$$L \equiv \sum_{t=1}^{T} (y_t - a_t)^2, \tag{28}$$

where a_t is the desired target for y_t

For the specification in (26)-(27) and a class of loss functions that includes the special case in (28), Prescott obtains several theoretical results. With $|S_t| \equiv |m_t h_t^{1/2}|$ as an informational measure (S_t is essentially a t-ratio), Prescott shows that the expected loss is decreasing in $|S_t|$. As expected, it is always desirable to have more rather than less information. Prescott also shows that in absolute magnitude, the optimal decision exceeds that which minimizes expected loss in the current period. Intuitively, from (27), a larger setting of the control variable will decrease the estimation risk on β (by increasing the precision) in subsequent periods. Consequently, since the optimal decision reflects the effects of this learning about the value of β, it exceeds in absolute magnitude the current minimum expected loss decision.

To provide additional insight into the role of estimation risk, Prescott also examines a numerical example for which he compares three decision rules. The first of

---

sensitivity to estimation risk was high.

15. In addition to the papers summarized here, see also, for example, Albright (1977), Barry

these, which we will term the modified parameter certainty equivalent (MCE) rule, is defined by:

$$x_t^{MCE} = \begin{cases} a_t/m_t \text{ if } |S_t| \equiv |m_t h_t|^{1/2} > 1 \\ 0 \qquad \textit{otherwise.} \end{cases} \tag{29}$$

The motivation behind this rule can be seen by examining the parameter certainty equivalent (CE) rule. For the CE rule, let m_t estimate β and replace β by m_t in the loss function (thereby ignoring estimation risk). The CE control setting is then given by:

$$x_t^{CE} = a_t/m_t. \tag{30}$$

Since this rule ignores estimation risk, Prescott shows that it can be modified as in (29) to reduce the expected loss.

The second decision rule is termed Sequential Updating (SU). This rule is the myopic one which minimizes expected loss in the current period. Since the expectation is taken over the updated predictive distribution for y_t in the current period, estimation risk is taken into account. Using this rule, the control setting is given by:

$$x_t^{SU} = a_t m_t/(m_t^2+1/h_t). \tag{31}$$

Before continuing, it is interesting to note how the SU and CE rules compare with each other. From (30) and (31), in absolute magnitude, the SU control is less than the CE control:

$$|x_t^{CE}| - |x_t^{SU}| = |a_t/m_t|[1-c] > 0, \tag{32}$$

where

$$c \equiv 1/[1+1/(m_t^2 h_t)].$$

Intuitively, because of estimation risk, the SU rule is more conservative than the CE rule and sets a control setting that is smaller in absolute value. Moreover, the difference between two rules, as shown in (32), decreases as $m_t^2 h_t$ increases. This result becomes intuitive when it is recognized that $m_t^2 h_t$ (also Prescott's informational measure) is essentially a squared t-statistic.

The third decision rule is the optimal one, where the vector of control settings, x_t, $t = 1,\ldots, T$, is chosen to minimize the expected value of the multiple period expected loss function in (28). As in the SU rule, this rule clearly takes estimation risk into account. However, unlike the SU rule, the optimal rule also incorporates experimentation. Here, we are concerned not only with expected loss in the current period, but also in a control setting that will increase our knowledge (precision) of β for subsequent periods. The impact of the control setting on the precision is shown in (26).

Table 2.5 below shows the first period control for these three rules, as functions of $|S_1|$ and the horizon length, T.[16] The targets for all periods are 1.0.

Values Of First Period Control Settings:
All Targets Equal 1.0

			Optimal		
$\lvert S_1 \rvert$	MCE	SU	$T = 2$	$T = 4$	$T = 6$
.2	0.00	.19	.40	.69	.80
1.0	0.00	.50	.52	.58	.67
2.0	.50	.40	.41	.41	.42
4.0	.25	.24	.24	.24	.24

Table 2.5

From this table, it can be seen that there are several effects of experimentation. First, as expected, experimentation becomes more important as the horizon length, T, increases. Consequently, the optimal control setting is an increasing function of T (from (26), a larger control setting increases the precision). Second, the optimal control is smaller for high values of $|S_1|$ relative to low values. Intuitively, experimentation becomes less important as our knowledge ($|S_1|$) increases. Third, as a result of experimentation, the optimal control is never less than the SU control. Finally, and as expected, all decision rules are very similar when $|S_1|$ is high (a low degree of estimation risk).

The expected losses for the MCE and SU rules, as percentages of the minimum expected loss, are shown in Table 2.6.[17]

(1976), Chow (1973, 1976), Prescott (1971), and Zellner (1971, Ch. 11).

16. This table is taken from Table II in Prescott (1973; p. 1052).

17. This table is taken from Table III in Prescott (1972; p. 1053).

Expected Losses as Percentages of the Minimum:
All Targets Equal 1.0

$\lvert S_1 \rvert$	MCE			SU		
	$T = 2$	$T = 4$	$T = 6$	$= 2$	$T = 4$	$T = 6$
.2	104	111	118	101	106	112
1.0	134	136	140	100	101	102
2.0	104	104	104	100	100	100
4.0	100	100	100	100	100	100

Table 2.6

From this table, it is first clear that these relative expected losses increase with the horizon length. Intuitively, as the horizon increases, it is more costly to ignore experimentation. Second, the SU rule significantly outperforms the MCE rule and is nearly optimal over a wide range. In other words, it can be very costly to ignore estimation risk. Prescott shows that this dominance of the SU over the MCE becomes even more pronounced as the targets are increased. Intuitively, with a larger target, the control setting will increase, thereby magnifying the uncertainty due to estimation isk.

Large (Potential) Losses for Ignoring Estimation Risk

The example just considered suggests that it is important to account for estimation risk, Harkema (1975) analytically shows that the loss to ignoring estimation risk is not only finitely large, but can be infinite! Harkema considers a model identical to Prescott's in (24):

$$\tilde{y}_t = \beta x_t + \tilde{u}_t, \tag{33}$$

where $t = -N, \ldots, 0, 1, 2$, and x_t, $t = 1, 2$, is the control. The disturbance, $\tilde{u}_t$, is i.i.d normal with mean zero and known variance, σ^2. As in Prescott's example, the loss function is quadratic:

$$L = \sum_{t=1}^{2} (y_t - a_t)^2. \tag{34}$$

Before period t, $t = 1, 2$, the prior for β is taken to be normal with mean m_t and precision h_t:

$$m_t = \sum_{i=-N}^{t-1} x_i y_i \Big/ \sum_{i=-N}^{t-1} x_i^2 \tag{35}$$

$$h_t = \sum_{i=-N}^{t-1} x_i^2/\sigma^2.$$

For the parameter certainty equivalent (CE) rule the control setting is given as in (30) by:

$$X_t^{CE} = a_t/m_t,\ m_t \neq 0,\ t = 1,\ 2. \tag{36}$$

To determine the expected loss for this rule, note that the predictive distribution for $\tilde{y}_2$ (conditioned on all variables for $t < 2$) is normal with mean $x_2 m_2$ and variance $a_2^2/(h_2 m_2^2) + \sigma^2$. Therefore, since from (35), $E(\tilde{y}_2 - a_2)^2$ is the variance of $\tilde{y}_2$, Harkema shows that the expected loss of the CE rule (conditioned on $\tilde{y}_1$) is:

$$E[L^{CE}|y_1; x_2 = x_2^{CE}] = a_2^2/(h_2 m_2^2) + \sigma^2 + (y_1 - a_1)^2. \tag{37}$$

To calculate the unconditional expected loss of the CE rule, we must take the expectation of the expression in (37). This expectation is taken with respect to the predictive distribution of $\tilde{y}_1$, which is normal with mean $m_1 x_1^{CE}$, and variance $a_1^2/(h_1 m_1^2) + \sigma^2$. Recalling from (35) that m_2 in (37) depends on y_1, Harkema shows that this expectation is infinite. It should be noted that Harkema obtains this result for the certainty equivalent rule, as opposed to the modified certainty equivalent rule examined by Prescott (1972).[18]

Harkema further shows that the expected loss for the sequential updating (SU) rule (as discussed in (31)) is finite. Consequently, expected loss for the fully optimal rule must be finite. Therefore, in this simplified but important decision problem, it can be very costly to ignore estimation risk. Indeed the expected cost to ignoring such risk (employing the CE rule rather than a Bayesian procedure) can be infinite.

4. The Effect of Estimation Risk on the Predictive Distribution

Recall that in the mainstream von Neumann-Morgenstern-Savage expected utility paradigm being considered, a decision maker's utility function is defined (in part) over the random variables $\tilde{\mathbf{y}}$, whose probability distribution $f(\tilde{\mathbf{y}}|\boldsymbol{\theta})$, is not completely known. This distribution uncertainty has been defined earlier to be estimation risk. Also, as noted earlier, the predictive distribution of $\tilde{\mathbf{y}}$ reflects estimation risk and is the appropriate distribution to use in decision making. Thus, it is important to examine the effect of estimation risk on the predictive distribution

18. It can be shown for the specification in (33)-(35) that while expected loss for the certainty equivalent rule is infinite, expected loss for the modified certainty equivalent rule is finite.

in a general context, free from nuances of any particular decision problem. We now survey the literature that examines the impact of estimation risk on the predictive distribution in a very general setting.

To investigate this issue, it is appropriate to distinguish, and analyze, two basically distinct cases of distributional uncertainty or estimation risk. The first case is the parametric one in which the functional form, $f(\mathbf{y}|\boldsymbol{\theta})$, of the probability distribution of $\tilde{\mathbf{y}}$ is known. However, the parameter vector $\boldsymbol{\theta}$, which characterizes this distribution, is unknown. For example, f might be normal with parameter vector $\boldsymbol{\theta}$ consisting of the unknown elements of a mean vector and a variance-covariance matrix. The second case is the nonparametric one in which the functional form f is itself unknown.

We begin with the parametric case by examining whether or not it is appropriate to base decisions on the estimate of the unknown parameter vector $\boldsymbol{\theta}$. Utility, for a given decision, depends on a vector of random variables, $\tilde{\mathbf{y}}$, with distribution $f(\tilde{\mathbf{y}}|\boldsymbol{\theta})$. In determining the "optimal" decision, the certainty equivalent (CE) approach uses, as noted earlier, the distribution $f(\mathbf{y}|\hat{\boldsymbol{\theta}})$, where the value of the unknown parameter $\boldsymbol{\theta}$ is replaced by a point estimate $\hat{\boldsymbol{\theta}}$. Klein et al. (1978) obtain necessary and sufficient conditions under which the traditional CE approach is optimal (i.e. equivalent to the Bayes' approach). Thus, they provide conditions under which it is necessary to make a "special" correction for estimation risk in the parametric case.

To resolve this question, assume that the functional form of the estimator for $\boldsymbol{\theta}$ does not depend on the decision-maker's utility function. It seems that this assumption is made implicitly in most applications of the certainty equivalent approach for two reasons. First, the decision-maker's utility function, *U*, is not (directly) a function of $\boldsymbol{\theta}$. Perhaps as a result, estimators are typically proposed for use in decision problems without regard to the ultimate decision problem. Second, since the estimate $\hat{\boldsymbol{\theta}}$ is often supplied by someone far removed from the decision process, the form of the estimator will of necessity not depend on *U*.

With the above restriction, decisions can be based on $f(\mathbf{y}|\hat{\boldsymbol{\theta}})$ if and only if there exists $\hat{\boldsymbol{\theta}}$ such that:

$$f(\mathbf{y}|\hat{\boldsymbol{\theta}}) = g(\mathbf{y}) \tag{38}$$

where g is the predictive distribution for $\tilde{\mathbf{y}}$. The estimate $\hat{\boldsymbol{\theta}}$ is permitted to depend on prior information. For example, $\hat{\boldsymbol{\theta}}$ might be a posterior mean or a constrained maximum-likelihood estimate. However, the use of $\hat{\boldsymbol{\theta}}$ in decision-making has not in practice depended on any particular prior distribution. Therefore, permitting $\hat{\boldsymbol{\theta}}$ to depend on the prior distribution the question is to determine when (38) holds for all prior distributions of $\boldsymbol{\theta}$. When there exists $\hat{\boldsymbol{\theta}}$ such that (38) is satisfied, Klein et al. term $\hat{\boldsymbol{\theta}}$ a proper summary value. Under conditions that hold for most, if not all probability distributions in common use, Klein et al. (1978; Theorem 1) show that a proper summary value exists if and only if $f(\mathbf{y}|\boldsymbol{\theta})$ can be written in a form that satisfies the separability condition:

$$f(\mathbf{y}|\boldsymbol{\theta}) = \sum_{i=1}^{r} h_1^i(\boldsymbol{\theta})h_2^i(\mathbf{y}) + t(\mathbf{y}), \tag{39}$$

where, with n as the dimension of $\boldsymbol{\theta}$, r is any integer that does not exceed n. The functions h_1^i, h_2^i, and t are any functions such that the set $\{h_1^i(\theta), i=1,...,r\}$ is convex, $h_2^i(\mathbf{y})$ integrates to zero for $i = 1,...,r$, and $t(\mathbf{y})$ integrates to one.

The separability condition above has an intuitive interpretation. Since utility is defined (in part) over $\mathbf{y}$ and not $\boldsymbol{\theta}$, $\hat{\boldsymbol{\theta}}$ will be a proper summary value if the estimation problem can in some sense be separated from the ultimate decision problem. In such circumstances, it is valid to estimate $\boldsymbol{\theta}$ without taking into account how the estimate will be used.

As is apparent and can be shown formally, few distributions satisfy the separability condition in (38). Accordingly, in a parametric framework, it is necessary to make a special correction for estimation risk. The distribution obtained, by replacing $\boldsymbol{\theta}$ with $\hat{\boldsymbol{\theta}}$ is seldom the predictive distribution.

There is one, and probably only one, frequently employed distribution, the multinomial, which satisfies the separability condition in (38) and is therefore worth noting.[19] Howard et al. (1972) employ this distribution to study the hurricane seeding problem. In this study, Howard et al. partition wind velocity into five categories, and associate an amount of damage with each category. The (multinomial) probabilities for these categories depend on whether or not the hurricane is seeded. To make an optimal decision, Howard et al. estimate these probabilities and calculate and compare expected losses for the decision to seed or note to seed. In this instance, decisions can legitimately be based on parameter (cell probability) estimates. The separability result of Klein et al. ensures that it is not necessary to make a separate correction for estimation risk in this case.

Other than the multinomial distribution, there do not appear to be any commonly employed distributions that satisfy (39). In otherwords, proper summary values seldom exist. Moreover, satisfactory approximations to these summary values are typically difficult to obtain.[20]

Turning to the nonparametric case, we note that unlike the parametric case, the literature dealing with the nonparametric case, as it pertains to estimation risk and optimal choice under uncertainty, is indeed very sparse. It essentially consists of three papers by Bawa (1977a, 1979, 1979b) that are based on recent fundamental papers on nonparametric Bayesian inference by Ferguson (1973, 1974). This sparsity has perhaps been due to difficulty in choosing an appropriate prior distribution and to analytical difficulties in deriving the posterior and predictive distributions of returns for a sufficiently general family of distributions.

As stated above, one difficulty in the nonparametric context lies in choosing a

19. For purposes of illustration, consider the special case of a binomial distribution. Let $\tilde{y}$ be distributed as binomial such that: $P(\tilde{y}=1) = \theta$, $P(\tilde{y}=0) = 1 - \theta$. Then, letting $I_j(y)$ be an indicator function, $j = 0, 1$, such that $I_j(k) = 1$ if $j = k$ and 0 otherwise:

$$\begin{aligned} f(y|\theta) &= I_1(y)\theta + I_0(y)(1-\theta) \\ &= [I_1(y) - I_0(y)]\theta + I_0(y), \end{aligned}$$

which with $h_1(\theta) = \theta$, $h_2(y) = I_1(y) - I_2(y)$, and $t(y) = I_0(y)$, satisfies (38).

20. Klein (1978) provides a counter example to the supposition that as the estimator of $\boldsymbol{\theta}$, $\hat{\boldsymbol{\theta}}$ improves in some reasonable and well defined sense, the decision based on $\hat{\boldsymbol{\theta}}$ uniformly converges to the Bayes decision.

specification of prior information. Indeed, it is not altogether clear over what parameter space to define the prior, because we are essentially dealing with a case not characterized by a finite number of parameters. To choose a specification of prior information, Ferguson (1973) and Bawa (1977a) note that it is important that the class of priors have the following desirable properties:

(i) The class of priors is rich enough to incorporate varying degrees of prior information (i.e., the support of the prior is large with respect to some suitable topology on the space of all probability measures).

(ii) The posterior distribution is manageable analytically.

(iii) The class of priors is parameterized in a manner that allows for direct incorporation and interpretation or prior information.

To formulate a prior satisfying these criteria, we might, as in the hurricane example discussed above, begin by considering a multinomial distribution for the random variable of interest, $\tilde{y}$.[21] We would allow the random variable to belong to K disjoint categories (intervals) that cover the entire sample space (real line). Then, we could proceed by associating probabilities, $P_1, \ldots, P_K$ (with $P_K \equiv 1 - \sum_{k=1}^{K-1} P_i$) to these categories. This specification has a nonparametric flavor in that $K - 1$ cells are being assigned $K - 1$ probabilities that are arbitrary except that their sum over all k cells cannot exceed one.

It is now natural to assign a Dirichlet prior distribution to these probabilities. Since this distribution is conjugate to the multinomial,[22] the posterior distribution is also a Dirichlet distribution; criterion (ii) above is immediately satisfied. Furthermore, the multinomial-Dirichlet specification also provides for a direct interpretation of prior information [criterion (iii)]. The Dirichlet distribution is characterized by K parameters, $\alpha_1, \ldots, d_K$, where α_k is associated with cell k, $k = 1,\ldots,K$. These K parameters, when properly normalized, can conveniently be interpreted as prior probabilities. Specializing Ferguson's (1973) argument to this case, it can be shown that the prior probability that $\tilde{y}$ is in cell or category $\mathbf{C}_k$ is given by:

$$P_0(\tilde{y} \in \mathbf{C}_k) = \alpha_k / \sum_{i=1}^{K} \alpha_i. \tag{40}$$

Unfortunately, this multinomial-Dirichlet specification is not very rich so that criterion (i) is not satisfied. With an arbitrarily fixed partition of the sample space (i.e., $\mathbf{C}_k$, $k = 1,\ldots,K$), we are implicitly assigning prior probability one that $\tilde{y}$ has a particular type of distribution. To retain the desirable features of the multinomial-Dirichlet specification and satisfy criterion (i) above, Ferguson (1973) extends the multinomial-Dirichlet framework. Rather than considering any given and arbitrary partition, Ferguson considers all possible partitions. For each and every partition, we have a multinomial distribution for which a Dirichlet prior distribution is assigned. Ferguson uses the term, Dirichlet *process* prior in referring

21. Ferguson (1973) notes that all results presented for this nonparametric case can easily be extended when $\tilde{y}$ is a vector of random variables.

22. With $K = 2$ cells or possibilities, the multinomial distribution specializes to binomial and the Dirichlet to the beta, the well known conjugate distribution for the binomial.

to the set of Dirichlet prior distributions assigned in this manner.

This Dirichlet process prior is intuitively "rich" in terms of criterion (i) above, a point that we will clarify and qualify below. As should be expected, this process retains the desirable features of the less general multinomial-Dirichlet formulation. The posterior distribution has a convenient analytical form in that it is also (not surprisingly) a Dirichlet process. In otherwords, the Dirichlet process may be viewed as a conjugate family. Moreover, as for a given Dirichlet distribution, the Dirichlet process admits a convenient interpretation of information. For the Dirichlet process, we must now conceptually consider all possible $\boldsymbol{\alpha}$ parameters of the Dirichlet distributions. Formally, $\boldsymbol{\alpha}$ must now be interpreted as a measure. In the same spirit of (40), Ferguson shows that under the appropriate normalization, $\boldsymbol{\alpha}$ is a probability measure. For any set **C**, with assigned measure $\alpha(\mathbf{C})$, Ferguson shows (analogous to (40)) that:

$$P_0(\tilde{y} \in \mathbf{C}) = \boldsymbol{\alpha}(\mathbf{C})/\boldsymbol{\alpha}(\mathbf{R}), \tag{41}$$

where $P_0(\tilde{y} \in \mathbf{C})$ denotes the prior probability that the random variable is in set **C** and $\boldsymbol{\alpha}(\mathbf{R})$ is the measure for the entire space.

Given that the posterior distribution is a Dirichlet process with prior probabilities interpreted as in (40), the predictive distribution function is given as:[23]

$$G(y) \equiv E(F) = P_n F_0(y) + (1-P_n)F_n(y), \tag{42}$$

where E denotes an expectation over the posterior (process) distribution, $F_0(y) = \boldsymbol{\alpha}[(-\infty,y)]/\boldsymbol{\alpha}(\mathbf{R})$ is the prior guess of $F(y)$, $F_n(y)$ is the empirical distribution function for a random sample of size n, and **R** denotes the real line. The quantities P_n and $1-p_n$ are the weights attached to the prior guess and the empirical distribution function, where

$$P_n \equiv \boldsymbol{\alpha}(\mathbf{R})/[\boldsymbol{\alpha}(\mathbf{R})+n]. \tag{43}$$

As is to be intuitively expected, the weights in (42) depend on the relative importance of prior and sample information. When the sample size, n, decreases the weight on prior guess of F increases. On the other hand, when n increases the weight on the empirical distribution F_n increases.

It should be noted that although the Dirichlet process has many desirable features, it has an undesirable discreteness property. Namely, this process places probability one on the true distribution being discrete [Ferguson (1973), Blackwell (1973)]. Nevertheless, when $n \to \infty$ in (42), $P_n \to 0$ and $F_n \to F$, implying that $G \to F$ [see Ferguson (1973, p. 223)]. In otherwords, the predictive distribution converges (as the sample size increases) to the true distribution F. This result provides one illustration of the "richness" of the Dirichlet process prior (criterion (i) above). This convergence result would not follow if this class were in some sense

23. Ferguson (1973) derived the estimate of F, $\hat{F}$ by minimizing the expected value of the quadratic loss $(\hat{F}-F)^2$. The solution to this minimization is $\hat{F} = E(F)$ as given in (41) where the expectation is taken over the posterior. Bawa (1977a, 1979a) notes that $\hat{F} = E(F)$ is actually the predictive distribution function $G(y)$, required for decision making.

too restrictive.[24] One intuitive implication of this result is that the effect of estimation risk disappears when the sample size becomes sufficiently large. In contrast, in the parametric context it is necessary to assume that the true distribution belongs to a given family (e.g., normal). If this assumption is incorrect, then estimation risk need not disappear even for infinite sample sizes.

It is also of particular interest in (42)-(43) to examine the special case in which $\boldsymbol{\alpha}$ tends to zero (the "noninformative" Dirchilet process prior).[25] From (42)-(43), it follows that the predictive distribution function, $G(y)$, converges to the empirical distribution function, $F_n(Y)$, as $\alpha \rightarrow 0$. Interestingly, unlike the parametric case (Klein et al. (1978)), for the "noninformative"-nonparametric case, the traditional method of using the distribution functions is invariant to estimation risk: Estimation risk is indeed present, but is properly incorporated directly into the empirical distribution function; no further "special" corrections are needed.[26]

To summarize, we have seen that whether or not it is necessary to make a correction for estimation risk depends crucially on the prior information. With no information on the functional form of the distribution of interest (a nonparametric setting) and minimal prior information, the traditionally used empirical distribution function is appropriate for decision making. With some information on the functional form of the distribution of interest (a parametric setting), it will usually be necessary to make a "special" correction for estimation risk and the traditional method of using point estimates will be generally inappropriate. These results hold for problems of optimal choice under uncertainty problems in their full generality.

5. Summary

To summarize this review, in a nonparametric context just with minimal prior information, we have seen that there is no need to make a special correction for estimation risk [Bawa (1977a, 1979a, 1979b)]. In a parametric context, which presumes more information, it is generally necessary to make such a correction [Klein et al. (1978)]. Within the parametric context, the loss to ignoring estimation risk (or the advantage to taking it into account) can be considerable, even infinite [Harkema (1975)]. When this loss is finite, its size depends, as might be expected, on the degree of estimation risk [Bowman and Laporte (1972), Klein et al. (1978), Prescott (1972), Varian (1975), and Zellner and Geisel (1968)]. This loss also depends in some sense on the sensitivity of the objective function to estimation risk [Bowman and Laporte (1972) and Klein (1978)]. Even when the

---

24. To illustrate a prior distribution that is too "restrictive" to permit this convergence, let the true distribution for $\tilde{y}$ be normal with mean zero and variance one. Assume that the marginal prior distribution for the mean places no probability inside some neighborhood of the true mean: $[-a,a]$, $a \neq 0$. Then, the predictive distribution will not converge to the true distribution.

25. For purposes of illustration, consider a particular Dirichlet distribution, the specialized Beta, for which there are two α parameters: α_1, α_2. As $\alpha_i \rightarrow 0$, $i = 1, 2$, the variance of this distribution becomes infinite. In the limit, this distribution converges to a distribution discussed by Jeffreys (1961) and employed by Zellner (1971; p. 39-40) to represent minimal information.

26. The traditional method of using the empirical distribution function in the nonparametric case involves, unlike the parametric cases, the use of an entire distribution function and not point estimates of unknown parameters. This is indeed in keeping with the spirit of the discussion in the previous chapter that in the presence of estimation risk, the entire distribution functions, and not simply point estimates, should be used.

objective function is misspecified, the advantage to taking estimation risk into account can be considerable [Zellner and Geisel (1968)].

In conclusion, the effect of estimation risk can be large and there can be a considerable gain to taking it into account. Accordingly, it is worthwhile to further examine the impact of estimation risk in a decision problem that is of inherent interest and that is representative of a wide range of decision problems. The portfolio choice problem is such a decision problem, and it is to this problem that we turn in the succeeding chapters.

CHAPTER 3

ESTIMATION RISK AND OPTIMAL PORTFOLIO CHOICE: A SELECTIVE REVIEW

1. Introduction

In this chapter, we selectively review the literature on portfolio choice with focus on the issue of estimation risk. In Section 2, we provide a brief overview of portfolio theory, its use in the development of capital asset pricing models, and note its importance in the modern development of financial economics. We note in Section 3 that the issue of estimation risk was recognized early in the portfolio choice literature and selectively review attempts to assess its role in portfolio theory.

In Section 4, first we discuss and examine sources of information for the predictive distribution of security returns. Accordingly, in the portfolio context, we discuss the appropriate model for the observations and the types of prior information that one could employ for the parameters of the model. Second, in this section we review the literature that attempts explicitly to take estimation risk into account in the portfolio choice problem. In so doing, we will find that while important and substantial progress has been made, even in a single period context there are still many unresolved questions.

2. Portfolio Choice Under Uncertainty

The portfolio choice problem is a canonical representation of an important special class of problems involving choice under uncertainty. The decision-maker's choice set consists of not only the basic investment choices available in the market, but also all portfolios (i.e., convex linear combinations) of these basic choices.[1] In the context of single period decision problems, which are the focus of this book,[2] the problem is to allocate the initial wealth among the set of feasible portfolios so as to maximize the expected utility of final wealth. Let $\tilde{\mathbf{R}}$, with $\tilde{\mathbf{R}}' \equiv (\tilde{R}_1, \tilde{R}_2, \ldots, \tilde{R}_n)$, denote the random rates of return on the basic

1. There are several economic decision problems wherein the decision problem is an allocation problem and the choice set is a convex set of alternative probability distributions. The results obtained in this book for the portfolio choice problem are clearly germane to these decision problems as well.

2. The portfolio choice problem has also been posed and solved in a multiperiod context, as an investment problem or as part of a consumption investment problem. See, for example Hakansson (1970), Fama (1970) for a discrete time formulation and Merton (1971) for a continuous time formulation. Apart from the work of Winkler and Barry (1975) which addressed this issue, there has been, to our knowledge, no satisfactory resolution of the estimation risk issue in the multiperiod framework for general classes of utility functions. The results in the book will hopefully motivate research on the estimation risk issue in the multiperiod portfolio problem.

securities,[3] and $\mathbf{X}$, with $\mathbf{X}' \equiv (X_1, X_2, \ldots, X_m)$, denote the proportional allocations of initial wealth invested in the basic securities.[4] Then, optimal portfolio choice is determined by choosing $\mathbf{X}$, the decision vector, as a solution to the following optimization problem:

$$\max_{\mathbf{X} \in \mathbf{C}} E_{\tilde{\mathbf{R}}} U[w_o(1+\mathbf{X}'\tilde{\mathbf{R}})], \tag{1}$$

where U denotes the decision-maker's utility function, $E_{\tilde{\mathbf{R}}}$ denotes the expectation (of the utility function) over the joint distribution f of the random vector $\tilde{\mathbf{R}}$ (the rate of return vector), and $\mathbf{C}$ is the set of feasible allocations. It is commonly assumed that f is known to the individual decision maker.

If a riskless asset exists, i.e., an asset that yields a certain (or riskless) one period rate of return, then the optimal portfolio is determined as follows:

$$\max_{\bar{\mathbf{X}} \in \mathbf{C}} E\{U[w_o(1+X_oR_f+\mathbf{X}'\tilde{\mathbf{R}})]\}, \tag{1'}$$

where $\bar{\mathbf{X}}$ represents a portfolio including investment in the riskless asset yielding known return R_F: $\bar{\mathbf{X}}' \equiv (X_o, \mathbf{X}')$.

Optimal portfolio choice, a solution to (1) or (1') as appropriate, may be viewed as being determined in a two-stage process. In the first stage, one obtains the admissible set of portfolios. This set is derived from the feasible set, $\mathbf{C}$, by deleting from $\mathbf{C}$ all alternatives or allocations that are not candidates for the optimal choice. These allocations are excluded on the basis of utility function restrictions that follow from prevalent and appealing modes of economic behavior. The admissible set of portfolios so generated is useful in two respects. First, this set can be viewed as being based on certain acceptable properties of a given individual's utility function. As such, without completely specifying the utility function, this set eliminates inferior alternatives. Second, while individuals may differ, it may be the case that they have utility functions belonging to a certain class. The admissible set corresponding to this class can be viewed as *containing* the optimal choices for all of these individuals. Once this set is determined, the optimal portfolio choice for an individual can then be derived in the second stage from among the smaller set of admissible portfolios.

Markowitz's (1952) seminal contribution to portfolio theory was to suggest a rigorous approach to portfolio theory and to propose, for risk averse investors, a mean-variance selection rule for determining the admissible set of portfolios. In this rule, to obtain the admissible set from among the feasible set of portfolios, first discard portfolios with a lower mean return and a higher variance than a

---

3. The rate of return R_i on asset i includes both price appreciation and dividends, i.e.,

$$R_i = \frac{(P_{1i}-P_{0i}) + Div_i}{P_{0i}}.$$

Generally taxes are neglected. Alternatively, R_i could be defined to be after-tax rate of return.

4. A negative X_i represents a short sale, that is, a promise to deliver asset i at the end of the period at the then current market price.

member of the feasible set. Second, if two feasible portfolios have the same mean return, discard one if its variance exceeds that of the other. Third, if two feasible portfolios have the same variance, discard one if its mean return is less than that of the other. Formally, to obtain the admissible set under this rule, let $\boldsymbol{\mu}$ denote the mean vector and $\boldsymbol{\Sigma}$ the variance-covariance matrix of the uncertain rates of return, $\tilde{\mathbf{R}}$. Consequently, the mean return on the risky portion of the portfolio is given by $\mathbf{X}'\boldsymbol{\mu}$, and the portfolio variance is given by $\mathbf{X}'\boldsymbol{\Sigma}\mathbf{X}$. Then, letting $\bar{\mu}$ denote a given value of $\mathbf{X}'\boldsymbol{\mu}$, the admissible set is given as parametric solutions over $\bar{\mu}$ in the following optimization problem:[5]

$$\min_{\mathbf{X}\in C} \mathbf{X}'\boldsymbol{\Sigma}\mathbf{X}, \qquad s.t.\ \mathbf{X}'\boldsymbol{\mu} \geqslant \bar{\mu}. \tag{2}$$

A major contribution of Markowitz in 1952 was to examine and reject the use of maximum expected return (mean) as a criterion for choice among alternatives, and to show the need for considering a risk measure. He proposed the use of variance as a risk measure, and hence the mean-variance portfolio selection rule to obtain the admissible portfolios. Later, Markowitz (1959) and Tobin (1958, 1964) noted that under certain conditions the mean-variance selection rule given by (2) does indeed provide the admissible set of portfolios for all risk averse investors [i.e., contains the optimal solutions to (1), (1') for all utility functions U that are monotonically increasing and concave]. The required conditions or assumptions are either that the joint probability distribution of security rates of return is multivariate normal or that the utility function of all investors is quadratic. The second condition may be deemed unacceptable, as the quadratic utility function has the unsatisfactory property of increasing absolute risk aversion [absolute risk aversion being as defined by Arrow (1965) and Pratt (1964)]. Accordingly, the first condition provides the rationale for the use of mean-variance selection rules within the von Neumann-Morgenstern expected utility paradigm.[6]

However, as noted in Fama (1965a) in reference to symmetric stable distributions and Bawa (1975, 1977b), it is possible to weaken this condition by considering the probability distribution restricted to a location-scale family.[7] This family includes the multivariate normal, Student-*t*, and stable distributions as special cases.[8] Then, using the Stochastic Dominance apparatus [Bawa (1975)], one can apply the same type of analysis as in the mean-variance case, replacing mean and

5. This provides the admissible set of portfolios of risky assets only. If a riskless asset is assumed to exist and one can borrow or lend freely at this rate, the admissible portfolios (in the mean variance framework) of all assets provide the well known mutual fund separation property. For a detailed discussion of this, including references to the literature, see Chapter 7 of this book.

6. See Bawa, Goroff, and Whitt (1978) for references to the literature on an asymptotic justification of mean-variance selection rules.

7. For this family, for all $\mathbf{X}$, $\mathbf{X}'\mathbf{R}$ has the same distribution as: $l_{\mathbf{X}} + S_{\mathbf{X}}\tilde{Z}$, where $l_{\mathbf{X}}$ and $S_{\mathbf{X}}$ are location and scale parameters respectively that depend on $\mathbf{X}$ and $\tilde{Z}$ is a random variable whose distribution does not depend on $\mathbf{X}$.

8. For related discussions, see Fama (1965a), Press (1972), and Samuelson (1967) for discussions of symmetric stable distributions and Blattberg and Gonedes (1974) and Praetz (1972) for discussions of Student-*t* distributions.

variance with mean and scale respectively.[9]

This approach pioneered by Markowitz, may be viewed as a major breakthrough in modern finance theory and has spawned a considerable body of literature. It suggested that portfolio management, heretofore an art, might become a science with a strong foundation and susceptible to rigorous analysis. It provided an explicit role for diversification. Finally, and perhaps most importantly, its characterization of the optimal portfolio choices of individual investors led Sharpe (1964), Lintner (1965), and Mossin (1966) to develop a theory of capital market equilibrium by aggregating individuals' optimal portfolio choices and invoking market clearing conditions. The capital asset pricing model (CAPM) developed in these papers and the implied linear risk return relationship has been extensively used in finance theory, and generalized in various ways.

Given its important implications, the location-scale type analysis has been extended in a number of ways to relax its more restrictive assumptions. The extensions reflect institutional considerations (e.g., constraints on borrowing and lending and taxes), nonmarketable assets, and other constraints on portfolio choices.[10] However, a maintained assumption in most of this analysis is that individual investors know completely the probability distribution of returns; estimation risk considerations are ignored. It is to these considerations that we now turn.

3. The Recognition of Estimation Risk for the Portfolio Choice Problem

The existence of estimation risk, or "measurement error" as it is sometimes termed, for the portfolio choice problem has been well documented both in the portfolio theory and capital market equilibrium theory literature. Indeed, Markowitz (1952) recognized this problem and concluded his paper by noting:

> "To use the E-V rule in the selection of securities, we must have procedures for finding reasonable μ_i and σ_{ij} ... One suggestion as to tentative μ_i, σ_{ij} is to use the observed μ_i, σ_{ij} for some period of the past. I believe that better methods, which take into account more information can be found. I believe that what is needed is essentially a 'probabilistic' reformulation of security analysis. I will not pursue this subject here, for this is 'another story'. It is a story of which I have read only the first page of the first chapter"[11]

This succintly summarizes the estimation risk issue and yet has received scant attention in the literature in the past twenty-seven years. Indeed, Markowitz's tentative proposal to use point estimates of means and a covariance matrix has been extensively used in spite of the stringent and unattainable data requirements it

9. When no assumptions are made about the family of distribution functions, it is difficult to determine the admissible set of portfolios. Bawa, Goroff, and Whitt (1978) demonstrate that a reasonable approximation may be provided by a two parameter mean-lower partial moment rule.

10. For an excellent review of the literature on these results, see Jensen (1972a).

11. In this quote from Markowitz (1952), the E-V rule refers to the mean-variance selection rule, $\mu_i = E(\tilde{R}_i)$ and $\sigma_{ij} = Cov(\tilde{R}_i,\tilde{R}_j)$.

imposes. For a thousand security example, one would need at least a thousand observations on each security to obtain a nonsingular estimate of the covariance matrix, let alone a very precise estimate of the whole covariance structure, as would be required to evaluate precisely portfolio variance for all possible portfolio allocations.[12]

Other difficulties with the use of sample estimates have also been noted in the literature. For example, Joyce and Vogel (1970) point out that the variance estimates are sensitive to the period of data and the unit of time under consideration. Frankfurter, Phillips and Seagle (1971) consider a very simple three asset example and show that the sample admissible set could differ considerably from the true admissible set. Finally, by considering the probability distribution of the portfolio that minimizes sample variance, Dickinson (1974) shows that for a two asset example, an optimal portfolio for the sample distribution of returns would be an unreliable approximation to the optimal portfolio for the true parameter values.

In the literature that tests for the empirical implications of capital asset pricing models,[13] the problem of estimation risk is well known. It is assumed implicitly in this literature that individual investors act as if they determined their optimal portfolios by replacing the true parameter values with sample estimates. The aggregate of individuals representing the market then determines prices of assets on this basis. Miller and Scholes (1972) discuss some of the biases that can result from tests of this nature.

The problem of estimation risk is very prominent in the closely related literature on option pricing. As Black and Scholes (1972, p. 405) note:

> "One possible explanation for these findings is that the price we would compute for the option, if we knew the variance that would apply over the option period, tends to fall between the model price we actually computed and the market price. The variances computed using past data are subject to measurement error so that the spread in the distribution of estimated variances is larger than the true spread in the variances. Thus the model using noisy estimates of the variance will tend to overprice options on high variance securities and underprice options on low variance securities."

Be this as it may, the investor is still urged to use the sample estimate in place of the true variance in pricing security options (e.g., Merton, Scholes and Gladstein, (1978)). To date this prescription to a large extent reflects the state of the art in the finance literature.

As we have noted earlier, the Bayesian approach for dealing with estimation risk is to use the predictive distribution. Before we review the portfolio choice

12. To give a graphic illustration of this problem, suppose there were available 999 observations. Then while it might be possible to obtain "good" estimates of particular variance and covariance terms, it would be possible to find a portfolio with an estimated variance of zero, clearly an absurd result. This observation also applies to capital asset pricing models, where the true parameters are replaced by sample estimates based on a sample of size smaller than the total number of securities that enter the market portfolio.

literature on attempts to do this, we review the literature that attempts to minimize estimation risk and hence its effects and importance in a practical sense.

The first simplification, designed to reduce the dimensionality of the portfolio choice problem, was a simple structural model introduced by Sharpe (1963).[14] He postulates that the returns on all securities are related to each other only to the extent that they are all related to some general index of market activity, I_t:

$$\begin{aligned}
\tilde{R}_{1t} &= \alpha_1 + \beta_1 \tilde{I}_t + \tilde{\epsilon}_{1t} \\
R_{2t} &= \alpha_2 + \beta_2 \tilde{I}_t + \tilde{\epsilon}_{2t} \\
&\cdot \quad \cdot \quad \cdot \cdot \quad \cdot \\
\tilde{R}_{mt} &= \alpha_m + \beta_m \tilde{I}_t + \tilde{\epsilon}_{mt} \\
\tilde{I}_t &= \mu_M + \tilde{\epsilon}_{Mt},
\end{aligned} \tag{3}$$

where the zero mean error terms $\tilde{\epsilon}_1, \ldots, \tilde{\epsilon}_m, \tilde{\epsilon}_M$ are distributed independently of one another. The vector of means is given by

$$E\tilde{\mathbf{R}}_t \equiv \boldsymbol{\mu} = \boldsymbol{\alpha} + \boldsymbol{\beta}\mu_M \tag{4}$$

and the covariance matrix by

$$\boldsymbol{\Sigma} = \boldsymbol{\beta\beta}'\sigma_M^2 + D_{\sigma^2}, \tag{5}$$

where σ_M^2 is the variance of $\tilde{\epsilon}_{Mt}$ and D_{σ^2} represents a diagonal matrix with the variances of $\tilde{\epsilon}_{1t}$ through $\tilde{\epsilon}_{mt}$ on the diagonal.

Sharpe himself (1963, 1968) is not very explicit about how one would obtain values of the Sharpe model coefficients. By writing the Sharpe model as a multivariate regression model, it is common to estimate the parameters of this model by Ordinary Least-Squares (OLS). These estimates, which are computed either on the basis of actual sample data or on the basis of information equivalent to a given set of hypothetical sample data, represent minimum variance linear unbiased esti-

13. For a review of this literature see Jensen (1972a).

14. Not only does the model yield an evident reduction in dimensionality, but the structure of the covariance matrix also yields simple rules to compute the admissible set [see Bawa, Elton and Gruber (1978) and references therein] that do not require quadratic programming algorithms.

15. There has been some dispute in the literature concerning the extent to which this model is consistent with multivariate normality. This problem arises where I_t is interpreted as a linear combination of the m security returns. Clearly, the multivariate distribution of returns is degenerate in this case, and certainly not normal, although early writers (Fama 1968) believed the problem was due to the correlation between $\tilde{\epsilon}_M$ and the other errors. As Fama himself (1973) later pointed out, it is sufficient that just one security be excluded from consideration to correct for this anomaly. Indeed it is possible to show in this case, if we generalize the model slightly to account for a general covariance matrix of the errors, this model is *implied by* multivariate normality.

mates of the true parameter values.[15] While these estimates are not in general the true parameter values, it is widely believed (e.g., Black and Scholes 1972) that the problem of estimation risk is greatly reduced by using the Sharpe model, as opposed to estimating the distinct elements of a general covariance matrix for returns.

Indeed, it is sometimes argued that these estimates *are* the true parameter values. The argument runs as follows [e.g., Blume (1970)]: The time period for which returns are defined is somewhat arbitrary. By cutting up the the interval into successively finer segments -- from months to days to even minute by minute observations, the number of observations increases without limit and the estimates will converge in probability to the true parameter values. This would be consistent with prices that follow a geometric Brownian motion [e.g., Merton (1971)]. Unfortunately, stocks are not continuously traded, so there may be some problem in observing this process continuously. The results of Blattberg and Gonedes (1975) demonstrate that, as the unit of time decreases, the distribution of finite period returns approaches a Cauchy distribution. That is, if we approximate the distribution by a symmetric stable distribution, the characteristic exponent approaches unity. If we approximate the distribution by a Student-t, the degrees of freedom approaches unity. In either case, this implies a Cauchy distribution. A well known property of this distribution is that observations from the process have the same distribution as sample means of observations [e.g., Johnson and Kotz (1970 p. 156)], and hence nothing is gained by so subdividing the periods. This is not to say that prices do not follow a geometric Brownian motion, but rather that we may never *observe* this process continuously on the basis of prices derived from trades at finite periods of time. In addition, this point of view does not allow for the acquisition of information that would change the distributions in the course of time.

Blume (1970) suggests another procedure for avoiding estimation risk in this context. He points out that by taking portfolios of securities and estimating the appropriate linear combination of the coefficients, the precision of such estimates can be arbitrarily improved. This follows if the errors for the different equations are indeed independent, although in his empirical work Blume finds that the precision of the estimates can be improved by taking dependence into account. Thus he argues that estimates for portfolios should be used in place of estimates for individual securities. This suggestion was very influential, particularly in the literature on testing asset pricing models [Black, Jensen and Scholes (1971), Fama and McBeth (1973)]. However, there is a fundamental problem here. The improvement in precision ignores individual differences and hence comes at the cost of sacrificing information. His procedure can be justified on the assumption that securities are identical within certain groups. Not surprisingly, with this additional information (assuming it is correct), estimation risk can be reduced.

4. The Bayesian Approach to Incorporating Estimation Risk in the Portfolio Choice Problem

As noted earlier, the predictive distribution of returns reflects all the available information and properly accounts for estimation risk. Thus, for the portfolio choice problem as Zellner and Chetty (1965) clearly noted, one first needs to determine the joint predictive distribution of security rates of return. This in turn, determines the predictive distribution of portfolio returns for all feasible portfolios i.e., all feasible linear combinations of security rates of return. Accordingly, the first objective of this section is to discuss, in a portfolio context, the types of information available to determine the predictive distribution. With this distribution, one can analyze such issues as the effect of estimation risk on the set of admissible portfolios, on optimal portfolios for individual investors, and consequently on capital market equilibrium conditions. The second objective of this section is to examine the portfolio literature that takes estimation risk into account in dealing with these issues.

Derivation of the Predictive Distribution and Sources of Prior Information. There is much information available to investors who wish to assess future price movements or rates of return on individual securities. This information is not limited to the past history of observed rates of return but can include a vast amount of information, ranging from accounting information, earnings announcements, economic news and the like, to theories of stock price determination.

Indeed, the task of security analysts is to integrate this variety of information and to process it in order to determine how well or how poorly a particular security will perform over a given investment horizon. There have been several studies reported in Winkler (1972) that have had security analysts assess predictive distributions of future stock price movements. The subjects in these experiments apparently understood the assessment techniques and had little difficulty assessing predictive distributions.

These experiments have been limited to assessing predictive distributions on a security by security basis. In the portfolio context it is necessary to consider the multivariate predictive distribution of returns. In addition, it is not clear how sensitive these direct assessment procedures are to the acquisition of new information in the form of data, or other information. By postulating a model for observed returns, and considering information relating to the structure and parameters of this model, a less direct Bayesian approach simplifies the assessment procedure, provides for the acquisition of new information and can readily handle the multivariate problem.

To derive the predictive distribution of returns using this approach, one must consider both the appropriate model for the observations and the parameters that enter such a model. That is, the investor must first determine a model for the observations. Then given that model he must assess a prior distribution for the parameters that enter such a model. This prior distribution may be updated upon acquisition of sample data to form a posterior distribution, which as noted in Chapter 1 can be used to derive the predictive distribution. The available information pertains to both the model for the observations and the assessment of the prior distribution. As noted before, this information can take many forms.

In the polar case where the information set is restricted to a given set of sample data, and little information is available regarding the appropriate model for the observations, then as indicated in Section 4 of Chapter 2 and in Chapter 7 of this book, a diffuse Dirichlet process prior might be used to model the uncertainty relating to the form of the distribution function, and the predictive distribution is simply the empirical distribution function. However, in other cases, there is information about the form of the distribution function. Indeed there has been a large literature that has concentrated on developing an appropriate model for the observations and it is to this literature that we now turn.

The simplest model is of course the normal distribution which has convenient portfolio implications. In addition, it is a simple matter to derive the predictive distribution for this model of the observations. However, as Fama (1965b) notes, the historical data do not fully support this model and he argues that a nonnormal member of the class of symmetric stable distributions appears to better explain the available data. There have been a number of studies that have attempted to account for this observed nonnormality in other ways. Officer (1971) provides extensive evidence of the nonstationarity of the standard deviation of the market factor as it relates to the returns on individual securities. Praetz (1972) observes that modeling the standard deviation as an inverted gamma distribution would give rise to a Student-*t* distribution of returns. Blattberg and Gonedes (1974) demonstrate that a Student-*t* distribution with small degrees of freedom better explains the observed data than does a member of the class of stable distributions.[16] For ease of exposition, in the remainder of the book we shall concentrate on the normal distribution as a model for the observations. For certain classes of prior information, the predictive distribution is a Student-*t*, a distribution which has convenient portfolio implications.[17] In any event, incorrectly specifying the model for the observations as a normal distribution does not appear to significantly degrade the performance of the optimal Bayes portfolio choice where the distribution is in fact as described in Blattberg and Gonedes (1975) (Brown, 1976).[18]

Once the appropriate model for the observations is determined, it is possible to derive the predictive distribution for a given set of prior and sample information. In the case where the distribution of returns is multivariate normal and the information set is limited to sample data in the sense that prior to observing the data, the investor has an informationless or diffuse prior distribution on the parameters of this multivariate normal distribution, the joint predictive distribution of security rates of return is a multivariate Student-*t* distribution [Zellner and Chetty (1965)]. Zellner and Chetty (1965) also show that the predictive distribution of portfolio returns is univariate Student-*t* with mean and variance being linear and quadratic functions respectively of the portfolio weights.

It is possible to extend this result in an obvious way to consider informative conjugate prior distributions, where a possible interpretation of this conjugate prior assumption is that available information can be represented as sufficient statistics from hypothetical samples drawn from the multivariate normal distribution of returns. [Raiffa and Schlaifer, (1961), Ando and Kaufman, (1965)]. The papers of Klein and Bawa (1976, 1977)[19] illustrate the application of informative

16. A problem common to normal, stable and Student models is the fact that these distributions admit returns below -1, inconsistent with the institutional constraint of limited liability. However, depending on the particular application, this problem may only be apparent, since in characterizing expected utility, one can equivalently assume a non-truncated probability distribution with a utility function defined to be zero for returns less than -1.

17. As the work of Brown (1977) (a revised version of which appears as Chapter 9 of this book) indicates, even where the predictive distribution does not have a closed form representation, it is frequently possible to characterize optimal portfolio choices using standard stochastic dominance arguments [Bawa, (1975)].

18. See Chapter 8 of this book.

conjugate priors in the context of the portfolio problem.

In a formal sense the informative conjugate prior takes account of information not contained in the data. But this does not necessarily imply that it is a particular convenient vehicle for this information. Ando and Kaufman (1965) point out that the informative conjugate prior for the multivariate normal process implies a dependence in the prior that may not adequately reflect the available information. From a practical viewpoint a more serious difficulty presents itself. While there have been several very interesting proposals for the elicitation of prior information about covariance matrices [e.g., Abowd and Zellner (1977), Kadane et al. (1977)], these procedures have yet to be applied in a context where the dimensionality of the covariance matrix is as great as in the portfolio problem. Since information generally arrives on a firm by firm or industry by industry basis, it is useful to consider covariance structures that take this factor into account.

By representing the multivariate normal distribution in terms of the Sharpe index model [Sharpe (1963)] introduced earlier, we obtain a likely candidate for a simplified covariance structure. Capital asset pricing theory [Sharpe (1964), Lintner (1965)] emphasizes the central importance of the $\boldsymbol{\beta}$ slope parameters and imposes restrictions on the intercepts, the $\boldsymbol{\alpha}$.[20] Institutional factors and past empirical work [King (1966)] have bearing on the structure of the covariance matrix of the errors. Moreover, due to the interpretation of beta as risk, several studies use accounting based measures of risk to improve the estimation of beta [Beaver et al., (1970), Rosenberg and McKibben, (1973), Rosenberg and Guy, (1975)], though none have done so in an explicitly Bayesian way, using the accounting data as a source of prior information.

It would appear that the Sharpe model is a very useful construct for representing prior information in this multivariate context. Not only does it utilize non data based information of a type generally available and commonly used in this context, but also, it allows for this information to be processed on a security by security basis. However, the only explicitly Bayesian (estimation) study in this area is that of Vasicek (1973) who proposes using a cross section of the time series estimates of beta to construct a data based prior for this parameter. Note, however, that Vasicek does not derive the predictive distribution, but rather the posterior mean of beta as an estimate of the value of this parameter. The predictive distribution of portfolio returns for this Sharpe index model is derived by Brown (1977), a revised version of which appears as Chapter 9 in this book. As noted therein, despite the fact that the predictive distribution is not amenable to closed form representation, this distribution gives rise to a portfolio choice rule only marginally more complex than the familiar mean-variance procedure. Optimal portfolio choice in this context is characterized by three, not two, parameters--namely the mean, variance, and the beta of the portfolio. The mean and variance are defined as before, whereas the portfolio beta represents a weighted average of estimates of security beta parameters appearing in the definition of the Sharpe index model.

Implications of the Predictive Distribution for Portfolio Theory. Once the predictive distribution of portfolio returns is determined explicitly, the implications for

18. See Chapter 8 of this book.

19. These papers appear as Chapters 4 and 5 of this book.

portfolio theory can be addressed directly. As will become clear in the following review of the portfolio literature, in the estimation risk environment these issues have not been completely resolved, and are the focus of the rest of the book.

Mao and Sarndal (1966) were among the first to characterize optimal portfolios in this estimation risk environment. They consider a particularly simple example in which the joint distribution of security rates of return is multivariate normal. The underlying parameters take on one of two possible sets of values, depending upon the state of nature (e.g., good or bad condition of the economy). Thus, the underlying model is a mixture of normals: f_I with posterior probability p_I and f_{II} with posterior probability p_{II}, with $p_{II} = 1-p_I$. The predictive distribution in this case is simply

$$f^* = p_I f_I + p_{II} f_{II}. \tag{6}$$

Then, expected utility of wealth, $\tilde{w}$, where the expectation is taken with respect to the predictive distribution in (6), can conveniently be expressed as:

$$EU[\tilde{w}] = p_I \underset{I}{E} U[\tilde{w}] + p_{II} \underset{II}{E} U[\tilde{w}], \tag{7}$$

where $\underset{I}{E}$ and $\underset{II}{E}$ represent expected utility for f_I and f_{II} respectively. Thus an interpretation of using the predictive distribution is that the decision maker should maximize the expectation of expected utility over the different regimes.[21] Mao and Sarndal (1966) express expected utility as a function of the mean and variance of portfolio return:

$$E_I U[\tilde{w}] = \mu_{pI} - A\sigma_{pI}^2, \tag{8}$$

where

$$\mu_{pI} = \sum_{i=1}^{m} X_i \mu_{iI} = \mathbf{X}' \boldsymbol{\mu}_I \tag{9}$$

and

$$\sigma_{pI}^2 = \sum_{i=1}^{m} \sum_{j=1}^{m} X_i X_j \sigma_{ijI} = \mathbf{X}' \Sigma_I \mathbf{X}, \tag{10}$$

for a given set of portfolio weights $\mathbf{X}' = \{X_1, \ldots, X_m\}$. Defining parameters μ_{pII} and σ_{pII}^2 similarly, one can analogously derive expected utility in regime II. Then expected utility under the predictive distribution is[22]

20. $\boldsymbol{\alpha} = R_f(1-\boldsymbol{\beta})$ where R_f is the rate of return on a risk free security.

21. It is sufficient that the sum of the posterior probabilities be bounded by unity for this reinterpretation of the expected utility over the predictive distribution to hold.

22. Note that the expression in (11) is inconsistent with the negative exponential utility function most commonly associated with the maximand $\mu_p - A\sigma_p^2$, since this maximand represents

$$EU[w] = p_I \mu_{pI} + p_{II} \mu_{pII} - A\{p_I \sigma_{pI}^2 + p_{II} \sigma_{pII}^2\}, \tag{11}$$

and the authors proceed to characterize optimal solutions as a function of p_I and p_{II}. They illustrate an optimal choice algorithm in terms of a simple three asset example.

Mao and Sarndal consider a very simple model, which applies only when the utility function is of a special form. Kalymon (1971) analyzes the portfolio choice problem with a multivariate normal distribution of security rates of return with parameters having unknown values. He considers three special cases, the first of which involves unknown means but known covariance matrix. For this example, the predictive distribution is normal and mean-variance analysis still applies. In the second and third cases, the means are unknown and the Sharpe index model defines the covariance structure, with the underlying variances being known and unknown respectively. Only the mean and variance of the predictive distribution are obtained for these two cases, though as Kalymon notes, these predictive distributions are not normal and hence variance may be an incomplete measure of risk. We note that in this case, the variance of the predictive distribution will be the appropriate risk measure if and only if investors' utility functions are quadratic. For more general risk averse utility functions, variance alone is not enough to characterize risk. As Brown (1977) shows, both the variance and beta of the portfolio are the relevant risk measures in this context.

It was not until the doctoral dissertation of Barry (1973) and the work of Winkler (1973) that attempts were made to characterize optimal solutions to the portfolio choice problem in an estimation risk environment under somewhat more general circumstances. In this work and in several subsequent papers [Barry (1974), Winkler and Barry (1975), and Barry and Winkler (1976)], it is generally assumed that the security rates of return have a multivariate normal distribution with unknown parameter values (with means assumed unknown and covariance matrix usually assumed known). The investor is generally assumed to have linear, quadratic or negative exponential utility functions. The predictive distribution of portfolio returns is known to be normal or Student-t, depending upon whether the covariance matrix is known or unknown, where conjugate priors are used for the unknown parameter values. Within this framework, Barry and Winkler study admissible portfolios and optimal portfolio choice.

Barry (1974) assumes that the joint distribution of security returns is multivariate normal with mean vector $\boldsymbol{\mu}$ and variance-covariance matrix $\boldsymbol{\Sigma}$. Letting $\hat{\boldsymbol{\mu}}$ and $\hat{\boldsymbol{\Sigma}}$ be the estimates of $\boldsymbol{\mu}$ and $\boldsymbol{\Sigma}$, Barry examines three cases:[23]

(i) The parameter certainty equivalent approach, conditioned on $\boldsymbol{\Sigma} = \hat{\boldsymbol{\Sigma}}$ and $\boldsymbol{\mu} = \hat{\boldsymbol{\mu}}$.

---

the *logarithm* of expected utility for the negative exponential utility case. Since the predictive distribution f^* is bimodal in this case, the use of mean-variance analysis in Mao and Sarndal (1966) can be justified only for the case of quadratic utilities. For this case, the expected utility would involve terms like μ_{pI}^2 and μ_{pII}^2 and with suitable adjustments, mean-variance analysis can be justified in determining admissible and optimal portfolios.

23. Here, $\hat{\boldsymbol{\mu}}$ is a vector of sample means, and $\hat{\boldsymbol{\Sigma}}$ is the maximum likelihood estimate of $\boldsymbol{\Sigma}$

(ii) The Bayesian approach, conditioned on $\boldsymbol{\Sigma} = \hat{\boldsymbol{\Sigma}}$ and a conjugate prior for $\boldsymbol{\mu}$.

(iii) The Bayesian approach with a conjugate prior for $\boldsymbol{\Sigma}$ and $\boldsymbol{\mu}$.

Assuming quadratic utility in case (iii), Barry argues that the efficient set is invariant to estimation risk (i.e., it is the same in (i)-(iii)), but that the optimal choice may change. Furthermore, he shows the intuitive result that expected portfolio return decreases *(ceteris paribus)* as we move from case (i) to (iii).[24]

Winkler and Barry (1975) extend the Bayesian analysis to the multiple period case. They consider a two security problem with one security risky and the other riskless. The risky security is normally distributed with known variance, σ^2, and unknown mean, μ. Then, with a diffuse ("noninformative") prior for μ, they examine optimal portfolio choice under linear and quadratic utilities. The single period solution is shown to be very different from the multiple period solution.

In all of the above studies, it is implicitly assumed that the underlying probability distribution of returns is stationary. Barry and Winkler (1976) relax this assumption and examine a Bayesian approach to nonstationarity. In a two security world, one security riskless and the other risky, the risky security is assumed to have a normally distributed return. The variance is known, but the mean is unknown and nonstationary. Then, for a particular type of nonstationarity, they show that this nonstationarity increases the posterior variance of μ. As a result, they show that under quadratic and exponential utility, nonstationarity causes the risk averse investor to switch out of (though not completely) the risky security. This impact of nonstationarity and estimation risk is further examined by Barry (1978) in a study of capital market equilibrium.

From the above studies, it is apparent that substantial progress has been made in examining the impact of estimation risk in a portfolio context. There remain, however, many issues that need to be explored. Many of the results reported are derived for special and somewhat restrictive classes of utility functions. It is possible to use the Stochastic Dominance apparatus [Bawa (1975)] to derive qualitative results that apply for quite general classes of utility functions, as illustrated in the paper by Klein and Bawa (1976), reproduced as Chapter 4 of this book. None of the studies reported have considered the quantitative impact of estimation risk. It is also important to consider other specifications of prior information than those that have been considered in the literature, and the effect that such specifications have on optimal portfolio choice. Finally, we need to know something more about the effect of estimation risk on capital market equilibrium conditions. It is the purpose of the remainder of this book to address these and related issues.

---

multiplied by a degrees of freedom correction.

24. Williams (1977) replicates Barry's results for the continuous time case and provides some justification in this context for model (ii).

CHAPTER 4

THE EFFECT OF ESTIMATION RISK ON OPTIMAL PORTFOLIO CHOICE*

Roger W. KLEIN and Vijay S. BAWA**

1. Introduction

The problem of portfolio choice under uncertainty has been traditionally viewed as choosing among alternative known probability distributions of returns. An individual chooses among them according to a consistent set of preferences. In practice, the distributions are assumed to belong to a certain family of distributions. Since the values of the parameters characterizing each distribution are not ordinarily known, they are estimated using available economic data. The traditional approach is to use the distribution with the estimated parameter values treated as if they were the values of the true parameters to obtain an individual's optimal choice. By treating estimated parameter values as the true parameter values, estimation risk is ignored. Our purpose is to incorporate estimation risk directly into the decision process and determine its effect on optimal portfolio choice under uncertainty.

Under the von Neumann-Morgenstern (1944) axioms, the optimal portfolio choice for an individual is a portfolio that maximizes the expected utility of returns, where the individual's utility function is determined uniquely, up to a positive linear transformation, by his preferences. In the traditional analysis, one assumes that the estimated values of the parameters of the distribution are the true parameters values. In the Bayesian analysis, which explicitly considers estimation risk, we note that the von Neumann-Morgenstern-Savage (1944, 1954) postulates allow us to solve the problem by using the predictive distribution of portfolio returns. We consider the case where the joint distribution of security returns is multivariate normal, determine the predictive distribution for several important prior distributions on the parameters whose values are unknown, and determine the effect of estimation risk on both the admissible set of portfolios and on the optimal portfolio choice.[1]

Section 2 outlines the traditional method of analysis by which the optimal portfolio choice is based on estimates of the parameter values, as well as the

* Except for minor notational changes made to keep the notation as consistent as possible throughout this book and for several expository changes, this paper appeared in *Journal of Financial Economics* 3(1976)215-231.

** We acknowledge helpful discussions with our colleague R. D. Willig. We thank members of the Holmdel Economic Theory Workshop at Bell Laboratories for stimulating discussions. We also thank Martin S. Geisel, and M. C. Jensen for helpful comments.

1. The importance of estimation risk for portfolio choice is also discussed by Black and Treynor (1973).

alternative Bayesian procedure that incorporates estimation risk directly into the decision process. The Bayesian method of analysis is not foreign to economists and has been applied elsewhere [see for example Zellner (1971), Zellner and Geisel (1968), Chow (1973), and Prescott (1972)].

Section 3 examines optimal portfolio choice when there are an equal number of observations on each security's return and individuals have "noninformative" or "invariant" priors on the distribution's parameters. We show that the admissible set for all individuals is the same under the two procedures. However, more importantly, we show that the optimal choice for an individual, a point in this admissible set, will in general not be the same for the two procedures. As intuitively expected, for most risk-averse individuals, the optimal choice is likely to be a portfolio with lower expected portfolio return when the estimation risk is explicitly considered. An illustrative example is provided to demonstrate the extent to which decisions can differ under these two decision procedures.

Section 4 considers the portfolio choice problem for several general types of informative priors that one is likely to encounter. Two illustrative cases show that under the Bayesian procedure the admissible set can still be obtained by a very intuitive 'mean-variance' type selection rule. However, this rule differs (in a very intuitive way) from the mean-variance selection rule that one obtains under the traditional procedure. Our conclusions are stated in section 5.

2. The method of analysis

To apply the methods of analyses discussed in Chapter 1, denote $\tilde{R}_i$ as the (future) return to security i and X_i as the proportion of wealth invested in security i, $i = 1, \ldots, m$. Then, with $\mathbf{X}' \equiv (X_1, \ldots, X_m)$ and $\tilde{\mathbf{R}}' \equiv (\tilde{R}_1, \ldots, \tilde{R}_m)$, the return on portfolio $\mathbf{X}$ is $\tilde{P}_{\mathbf{X}} \equiv \mathbf{X}'\tilde{\mathbf{R}}$. With U and $f(\mathbf{R}|\boldsymbol{\theta})$ denoting the investor's utility function and the conditional distribution of $\tilde{\mathbf{R}}$ (conditioned on $\boldsymbol{\theta}$), respectively, the conditional expected utility of portfolio $\mathbf{X}$ is given by

$$E_{\tilde{\mathbf{R}}|\theta}[U(\mathbf{X}'\tilde{\mathbf{R}})] \equiv \int_{\mathbf{R}} U(\mathbf{X}'\mathbf{R}) f(\mathbf{R}|\boldsymbol{\theta})\, d\mathbf{R}. \tag{1}$$

In practical applications, the value of $\boldsymbol{\theta}$ is unknown, implying that $f(\mathbf{R}|\boldsymbol{\theta})$ is not completely specified. In the traditional analysis one assumes that $\boldsymbol{\theta}$ equals its estimate, $\hat{\boldsymbol{\theta}}$. If we make this questionable assumption, it is consistent with the von Neumann-Morgenstern axioms for the investor's optimal portfolio to be given as the solution to the following:

$$\text{(I)} \qquad \underset{X}{Max} E_{\tilde{\mathbf{R}}|\theta=\hat{\theta}}[U(\mathbf{X}'\tilde{\mathbf{R}})] = \int_{\mathbf{R}} U(\mathbf{X}'\mathbf{R}) f(\mathbf{R}|\hat{\boldsymbol{\theta}})\, d\mathbf{R},$$

subject to

$$\mathbf{X} \in \mathbf{C} = \left\{\mathbf{X}: \sum X_i = 1,\ X_i \geqslant 0\right\}.^2$$

2. We note that the analysis in this paper is not affected if the set of feasible portfolios $\mathbf{C}$ is modified to include additional constraints of the type generally considered in the portfolio theory literature [e.g., Sharpe (1970)].

Since the solution in (I) is based on $f(\mathbf{R}|\hat{\boldsymbol{\theta}})$, the distribution of $\tilde{\mathbf{R}}$ conditioned on $\boldsymbol{\theta} = \hat{\boldsymbol{\theta}}$, we call it the Estimated Conditional Solution, ECS.

It is important to note that in conditioning on $\boldsymbol{\theta} = \hat{\boldsymbol{\theta}}$, the ECS ignores estimation risk. In contrast, in the Bayesian procedure let

$$g(\mathbf{R}) \equiv \underset{\boldsymbol{\theta}}{E}[f(\mathbf{R}|\boldsymbol{\theta})] \tag{2}$$

denote the unconditional (predictive) distribution of $\tilde{\mathbf{R}}$, where in (2) the expectation is taken over $\boldsymbol{\theta}$ with respect to the posterior distribution of $\boldsymbol{\theta}$, $p(\boldsymbol{\theta})$. As will become clear below, $g(\mathbf{R})$ incorporates estimation risk. In accordance with von Neumann-Morgenstern-Savage axioms, the investor's optimal portfolio is now given as the solution to the following:

(II) $\quad \underset{\mathbf{X}}{Max} \underset{\boldsymbol{\theta}}{E}\left[\underset{\tilde{\mathbf{R}}|\boldsymbol{\theta}}{E}[U(\mathbf{X}'\tilde{\mathbf{R}})]\right] = \underset{\mathbf{X}}{Max} \int_{\mathbf{R}} U(\mathbf{X}'\mathbf{R})g(\mathbf{R})\,d\mathbf{R},$

subject to

$$\mathbf{X} \in \mathbf{C}.$$

Since the method in (II) is based on the unconditional (predictive) distribution of $\tilde{\mathbf{R}}$, we will call it the Unconditional Solution, UCS.[3]

In this paper, we assume that the security returns $\tilde{\mathbf{R}}$ have a multivariate normal probability distribution, i.e., $f(\mathbf{R} \mid \boldsymbol{\theta})$ is multivariate normal with $\boldsymbol{\theta} = (\boldsymbol{\mu}, \boldsymbol{\Sigma})$, where $\boldsymbol{\mu}' \equiv (\mu_1, \ldots, \mu_m)$ denotes the mean vector and $\boldsymbol{\Sigma}$ denotes the variance-covariance matrix. Then, portfolio return $\tilde{P}_{\mathbf{X}} \equiv \mathbf{X}'\tilde{\mathbf{R}}$ is normally distributed with mean $\mu_{\mathbf{X}} = \mathbf{X}'\boldsymbol{\mu}$ and variance $\sigma^2_{\mathbf{X}} = \mathbf{X}'\boldsymbol{\Sigma}\mathbf{X}$. Under these assumptions and others provided below, the optimization problems (I) and (II) reduce to the following:

(I′) $\quad \underset{\mathbf{X}}{Max} \int_z U(\mathbf{X}'\hat{\boldsymbol{\mu}} + \hat{\sigma}_{\mathbf{X}} \cdot z)\phi(z)\, dz,$

subject to

$$\mathbf{X} \in \mathbf{C},$$

and

(II′) $\quad \underset{\mathbf{X}}{Max} \int_y U(u^*_{\mathbf{X}} + s^*_{\mathbf{X}} \cdot y)\eta(y)\, dy,$

subject to

$$\mathbf{X} \in \mathbf{C}.$$

In (I′), with $\hat{\boldsymbol{\mu}}$ and $\hat{\boldsymbol{\Sigma}}$ denoting estimates of $\boldsymbol{\mu}$ and $\boldsymbol{\Sigma}$, respectively,

3. This terminology, ECS and UCS, was introduced by Klein, Rafsky, Sibley, and Willig, and appears in Klein et al. (1978).

$\hat{\boldsymbol{\mu}}_X = \mathbf{X}'\hat{\boldsymbol{\mu}}$, $\hat{\sigma}_{\mathbf{X}} = (\mathbf{X}'\hat{\boldsymbol{\Sigma}}\mathbf{X})^{1/2}$, and $\tilde{z}$ is a random variable with standard normal density function ϕ. In (II′), $\boldsymbol{\mu}^*_{\mathbf{X}}$ and $s^*_{\mathbf{X}}$ are parameters that depend on the portfolio allocation X, and $\tilde{y}$ is a random variable with p.d.f. η. We show that η is either a standard normal or a standard Student-t depending upon the prior employed. In the following sections, we obtain the solution to (II′) for several type of priors and compare it with the solution to (I′) to determine the effect of estimation risk on optimal portfolio choice.

3. Optimal portfolio choice: "Noninformative" or "invariant" priors

3.1 Theoretical analysis

In this section we consider the case of "noninformative" or 'invariant' priors and obtain the optimal portfolio choice. We recall that the joint probability distribution of security returns $\tilde{\mathbf{R}}$ is assumed to be multivariate normal with mean $\boldsymbol{\mu}$ and variance-covariance matrix $\boldsymbol{\Sigma}$. Let r_{it} denote the (observed) return on security i, $i = 1, 2, \ldots, m$, at time t, $t = 1, 2, \ldots, T$, and assume that the data, $(r_{11}, r_{12}, \ldots, r_{1T}; r_{21}, \ldots, r_{2T}; \ldots; r_{m1}, \ldots, r_{mT})$:$1 \times mT$, consist of observations drawn from a multivariate normal distribution with mean vector $(\mu_1, \ldots, \mu_1; \mu_2, \ldots, \mu_2; \ldots; \mu_m, \ldots, \mu_m)'$:$1 \times mT$ and variance-covariance matrix $\boldsymbol{\Sigma} \otimes \mathbf{I}$ (where I is a $T \times T$ identity matrix). Also, recall that for portfolio $\mathbf{X}$, the portfolio return $\tilde{P}_{\mathbf{X}} \equiv \mathbf{X}'\tilde{\mathbf{R}}$ is normally distributed with mean $\mu_{\mathbf{X}} = \mathbf{X}'\boldsymbol{\mu}$ and variance $\sigma^2_{\mathbf{X}} = \mathbf{X}'\boldsymbol{\Sigma}\mathbf{X}$. Finally, we note that with $\boldsymbol{\theta} = (\boldsymbol{\mu}, \boldsymbol{\Sigma})$ denoting the parameters whose values are unknown and with α denoting 'proportional to', the 'noninformative' or 'invariant' prior, $p_o(\boldsymbol{\theta})$, is given as

$$p_o(\boldsymbol{\theta}) \;\alpha\; |\boldsymbol{\Sigma}|^{-(m+1)/2}. \tag{3}$$

We now define the parameters $\hat{\mu}_{\mathbf{X}}$ and $\hat{\sigma}_{\mathbf{X}}$ used in Theorem 1. Letting $\hat{\boldsymbol{\mu}}' \equiv (\hat{\mu}_1, \ldots, \hat{\mu}_m), \hat{\mu}_i \equiv \sum_{i=1}^{T} r_{it}/T$, $\hat{\mu}_{\mathbf{X}}$ is given by

$$\hat{\mu}_{\mathbf{X}} = \mathbf{X}'\hat{\boldsymbol{\mu}}. \tag{4}$$

Letting $\mathbf{r}$ be the $T \times m$ matrix of T observations on the m securities, with row t given by $r'_{\mathbf{t}} \equiv (r_{1t}, r_{2t}, \ldots, r_{mt})$, and $\mathbf{1}$ a $T \times 1$ column vector of ones, define

$$\mathbf{S} \equiv (\mathbf{r} - \mathbf{1}\hat{\boldsymbol{\mu}}')'(\mathbf{r} - \mathbf{1}\hat{\boldsymbol{\mu}}') \tag{5}$$

and

$$\hat{\sigma}^2_{\mathbf{X}} \equiv \mathbf{X}'\mathbf{S}\mathbf{X}/(T-m). \tag{6}$$

Before stating Theorem 1, it should be emphasized that $\hat{\mu}_{\mathbf{X}}$ and $\hat{\sigma}^2_{\mathbf{X}}$, which may be viewed as estimates of $\mu_{\mathbf{X}}$ and $\sigma^2_{\mathbf{X}}$, respectively, are defined prior to Theorem 1 only for convenience. The derivation of these estimates and their role in portfolio choice are determined by Theorem 1 as part of the decision problem. It should also be emphasized that in Theorem 1 and in all other theorems that follow, the predictive distribution of portfolio return is an induced distribution. This distribution is not derived directly by assigning a prior to the parameters of the univariate portfolio return distribution. Rather, we begin with the multivariate distribution for individual securities, and employ a prior for the parameters of this distribution

($\boldsymbol{\mu}$ and $\boldsymbol{\Sigma}$) to derive the induced predictive distribution for portfolio return.

Theorem 1. Under the assumptions outlined above and for the "noninformative" prior given by (3), the standardized unconditional (predictive) distribution η *used in* (II′) *is a Student-t distribution with* $T - m$ *degrees of freedom. The parameters* μ_X^* *and* s_X^* *are given by*

$$\mu_X^* = \hat{\mu}_X, \qquad s_X^* = (1+1/T)^{\frac{1}{2}}\hat{\sigma}_X.$$

Theorem 1 is proved in the appendix.

Before using Theorem 1 to obtain the optimal portfolio choice, note that $\boldsymbol{\mu}$ and $\boldsymbol{\Sigma}$ are independent in the prior and the prior for $(\boldsymbol{\mu}, \boldsymbol{\Sigma})$ is "noninformative" in that small changes in the data on security returns will change greatly the posterior p.d.f. for $(\boldsymbol{\mu}, \boldsymbol{\Sigma})$.[4] In this sense, the data, as expressed through the likelihood function, play the major role in determining the posterior distribution for these parameters.

Theorem 1 enables us to obtain the optimal portfolio choice under the UCS and compare it with the optimal portfolio obtained using the ECS. Under the ECS(I′), the admissible set for all risk-averse individuals, as well as individuals with decreasing absolute risk-averse utility functions, is the well-known Markowitz-Tobin [Markowitz (1952, 1959), Tobin (1958)] mean-variance admissible boundary [see Bawa (1975) for details]. The admissible set for all individuals is the admissible set obtained by Bawa (1976). However, using our analysis, we see that with explicit consideration of estimation risk, the underlying distributions being compared are standardized Student-*t* distributions with parameters μ_X^* and s_X^*. Since $\mu_X^* = \hat{\mu}_X$, $s_X^* = (1+1/T)^{\frac{1}{2}}\hat{\sigma}_X$, and for Student-*t* distributions the admissible sets are still obtained with comparisons of μ_X^* and σ_X^*, it follows [see Bawa (1978b) for the proof] that the admissible set for the same group of individuals is the same under the ECS and the UCS.

As stated above, consideration of estimation risk does not change the admissible set. However, more importantly, as a result of estimation risk, an individual's optimal choice (a member of the admissible set) is likely to differ from that obtained via the ECS. To show this result, we note that for all risk-averse individuals, the optimal portfolio choice lies on the Markowitz-Tobin mean-variance boundary. If we let $\sigma(\mu_X)$ denote this admissible boundary [see, for example, Markowitz (1959) and Sharpe (1970) for a derivation of the boundary under several different sets of feasible sets **C**], then it follows from Theorem 1 that the expected utility of return for the portfolio (on the admissible boundary) with expected return μ, denoted by $g(\mu_X)$, is given as

4. Formally, the marginal priors for $\boldsymbol{\mu}$ and $\boldsymbol{\Sigma}$ are Jeffreys' invariant priors [Jeffreys (1961)]. The properties of these priors are summarized in Zellner (1971, pp. 41-53). Zellner (1971, pp. 42-44) and Box and Tiao (1973, pp. 25-41) explain the sense in which $p_0(\boldsymbol{\mu}) \alpha c$ is non-informative. Geisser (1965, pp. 602-603) provides an explanation of the sense in which $p_0(\boldsymbol{\Sigma}) \alpha |\boldsymbol{\Sigma}|^{-(m+1)/2}$ is "non-informative".

$$g(\mu_X) = \int_{-\infty}^{\infty} U[\mu_X+(1+1/T)^{\frac{1}{2}}\sigma(\mu_X)y]\eta_{T-m}(y)\,dy, \tag{7}$$

where η_{T-m} denotes the standard Student-t distribution with $(T-m)$ degrees of freedom. Thus, the optimal portfolio choice is obtained in two stages by (i) determining μ_* that maximizes $g(\mu_X)$ over feasible μ_X, and (ii) selecting the portfolio $\mathbf{X}^*$ corresponding to the optimal choice μ_*.

For concave utility functions $(U'' < 0)$, μ_* is given by the following First-Order Condition:

$$g'(\mu_*) \equiv \int U'[\mu_*+\gamma\sigma(\mu_*)y][1+\gamma\sigma'(\mu_*)y]\eta_{T-m}(y)\;dy = 0, \tag{8}$$

where $\gamma \equiv (1+1/T)^{\frac{1}{2}}$ and $\mu_* \equiv \mu_*(T)$ both depend on T. We note that the optimal value of μ_X under the ECS [solution to (I')] is given by $\bar{\mu} \equiv \mu_*(\infty)$. Since $\mu_*(T)$ depends on T through the degrees of freedom $(T-m)$ of the Student-t distribution, for any finite T, $\mu_*(T) \neq \bar{\mu}$ for most utility functions. Moreover, one might intuitively expect that as a result of increased (estimation) risk, $\mu_*(T)$ would be less than $\bar{\mu}$. Formally, letting

$$h(Y) \equiv U'(\mu+\gamma\sigma Y)[1+\gamma\sigma'(\mu)Y], \tag{9}$$

then the First-Order Condition (8) reduces to

$$E_Y h(Y) = 0.$$

It follows from Bawa (1975, Theorem 13) that increasing the degrees of freedom $(T - m)$ of a Student-t distribution is equivalent to decreasing risk (for all increasing concave utility functions) as defined by Rothschild-Stiglitz (1971). Therefore, following the method of analysis in Rothschild-Stiglitz (1971, p. 67),

$$\mu_*(T) \lesseqgtr \bar{\mu} \quad \text{if} \quad h''(Y) \lesseqgtr 0. \tag{10}$$

Differentiating (9) and substituting $A \equiv -U''(w)/U'(w)$ and $R \equiv -wU''(w)/U'(w)$, the absolute risk-aversion and relative risk-aversion measures respectively, yields

$$h''(Y) = \gamma^2\sigma^2(\mu_X)\left[\left(1-\frac{\mu\sigma'(\mu_X)}{\sigma(\mu_X)}\right)(A^2-A') - \frac{\sigma'(\mu_X)}{\sigma(\mu_X)}[A(1-R)+R']\right]U'. \tag{11}$$

Summarizing the above results, from (10) and (11), the following theorem is immediately established:

Theorem 2. For all individuals that are risk-averse $(U''<0)$, $\mu_*(T) \leqslant \bar{\mu}$, *if*

$$U'\left\{\left[1-\mu_X\frac{\sigma'(\mu_X)}{\sigma(\mu_X)}\right](A^2-A') - \frac{\sigma'(\mu_X)}{\sigma(\mu_X)}[A(1-R)+R']\right\} \leqslant 0.$$

Theorem 2 immediately implies that $\mu_*(T) \leqslant \bar{\mu}$, if

(a) $U''' \leqslant 0$

or

(a′) $A' < 0$ (decreasing absolute risk–aversion),

(b′) $R \leqslant 1$ (relative risk–aversion does not exceed one),

(c′) $R' \geqslant 0$ (non–decreasing relative risk aversion),

and

(d′) $\mu_{\mathbf{X}}\sigma'(\mu_{\mathbf{X}})/\sigma(\mu_{\mathbf{X}}) \geqslant 1$ (over feasible $\mu_{\mathbf{X}}$).

This last condition $[\mu_{\mathbf{X}}\sigma'(\mu_{\mathbf{X}})/\sigma(\mu_{\mathbf{X}}) \geqslant 1]$ always holds when the available securities include a riskless asset. Thus, for many (and perhaps most) cases, it appears that $\mu_*(T) \leqslant \bar{\mu}$.

3.2 An illustrative example

The optimal portfolio choice $\mathbf{X}[\mu_*(T)]$ is the optimal portfolio allocation for the point $\mu_*(T)$ on the mean-variance admissible boundary. To illustrate the quantitative effect of estimation risk on optimal portfolio choice, i.e., on $\mathbf{X}[\{\mu_*(T)\}] - \mathbf{X}(\bar{\mu})$, we consider the case where $m = 2$ and the utility function is the quadratic[5]

$$U(y) \equiv 20y - y^2. \tag{12}$$

Then, using notation defined earlier, it can be shown easily from the first-order condition (9) that

$$X_1^*(T) \equiv X_1[\mu_*(T)]$$

$$\equiv \frac{10(\hat{\mu}_1-\hat{\mu}_2)-\hat{\mu}_2(\hat{\mu}_1-\hat{\mu}_2)-(\hat{\sigma}_{21}-\hat{\sigma}_{22})\alpha_T}{[(\hat{\mu}_1-\hat{\mu}_2)^2+(\sigma_{11}+2\hat{\sigma}_{21}+\hat{\sigma}_{22})\alpha_T]}$$

$$X_2^*(T) \equiv 1 - X_1^*(T). \tag{13}$$

In (13), $\hat{\mu}_i$ is the estimate of μ_i, $\hat{\sigma}_{ij}$ is the estimate of σ_{ij} (an element of the

5. We recognize the problems associated with quadratic utility functions (U' can be negative, absolute risk aversion is increasing). We employ the quadratic utility function to provide a simple example of the possible effect that estimation risk can have on optimal portfolio choice, as described in Theorem 2.

variance-covariance matrix) and α_T is given by

$$\alpha_T = \left(\frac{T+1}{T}\right)\left(\frac{T-m}{T-m-2}\right).^{6} \tag{14}$$

For $i = 1, 2$ let X_i^e denote $X_i^*(T = \infty)$; then X_i^e is the optimal allocation under the ECS [i.e., (13) with $\alpha_{T=\infty} = 1$]. The optimal allocation under the UCS is given by $X_i^* \equiv X_i^*(T)$ from (13) with α_T defined by (14). To compare X_i^* with X_i^e, consider the special case

$$\hat{\boldsymbol{\mu}}' = (12,\ 5), \qquad \hat{\boldsymbol{\Sigma}} = \begin{pmatrix} 25 & 1 \\ 1 & 1 \end{pmatrix}, \tag{15}$$

for which

$$X_1^*(T) = 35/(49+24\alpha_T). \tag{16}$$

Note that the estimated standard deviation of security 1 is 5, which is not unrealistically high. We can now compare X_i^* and X_i^e as functions of T.

As shown in Figure 4.1, X_1^* is smaller than X_1^e and, as expected, monotonically approaches X_1^e as $T \to \infty$. Similarly, X_2^* is larger than X_2^e and monotonically approaches X_2^e as $T \to \infty$. Intuitively, Figure 4.1 shows that explicit consideration of estimation risk can cause the investor to switch from the relatively "riskier" security 1 to (the less risky) security 2.[7] Figure 4.1 and the accompanying table also show that the impact of estimation risk can be substantial. Estimation risk results in a 22 percent reduction in the investment in security 1 when the sample size $T = 5$, a 3 percent reduction when $T = 20$, and a 0.24 percent reduction even when $T = 500$. It is not uncommon to have 20 observations (or fewer) per security (5 years of quarterly data), so that estimation risk is likely to be an important consideration in practice. Moreover, in practice the number of securities is much larger than 2, implying that the degrees of freedom $(T - m)$ may be small. Consequently, the impact of estimation risk, via α_T in (14), is likely to be even more pronounced than shown here.

4. Optimal portfolio choice: Informative priors

In section 3 we showed that when the prior on the parameters $(\boldsymbol{\mu}, \boldsymbol{\Sigma})$ is independent and "noninformative", estimation risk does not affect the admissible set of portfolios, but does affect the optimal portfolio choice. In this section, we consider two illustrative cases of informative and dependent priors and show that estimation risk alters the admissible set of portfolios.

We first consider an extreme case in which the means of $(m - n)$ securities are known with certainty. The priors on the remaining n means are

6. The estimate $\hat{\mu}_i$ is the sample mean as given in the discussion preceding (4). Letting $\hat{\boldsymbol{\Sigma}} \equiv \mathbf{S}/(T-m)$ be the estimated variance-covariance matrix, where $\mathbf{S}$ is given by (5), $\hat{\sigma}_{ij}$ is element $\{i,j\}$ of $\hat{\boldsymbol{\Sigma}}$.

7. This result is not due to the anamolies of quadratic utility functions. Letting P be any portfolio mean, $\partial E(U)/\partial P < 0$ for some P. However, with P^e and P^* as the ECS and UCS portfolio means respectively, in this example $P^* \leqslant P^e$ and $\partial E(U)/\partial P > 0$, $P \leqslant P^e$.

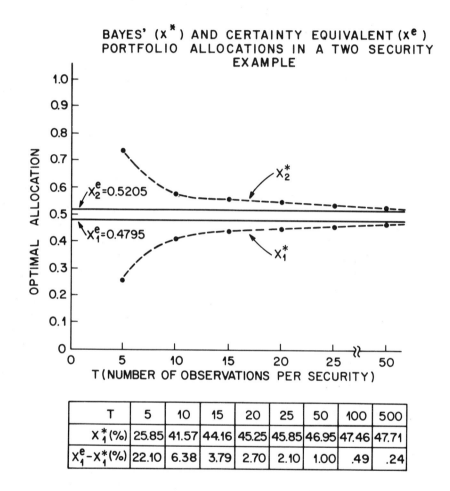

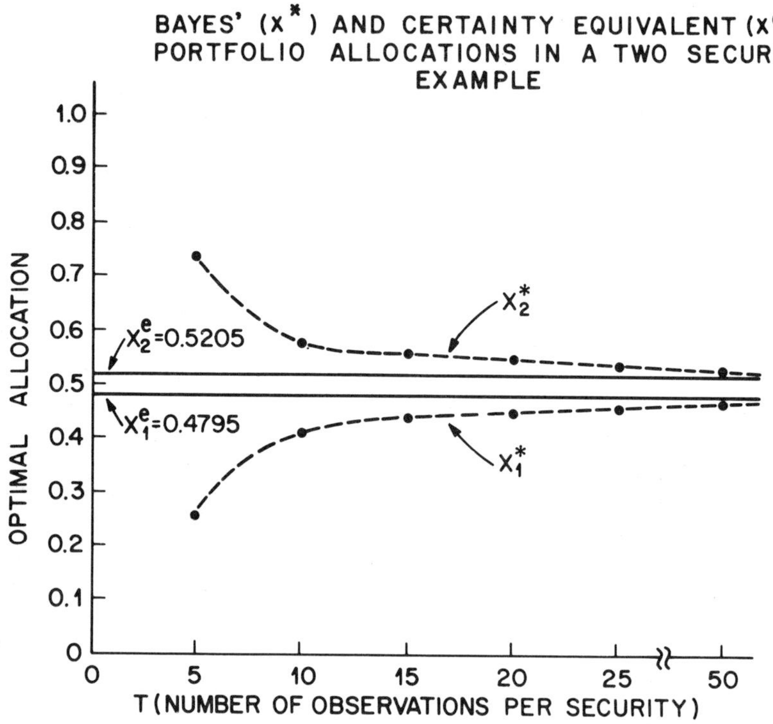

T	5	10	15	20	25	50	100	500
X_1^*(%)	25.85	41.57	44.16	45.25	45.85	46.95	47.46	47.71
$X_1^e - X_1^*$(%)	22.10	6.38	3.79	2.70	2.10	1.00	.49	.24

Figure 4.1

"noninformative". Before proceeding, it should be noted that this case would be approximated if much more data were available for some securities than for others. Loosely speaking, therefore, this example can be interpreted as showing how the admissible set changes when much more information (prior or sample) is available for some securities than for others. For simplicity, in this example, we also assume that the variance-covariance matrix, $\mathbf{\Sigma}$, is known to equal $\mathbf{\Sigma}^0$.

Partition the vector of means $\boldsymbol{\mu}$ and $\mathbf{V} \equiv \mathbf{\Sigma}^{-1}$ conformably as

$$\boldsymbol{\mu}' \equiv [\boldsymbol{\mu}'(1) \vdots \boldsymbol{\mu}'(2)], \boldsymbol{\mu}'(1){:}1 \times n, \ \boldsymbol{\mu}'(2){:}1 \times m - n,$$

$$\mathbf{V} \equiv \begin{bmatrix} \mathbf{V}_{11} & \mathbf{V}_{12} \\ \mathbf{V}_{21} & \mathbf{V}_{22} \end{bmatrix}.$$

Given $\mathbf{\Sigma} = \mathbf{\Sigma}^0$ and $\boldsymbol{\mu}(2) = \boldsymbol{\mu}^0(2)$, the prior is

$$p_0[\boldsymbol{\mu}(1) | \mathbf{\Sigma} = \mathbf{\Sigma}^0, \boldsymbol{\mu}(2) = \boldsymbol{\mu}^0(2)] \ \alpha \ c, \quad \text{a constant.} \tag{17}$$

Under these assumptions, Theorem 3, which is proved in the appendix, provides the standardized unconditional (predictive) distribution $\eta(y)$.

Theorem 3. Under the assumptions outlined in section 3 and for the prior p_0 given by (17), the standardized unconditional (predictive) distribution η used in (II′) *is normal. Denoting $\mathbf{X}_{(i)}$, $i = 1, 2$, as a partition of $\mathbf{X}$ conformable with $\boldsymbol{\mu}(i)$, the parameters $\overset{*}{\boldsymbol{\mu}}_X$ and $\overset{*}{s}_{\mathrm{X}}$ are given as*

$$\overset{*}{\mu}_X \equiv X'(1)[\hat{\mu}(1) - V_{11}^{-1}V_{12}\{\mu^0(2) - \hat{\mu}(2)\}],$$

$$\overset{*}{s}_{\mathrm{X}} \equiv [X'(1)(V_{11}^{-1}/T)X(1) + X'\Sigma X]^{\frac{1}{2}}.$$

Given the form of η in Theorem 3, the admissible set can again be obtained by a "mean-scale" type selection rule [Bawa (1978b)], where $\overset{*}{\mu}_{\mathrm{X}}$ and $\overset{*}{s}{}_{\mathrm{X}}^2$ are the appropriate mean and scale (variance in this case) measures, respectively. For example, for given $\overset{*}{\mu}_{\mathrm{X}}$, risk-averse individuals will minimize $\overset{*}{s}_{\mathrm{X}}$. However, since $\overset{*}{\mu}_{\mathrm{X}} \neq \mathbf{X}'(1)\hat{\boldsymbol{\mu}}(1) + X'(2)\hat{\boldsymbol{\mu}}(2) = \mathbf{X}'\hat{\boldsymbol{\mu}} = \hat{\mu}_{\mathrm{X}}$ and $\overset{*}{s}_{\mathrm{X}} \neq \sigma_{\mathrm{X}}$, decisions are no longer characterized by an estimated mean $\hat{\mu}_{\mathrm{X}}$, and the variance, σ_{X}^2, as they are in the ECS.

To explain Theorem 3 intuitively, consider the bivariate case in which the portfolio consists of two securities, with returns $\tilde{r}_{1t}$ and $\tilde{r}_{2t}$, $t = 1, \ldots, T$. Then, assuming the first security's mean, μ_1, is unknown while the second security's mean, μ_2, is known to equal μ_2^0 in the prior, it follows from Theorem 3 that

$$\overset{*}{\mu}_{\mathrm{X}} = \hat{\mu}_{\mathrm{X}} + X_1(\sigma_1/\sigma_2)\rho[\mu_2^0 - \hat{\mu}_2], \tag{18}$$

$$\overset{*}{s}_{\mathrm{X}} = [(1-\rho^2)\cdot X_1^2 \cdot \sigma_1^2/T + \sigma_{\mathrm{X}}^2]^{\frac{1}{2}}.$$

In (18), σ_1^2 and σ_2^2 are the variances of $\tilde{r}_{1t}$ and $\tilde{r}_{2t}$, respectively, and ρ is the correlation coefficient between the two security returns. Turning first to $\overset{*}{\mu}_{\mathrm{X}}$, since the second mean, $\mu_2 = \mu_2^0$, is known, we are not directly interested in its estimate. However, if the data are misleading as to the second mean, and the means are correlated, then the data are misleading as to the first mean. For example, if $\mu_2^0 > \hat{\mu}_2(\mu_2$'s estimate), then the data would understate the second mean (if one had employed the estimate rather than its known value, μ_2^0). If the returns are positively correlated ($\rho > 0$), then the data understate the first mean. Accordingly, the contribution of the first mean to expected portfolio return must be revised upward relative to its estimate (based solely on the data). The adjustment factor is given by

$$X_1(\sigma_1/\sigma_2)\rho(\mu_2^O - \hat{\mu}_2). \tag{19}$$

Turning now to s_X^{*2} in (18), note that it consists of two components, $(1-\rho^2)\cdot X_1^2\sigma_1^2/T$ and σ_X^2. The latter represents portfolio variance, while the former measures the impact of estimation risk. In a non-Bayesian analysis, σ_1^2/T would be the variance of μ_1's estimator, $\hat{\mu}_1$. Here, σ_1^2/T is the posterior variance of μ_1. It is essentially an additional risk element incurred as a result of not knowing the value of μ_1.

If estimation risk (σ_1^2/T) is ignored, then a risk-averse individual would behave in closer accordance with Theorem 1. For a given appropriate mean measure, μ_X^*, portfolios would be chosen to minimize the variance, σ_X^2. If the first security has a low variance, this decision rule may result in a high proportion of the portfolio being invested in the first security, i.e., a high X_1. However, once estimation risk is taken into account, it is clear from (18) that less weight will be given to the first security. In this manner, the impact of estimation risk is reduced by reducing the proportion of the portfolio invested in that security whose mean is unknown. Intuitively, other things being equal, a risk-averse individual will want to invest more heavily in those securities about which he has the most knowledge.

To examine the implications of removing the independence assumption, assume that we are interested in comparing several mutual funds. Each consists of a set of securities; the funds differ in the proportions invested in the various securities. Assume that we only observe the overall return to the funds at time t, $\tilde{f}_t^X$, $t = 1, \ldots, T$, and that $\tilde{f}_t^X$ is normally and independently distributed with mean μ_X and variance σ_X^2. Suppose that the mean, μ_X, is not independent of the variance, σ_X^2, in the prior. It may be, for example, that one initially believes that funds with a high mean have a high variance. In a simple formulation that captures this dependence, assume that

$$\mu_X = M(\sigma_X) + \epsilon, \tag{20}$$

where M is a known function (probably non-decreasing) and ϵ is a normally distributed error term with mean zero and known variance, σ_ϵ^2. Further, as stated above, for simplicity assume that σ_X^2 is known.

Employing these assumptions, the prior p_0 on the unknown mean μ_X is assumed to be normal with mean $M(\sigma_X)$ and variance σ_ϵ^2, i.e.,

$$p_0(\mu_X|\sigma_X) = N[M(\sigma_X), \sigma_\epsilon^2]. \tag{21}$$

Then, the standardized predictive distribution η is given by the following theorem.

Theorem 4. Under the assumption that portfolio returns at time t, $\tilde{f}_t^{\mathrm{X}}$, $t = 1,\ldots,T$, *are independently and normally distributed with mean* μ_{X} *and variance* σ_{X}^2 *and the prior* p_0 *given by (21), the standardized unconditional (predictive) distribution used in* (II′) *is normal. The parameters* μ_{X}^* *and* s_{X}^* *are given by*

$$\mu_{\mathrm{X}}^* = [\hat{\mu}_{\mathrm{X}}\sigma_\epsilon^2 + M(\sigma_{\mathrm{X}})\sigma_{\mathrm{X}}^2/T]/[\sigma_\epsilon^2+\sigma_{\mathrm{X}}^2/T],$$

$$s_{\mathrm{X}}^* = \{[\sigma_\epsilon^2\sigma_{\mathrm{X}}^2/T]/[\sigma_\epsilon^2+\sigma_{\mathrm{X}}^2/T]+\sigma_{\mathrm{X}}^2\}^{\frac{1}{2}},$$

where

$$\hat{\mu}_{\mathrm{X}} \equiv \sum_{t=1}^{T} f_t^{\mathrm{X}}/T.$$

Theorem 4 is proved in the appendix.

From Theorem 4 it is readily apparent that the admissible set is again given by a 'mean-scale' selection rule [see Bawa (1978b)], where μ_{X}^* and σ_{X}^2 are the appropriate mean and scale measures, respectively. However, decisions cannot be characterized in terms of the fund's estimated mean, $\hat{\mu}_{\mathrm{X}}$, and variance, σ_{X}^2, as they are in the ECS. For example, for risk-averse individuals $[U'' < 0]$, it is now possible that (assuming $M'(\sigma_{\mathrm{X}}) > 0$) expected utility is an increasing function of σ_{X}. Consequently, for the same estimated mean, $\hat{\mu}_{\mathrm{X}}$, a risk-averse individual, in choosing between two funds, might choose the fund with higher variance, σ_{X}^2. The problem here is that the relevant mean and variance measures are μ_{X}^* and s_{X}^{*2}, not $\hat{\mu}_{\mathrm{X}}$ and σ_{X}^2. Since μ_{X} depends on σ_{X} in the prior, increases in σ_{X} may increase the relevant mean measure, μ_{X}^*, which in turn may increase expected utility. Conditions under which this holds depend on the specific form of the utility function.

This example also has implications for risk behavior. If individuals believe that μ_{X} and σ_{X} are positively related $[M'(\sigma_{\mathrm{X}}) > 0]$, which is not unreasonable, then 'observed' risk-seeking behavior under the ECS may be really risk-averse behavior in terms of the appropriate mean and scale measures when estimation risk is explicitly considered in the decision process.

5. Conclusions

In the theory of choice under uncertainty, optimal decisions are typically formulated in terms of certain parameters of underlying probability distributions. However, the parameters' values are seldom known in practical situations. It is therefore important to incorporate the estimation problem (parameter uncertainty) and the accompanying estimation risk into the general decision problem. The purpose of this paper has been to examine the effect of estimation risk on optimal portfolio choice.

We have shown for the problem of optimal portfolio choice that for the normal distribution of returns and under "noninformative" or "invariant" priors, the admissible set is the same under the ECS and the UCS. However, as a result of estimation risk, the optimal member of this set under the UCS will differ from that under the ECS. For other types of priors that one is likely to encounter, the admissible set under the UCS was shown via illustrative examples to differ from that in the ECS. The method of analysis employed here could be extended to characterize capital market equilibrium when parameter values are unknown. In this manner, the impact of estimation risk on capital market equilibrium could be taken into account. Such an analysis would integrate the Sharpe-Lintner-Mossin (1964, 1965, 1966) Capital Asset Pricing Model (that assumes that the parameter values are known) with the econometric analysis [see, for example Jensen (1972a), Jensen (1972b) and references therein] done to estimate the unknown values of the parameters. These issues are addressed in Brown (1979) and Chapters 6 and 7 of this book.

Appendix: Proofs of Theorems

Proof of Theorem 1. Expected utility (unconditional) is given by

$$\underset{\tilde{\mathbf{R}}}{E}[U(\mathbf{X}'\tilde{\mathbf{R}})] = \int_{\mathbf{X}'\mathbf{R},\boldsymbol{\mu},\boldsymbol{\Sigma}} U(\mathbf{X}'\mathbf{R})\,h(\mathbf{X}'\mathbf{R}|\boldsymbol{\mu},\boldsymbol{\Sigma})\,p(\boldsymbol{\mu},\boldsymbol{\Sigma})\,d(\cdot),$$

where h is the conditional p.d.f. of $\mathbf{X}'\tilde{\mathbf{R}}$. From Zellner (1971, pp. 233-236, 383-385), the predictive distribution is in the t-form, where with

$$\hat{\boldsymbol{\mu}}' \equiv (\hat{\mu}_1,\ldots,\hat{\mu}_m), \qquad \hat{\mu}_i \equiv \sum_{t=1}^{T} r_{it}/T,$$

$$\mathbf{1}' \equiv (1,1,\ldots,1):1\times m, \qquad \mathbf{S} \equiv (\mathbf{r}-\mathbf{1}\hat{\boldsymbol{\mu}}')'(\mathbf{r}-\mathbf{1}\hat{\boldsymbol{\mu}}'),$$

$$s_{\mathbf{X}}^{*2} \equiv (1+1/T)\mathbf{X}'\mathbf{S}\mathbf{X}/(T-m),$$

the variable $(\mathbf{X}'\tilde{\mathbf{R}}-\mathbf{X}'\boldsymbol{\mu})/s_{\mathbf{X}}^{*}$ has a standardized Student-t distribution with $T-m$ degrees of freedom. Letting $\tilde{y} \equiv (\mathbf{X}'\tilde{\mathbf{R}}-\mathbf{X}'\hat{\boldsymbol{\mu}})/s_{\mathbf{X}}^{*}$, the theorem immediately follows.

Q.E.D.

The following lemma will be useful in proving Theorems 3 and 4.

Lemma 1. Define

$$E[U(\tilde{P}_{\mathbf{X}})|\mu_{\mathbf{X}},\sigma_{\mathbf{X}}] \equiv \int_{-\infty}^{\infty} U(\mu_{\mathbf{X}}+\sigma_{\mathbf{X}}\cdot z)\phi(z)\,dz,$$

where z is a standard normal variable. Partition $\mathbf{X}$ and $\boldsymbol{\mu}$ conformably as

$$\mathbf{X}' \equiv [\mathbf{X}'(1)|\mathbf{X}'(2)], \qquad \boldsymbol{\mu}' \equiv [\boldsymbol{\mu}'(1)|\boldsymbol{\mu}'(2)].$$

Assume that $\boldsymbol{\mu}(1)$'s posterior p.d.f., given $\boldsymbol{\mu}(2)$ and $\boldsymbol{\Sigma}$, is multivariate normal with mean $\bar{\boldsymbol{\mu}}(1)$ and variance-covariance matrix, $\boldsymbol{\Omega}$. Then, if $\boldsymbol{\Omega}$ depends only on $\boldsymbol{\Sigma}$,

$$E[U(\tilde{P}_{\mathbf{X}})|\boldsymbol{\mu}(2),\boldsymbol{\Sigma}] = \int_{-\infty}^{\infty} U[\mu_{\mathbf{X}}^{*}+s_{\mathbf{X}}^{*}y^{*}]\phi(y^{*})\,dy^{*},$$

where $\tilde{y}^{*}$ is a standard normal variable, and

$$\mu_{\mathbf{X}}^{*} \equiv \mathbf{X}'(1)\bar{\boldsymbol{\mu}}(1)+\mathbf{X}'(2)\boldsymbol{\mu}(2),$$

$$s_{\mathbf{X}}^{*} \equiv [\mathbf{X}'(1)\boldsymbol{\Omega}\mathbf{X}'(1)+\mathbf{X}'\boldsymbol{\Sigma}\mathbf{X}]^{\frac{1}{2}}.$$

Proof. Expected utility is given by

$$E[U(\tilde{P}_X)|\boldsymbol{\mu}(2),\boldsymbol{\Sigma}] = \int_{-\infty}^{\infty} U(\mu_X+\sigma_X\cdot z)\phi(z)p(\cdot)d(\cdot),$$

where p is $\boldsymbol{\mu}(1)$'s conditional (posterior) p.d.f. With $\mathbf{H}$ defined such that $\mathbf{H}'\mathbf{H} \equiv \boldsymbol{\Omega}^{-1}$ and $\mathbf{Z}^* \equiv \mathbf{H}[\boldsymbol{\mu}(1)-\bar{\boldsymbol{\mu}}(1)]$, expected utility becomes

$$E[\cdot] = \int_{\mathbf{Z}^*}\cdots\int_z U[\mu_X^*+\mathbf{X}'(1)\mathbf{H}^{-1}\mathbf{Z}^*+(\mathbf{X}'\boldsymbol{\Sigma}\mathbf{X})^{\frac{1}{2}}\cdot z]\phi(z)p_*(\mathbf{Z}^*)d(\cdot),$$

where $p_*(\cdot)$ is the multivariate p.d.f. of the independent standard normal variables $\tilde{\mathbf{Z}}^*$. Let

$$y \equiv \mu_X^* + \mathbf{X}'(1)\mathbf{H}^{-1}\mathbf{Z}^*(\mathbf{X}'\boldsymbol{\Sigma}\mathbf{X})^{\frac{1}{2}}\cdot \mathbf{z},$$

$$E[\cdot] = \int_y U(y)f_y(h)\,dy,$$

where $\tilde{y}$'s p.d.f., $f_y(\cdot)$ is normal with mean μ_X^* and variance $s_X^{*2} \equiv \mathbf{X}'(1)\boldsymbol{\Omega}\mathbf{X}(1) + \mathbf{X}'\boldsymbol{\Sigma}\mathbf{X}$. Therefore, with

$$y^* \equiv (y-\mu_X^*)/s_X^*,$$

the lemma follows immediately.

Q.E.D.

Proof of Theorem 3. The likelihood function for $\boldsymbol{\mu}(1)$, as a function of $\boldsymbol{\Sigma}^0$, $\boldsymbol{\mu}^0(2)$, and the data on security returns can be written as [see Zellner (1971, 380-383)] in the following form:

$$L \;\alpha\; exp[-\frac{1}{2}\{[\boldsymbol{\mu}'(1)-\hat{\boldsymbol{\mu}}^{*\prime}(1)]\,T\cdot\mathbf{V}_{11}[\boldsymbol{\mu}(1)-\hat{\boldsymbol{\mu}}^*(1)]\}],$$

where, with $\hat{\boldsymbol{\mu}}(1)$ and $\hat{\boldsymbol{\mu}}(2)$ denoting the appropriate vectors of sample means [estimates of $\boldsymbol{\mu}(1)$ and $\boldsymbol{\mu}(2)$ respectively],

$$\hat{\boldsymbol{\mu}}^{*\prime}(1) \equiv \hat{\boldsymbol{\mu}}'(1)-[\boldsymbol{\mu}^0(2)-\hat{\boldsymbol{\mu}}(2)]'\mathbf{V}_{21}\mathbf{V}_{11}^{-1}.$$

Therefore, the conditional posterior p.d.f. for $\boldsymbol{\mu}(1)$ is multivariate normal with mean $\hat{\boldsymbol{\mu}}^*(1)$ and variance-covariance matrix $\mathbf{V}_{11}^{-1}/T$. Accordingly, the proof follows from Lemma 1.

Q.E.D.

Proof of Theorem 4. Given σ_X, expected utility is given by

$$E[U(\tilde{P}_X)|\sigma_X] = \int_{\mu_X}\int_{z} U(\mu_X+\sigma_X\cdot z)\phi(z)p(\mu_X)\,dz\,d\mu_X,$$

where $\tilde{z}$ is standard normal random variable with p.d.p. ϕ and $p(\mu_X)$ is μ_X's posterior p.d.f. given data on fund returns over time, f_t^X, $t = 1, \ldots, T$. Since the prior for μ_X (given σ_X) is normal with variance σ_ϵ^2 and mean

$$M(\sigma_X),$$

the posterior p.d.f. of μ_X (given σ_X) will be normal [see Box-Tiao (1973, 15-18)], with mean

$$\mu_X^* \equiv \frac{\hat{\mu}_X\sigma_\epsilon^2+M(\sigma_X)\sigma_X^2/T}{\sigma_\epsilon^2+\sigma_X^2/T},$$

where

$$\hat{\mu}_X \equiv \sum_{t=1}^{T} f_t^X/T.$$

The variance is given by

$$s_X^{*2} = [\sigma_\epsilon^2\sigma_X^2/T]/[\sigma_\epsilon^2+\sigma_X^2/t].$$

The theorem now directly follows from Lemma 1.

Q.E.D.

CHAPTER 5

THE EFFECT OF LIMITED INFORMATION AND ESTIMATION RISK ON OPTIMAL PORTFOLIO DIVERSIFICATION*

Roger W. KLEIN and Vijay S. BAWA**

1. Introduction

In the previous chapter [reproduced from Klein and Bawa (1976)], we considered the portfolio choice problem where the joint distribution of security returns was multivariate normal and the values of the underlying parameters (means and variance-covariance matrix) were unknown. We determined the effect of estimation risk on optimal portfolio choice for the case of sufficient sample information (the number of observations per security exceeds the number of securities) and for a "noninformative" prior (on the unknown parameters), as well as for several illustrative cases of informative priors. We showed that for the "noninformative" prior, the admissible set of portfolios, taking estimation risk into account, is identical to that obtained using traditional mean-variance analysis. for all risk-averse investors, it is the well-known Markowitz-Tobin mean, minimum variance boundary. For all investors (including risk seekers and those with Friedman-Savage type utility functions) this admissible set is the Markowitz-Tobin boundary plus an additional set as given in Bawa (1976). However, as a direct result of estimation risk, an investor's optimal choice differs from that obtained by traditional analysis: Under assumptions provided in Chapter 4, for risk-averse investors, the optimal choice involves investing monotonically more in the riskless asset as the degree of (sample) information decreases. Brown (1979) has recently shown that for this case, with all investors having homogeneous beliefs, "noninformative" priors, and access to the same (sufficient) sample information, the traditional Sharpe-Lintner-Mossin Capital Asset Pricing Model [Sharpe (1964), Lintner (1965), Mossin (1966)] derived for the case of known parameter values remains intact.[1] Thus, the aforementioned result implies that the effect of estimation risk is for risk-averse investors to behave as if they exhibited additional risk aversion by investing more in riskless assets and less in the "market" portfolio of risky assets.[2]

* This paper, with the exception of notational changes made for purposes of consistency and several minor expository changes, appeared in *Journal of Financial Economics* 5(1977)89-111

** An earlier version of this paper was presented at the Bell Laboratories Symposium on Financial Economics, September 1976. We thank the participants of this symposium, especially Professors S. Ross and A. Zellner, for their helpful suggestions. We acknowledge helpful comments by T. Foregger and Kenneth Gaver, on an earlier draft.

1. More details of this are provided in the next Chapter.

2. Of course, as intuitively expected, the reverse would hold for risk-seekers.

In practice, it is quite common that the sample information is insufficient (i.e., the number of observations per security is less than the number of securities). Indeed most econometric analysis in capital markets is typically based on this type of small data sample [see, for example, Black, Jensen and Scholes (1972), Blume (1970), Miller and Scholes (1972), and Fama and MacBeth (1973)].[3]

Furthermore, even if it were hypothetically possible to gather additional data costlessly, there are two constraints that limit any advantage to increasing the sample size. First, one could increase the data sample by lengthening the observation period over which past data are collected. However, if the observation period is too long, then the assumption of stationary probability distributions becomes untenable. Second, one could increase the sample size by taking observations at more frequent intervals within a given observation period. However, if one assumes that returns are serially uncorrelated over time, then this assumption becomes unrealistic with finer partitions of the observation period. One could take such correlation into account. Yet, this could only be done at the expense of introducing additional parameters with unknown values and thereby possibly increasing the "estimation uncertainty".[4] Therefore, it is important to examine the portfolio choice problem with unknown parameter values when the data sample is small, i.e., insufficient sample information.

As in the previous Chapter, we assume throughout this Chapter that the joint distribution of the m risky security returns, $\tilde{\mathbf{R}}$, is multivariate normal with mean vector $\boldsymbol{\mu}$ and variance-covariance matrix $\boldsymbol{\Sigma}$. We will denote this distribution by $f(\mathbf{R}|\boldsymbol{\theta})$, $\boldsymbol{\theta} \equiv (\boldsymbol{\mu}, \boldsymbol{\Sigma})$. The investor's problem is to choose a vector of portfolio allocations (proportions of wealth), $\overline{\mathbf{X}} \equiv (X_0, \mathbf{X}')$, where X_0 denotes the investment in a riskless security and $\mathbf{X}'$ the vector of allocations to the risky securities. In making these allocations, the values of the parameters $\boldsymbol{\mu}$ and $\boldsymbol{\Sigma}$ are unknown.

We will focus primarily on the Bayesian procedure discussed in previous chapters to account for estimation risk. For reasons discussed in Chapter 4, we use the term Unconditional Solution (UCS) to refer to the Bayesian approach. We will also have occasion to refer to the (parameter) certainty equivalent approach in which decisions are made by replacing unknown parameter values with point estimates. As in Chapter 4, we refer to this method as the Estimated Conditional Solution, ECS.

To employ the UCS, we require the likelihood function for the observations and the prior distribution. As in Chapter 4, we assume that the data consist of a random sample of T observations drawn from the multivariate normal return distribution. The observed risky returns at time t are denoted by R_{it}, $i = 1,\ldots,m$, $t = 1,\ldots,T$[5] As to the prior distribution, since the results derived below are based on different priors, we will make the prior specification explicit in subsequent sections.

For several important prior distributions, we will determine the effect of limited information and estimation risk on both the admissible set of securities and the

3. Estimation risk is not explicitly considered in any of these studies.

4. There may be an important tradeoff between increasing the sample size in this manner and increasing the number of unknown parameters. This tradeoff, however, is beyond the scope of this paper.

5. Each return is a rate determined as the ratio of the price change plus dividends, during the period to the price level at the beginning of the period. There are no transactions costs or taxes in this formulation.

optimal portfolio choice. Section 2 examines the case of sufficient information (prior and/or sample) and provides conditions under which the optimal portfolio choice involves investing monotonically more in the riskless asset as the degree of information decreases. This result generalizes, and provides the link to, the result for sufficient sample information and "noninformative" prior information in Chapter 4. The results in section 2, as shown in Bawa (1977b) imply that in equilibrium, the traditional Capital Asset Pricing Model still holds: A risk-averse investor behaves as if his degree of risk aversion had increased by investing more in the riskless asset and less in the "market" portfolio for risky assets. These issues are also discussed in the next chapter.

In section 3, we consider two illustrative cases of insufficient sample information and minimal prior information (i.e., a prior arbitrary close to the well-known "noninformative" prior) and show that it is asymptotically optimal for a risk-averse investor to limit diversification to a subset of the securities. The first case considers minimal prior information on all risky assets and shows that it is asymptotically optimal to invest only in the riskless asset. This result has the intuitive appeal that in view of insufficient information, the risk-averse investor behaves as if the induced risk aversion is very large and asymptotically invests only in the safe asset. The second case involves differential amounts of information on two different security subsets. We consider the situation of sufficient information on the first security subset and minimal information on the second subset of the remaining securities. We obtain the intuitive result that the optimal portfolio asymptotically limits diversification among the first set of securities only. This admittedly extreme, but realistic, case is included to make explicit what seems to be done implicitly in many problems that involve decision-making under uncertainty. Namely, every time one specifies a set of alternatives, from among which an optimal element is chosen (e.g., all securities, stocks and bonds, traded in U.S. capital markets), one is implicitly eliminating all other available alternatives from consideration (e.g., securities in foreign capital markets). In this manner, one is implicitly imposing a special type of information structure on those alternatives not even considered. Our result is very much in this spirit and indicates that it is asymptotically optimal for an investor to limit diversification among a small subset of securities for which he has sufficient useful/relevant information. These theoretical results are in keeping with the observation that large groups of investors invest in either a (nominally) riskless asset or a subset of all securities. Some concluding remarks are provided in section 4.

2. Optimal portfolio choice: Sufficient information

To characterize a situation of sufficient information, we will employ two prior specifications and analyze the UCS under each one. First, letting $\boldsymbol{\iota}$ denote a vector of ones, assume that the prior on $(\boldsymbol{\mu}, \boldsymbol{\Sigma})$ is given by

$$p_0(\boldsymbol{\mu}, \boldsymbol{\Sigma}) \equiv p_0(\boldsymbol{\mu}|\boldsymbol{\Sigma})p_0(\boldsymbol{\Sigma}), \tag{1}$$

$$p_0(\boldsymbol{\mu}|\,\boldsymbol{\Sigma})\ \alpha\ c, \qquad -\infty\boldsymbol{\iota} < \boldsymbol{\mu} < \infty\boldsymbol{\iota},$$

$$p_0(\boldsymbol{\Sigma})\ \alpha\ |\boldsymbol{\Sigma}|^{-(m+1-d_0)/2}\exp\{-\frac{1}{2}tr[d_0\cdot\boldsymbol{\Omega}\cdot\boldsymbol{\Sigma}^{-1}]\}, \qquad |\boldsymbol{\Sigma}| > 0,$$

where c is a constant, $\boldsymbol{\Omega}$ is positive definite, and $d_o \geqslant 0$. Here d_0 is to be interpreted as the prior degrees of freedom. Note that $d_0 = 0$ corresponds to the "noninformative" prior on $\boldsymbol{\Sigma}$.[6] We can now establish the following theorem, which does not depend on the allocation constraint set, **C**. This theorem generalizes Theorem 1 of Chapter 4.

Theorem 1. Employing the prior in (1), assume that $d \equiv T - m + d_0 > 0$. *Let S be the unnormalized-sample variance-covariance matrix:*

$$\left[S_{ij} \equiv \sum_t (R_{it} - \bar{R}_i)(R_{jt} - \bar{R}_j) \right].$$

Then, under the assumptions on $f(\mathbf{R}|\boldsymbol{\theta})$ *and the likelihood function for* $\boldsymbol{\theta}$, *expected utility under the UCS is given as*

$$E[U(\tilde{P}_{\mathbf{X}})] = \int_{-\infty}^{\infty} U\Big\{ X_0\mu_0 + \mathbf{X}'\hat{\boldsymbol{\mu}} + [(1+1/T)|(T-m)|/d]^{1/2} \times [\mathbf{X}'(\mathbf{S}+d_0\cdot\boldsymbol{\Omega})\,\mathbf{X}/|(T-m)|]^{1/2}\cdot y\Big\}\eta(y)\,dy,$$

where $\hat{\mu}$ *is a vector of sample means and* $\tilde{y}$ *is a random variable with standardized Student-t distribution,* $\eta(y)$, *with d degrees of freedom.*

To prove this theorem, note that it can be shown from Zellner (1971, p. 224-229) that under the conditions outlined in Theorem 1, the predictive distribution of $\tilde{\mathbf{R}}$ is multivariate Student-t with d degrees of freedom. Therefore, Theorem 2 follows directly by employing the same transformation as in the proof of Theorem 1 in Chapter 4.

Theorem 1 enables us to obtain the admissible set of portfolios as well as the optimal portfolio choice for all investors under the UCS. We can now compare this portfolio to that obtained under the ECS. As shown in Chapter 4, expected utility under the ECS reduces to (for $T > m$)

$$\int_{-\infty}^{\infty} U(X_0\mu_0 + \mathbf{X}'\hat{\boldsymbol{\mu}} + [\mathbf{X}'\mathbf{S}\mathbf{X}/(T-m)]^{1/2}\cdot z)\phi(z)\,dz, \tag{2}$$

where $\tilde{z}$ is a random variable with a standard normal distribution ϕ. Thus, as noted in Chapter 4, one obtains (2) by replacing the unknown mean $\boldsymbol{\mu}$ by $\hat{\boldsymbol{\mu}}$ and the unknown variance-covariance matrix $\boldsymbol{\Sigma}$ by $\mathbf{S}/(T-m)$.[7] The admissible set of portfolios for all risk-averse investors is the Markowitz-Tobin mean-variance admissible boundary. Also, the set of admissible portfolios for all investors is this boundary plus an additional set of portfolios identified in Bawa (1976). From Theorem 1, under the UCS, the underlying distribution is a Student-t with

6. See Geisser (1965, p. 604) for an interpretation of $p_0(\boldsymbol{\Sigma})$ when $d_0 = 0$.

7. All results based on comparing the UCS with the ECS hold if in the ECS, $\boldsymbol{\Sigma} = \mathbf{S}/N, N > T - m$.

$d = (d_0+T-m)$ degrees of freedom and with location and scale parameters (μ_X^*, s_X^*) given by

$$\mu_X^* = X_0\mu_0 + \mathbf{X}'\hat{\mu},$$

$$s_X^* = \mathbf{X}'\mathbf{\Sigma}^*\mathbf{X}, \qquad \mathbf{\Sigma}^* \equiv (\mathbf{S}+d_o\cdot\mathbf{\Omega})/[d/(1+1/T]. \tag{3}$$

Thus, using the results in Bawa (1975), it follows that the admissible portfolios under the UCS are obtained by a "mean-variance" rule using (μ_X^*, s_X^*) instead of the unknown (μ_X, σ_X). However, from (3), since $\mathbf{\Sigma}^*$ is not proportional to $\hat{\mathbf{\Sigma}} \equiv \mathbf{S}/(T-m)$, the admissible set of portfolios for the UCS is distinctly different from that under the ECS. Therefore, in general, the optimal portfolio choice under these two procedures, a member of their respective admissible sets, will also be different. We note that for the special case where $T > m$ and $d_o = 0$, the case of the "noninformative" prior considered in Chapter 4, $\mathbf{\Sigma}^*$ is proportional to $\hat{\mathbf{\Sigma}}$. In this case, the admissible set under the UCS is identical to that under the ECS. Even in this case, the optimal portfolio choices are different (Theorem 2 of Chapter 4).

We now proceed to obtain the effect of the degree of information (as characterized by d) on the optimal portfolio choice under the UCS. Let

$$AR \equiv -U''(W)/U'(W) \quad \text{and} \quad RR \equiv -WU''(W)/U'(W) \tag{4}$$

denote the Arrow-Pratt absolute and relative risk-aversion indices respectively. Define the following class of utility functions:

$$\mathbf{U} = \{U: U' > 0,\ U'' < 0,\ AR' \leqslant 0,\ RR' \geqslant 0,\ RR \leqslant 1\}. \tag{5}$$

Then, the effect of changes in information is summarized by the following theorem:

Theorem 2. Assume that the allocation constraint set is given by the following:

$$\mathbf{C}_1 \equiv \left\{X_i: \sum_{i=0}^{m} X_i = 1\right\}.$$

Then, under the conditions outlined in Theorem 1 and for all utility functions in **U**, *the optimal allocation to the riskless asset under the UCS is:*

i. *strictly more than under the ECS if* $T > m$ *and* $(1+1/T)|(T-m)|/d \geqslant 1$.[8]

ii. *monotonically increasing as* $d > 0$ *decreases.*

8. We require $T > m$ for this comparison, because the ECS as shown in (2) is undefined if $T \leqslant m$. From Theorem 1 and (2), if we also have $(1+1/T)(T-m)/d \geqslant 1$, then investment in the risky securities is unambiguously a riskier proposition under the UCS than as perceived by the ECS. Consequently, part (i) of Theorem 2 is intuitive. The proof of this theorem is identical (except for obvious notational changes) To Theorem 2 of Chapter 4. With a positive riskless return, μ_p denoting the portfolio mean return, and $\sigma_p(\mu_p)$ the admissible boundary, $\mu_p\sigma'(p)/\sigma_p > 1$. The proof of Theorem 2 in Chapter 4 then shows that any decrease in the degrees of freedom of the predictive Student-t distribution (the degrees of freedom are infinite

The proof of this theorem is the same, except for obvious notational changes, as the proof of Theorem 2 of Chapter 4 and will not be repeated (see footnote 7). To explain this result intuitively, note that the posterior degrees of freedom, d, are decreased through a decrease in the sample size, T, or a decrease in the prior degrees of freedom, d_0. As the degree of prior and/or sample information (summarized in d) decreases, estimation risk increases. In this case, a risk-averse investor with $U \in \mathbf{U}$ will seek additional security.

The above results are applicable as long as $d = (T-m+d_0) > 0$. However, as argued above, it is likely that $T-m \ll 0$ (insufficient sample information), in which case there is no guarantee that $d > 0$. Unfortunately, if $d \leqslant 0$, the predictive distribution underlying the above theorems is undefined. To circumvent this insufficient sample problem, we will examine an alternative prior that is sufficiently informative to generate a well-defined predictive distribution.[9] As in Theorems 1-2, we will refer to this case as one of sufficient information (sample plus prior).

We note that it follows from Lemma 2 (Appendix) that when $T \ll m$, the predictive distribution is undefined, not due to a diffuse prior for $\boldsymbol{\mu}$, but due to an improper prior for $\boldsymbol{\Sigma}$. To analyze this case, we therefore require a proper prior for $\boldsymbol{\Sigma}$. We still want (in section 3) to analyze optimal portfolio choice when $T < m$ (for all securities or a security subset) and prior information is minimal. Accordingly, we will formulate a proper prior for $\boldsymbol{\Sigma}$ that can (in part) be characterized by a parameter vector, say $\boldsymbol{\epsilon}$, that reflects the degree of prior information. As $\boldsymbol{\epsilon} \rightarrow \mathbf{O}$, this proper prior will converge to the "noninformative" prior, which permits us to examine asymptotically optimal portfolio choice in a minimal information (sample plus prior) setting. Since $\boldsymbol{\Sigma}$ enters the portfolio choice problem as $\mathbf{X}'\boldsymbol{\Sigma}\mathbf{X}$,[10] we ultimately need the prior for $\mathbf{X}'\boldsymbol{\Sigma}\mathbf{X}$ that is implied or induced (exactly or as in our case approximately) by the proper prior for $\boldsymbol{\Sigma}$. The details of this formulation are discussed below, and our final prior specification, termed ϵ-informative, is shown in (9).

To formulate this proper prior for $\boldsymbol{\Sigma}$, note that the "noninformative" prior for Σ is given by [(3) with $d_0 = 0$]:

$$P_0(\boldsymbol{\Sigma}) \; \alpha \; |\boldsymbol{\Sigma}|^{-(m+1)/2}, \; \boldsymbol{\Sigma} \in \bar{\mathbf{A}} \equiv \{\boldsymbol{\Sigma}:|\boldsymbol{\Sigma}|>0\}. \tag{6}$$

In view of the prior in (6), it seems natural to obtain the desired proper prior for $\boldsymbol{\Sigma}$ by restricting its domain. Therefore, we restrict the eigenvalues of $\boldsymbol{\Sigma}$ to obtain the following:[11]

---

under the ECS) will strictly decrease the mean portfolio return (at the optimum). Consequently, investment in the riskless security will increase. Note that Theorem 2 in Chapter 4 precluded short sales, but implicitly assumed unconstrained borrowing and lending at a riskless rate; it also readily holds under $\mathbf{C}_1$ defined above.

9. For $T - m < 0$, one might attempt to examine a low information benchmark case for which $d_0 = m - T + 1$. However, this prior specification is unacceptable as it depends on the sample size.

10. The return of the risky portion of this portfolio, $\mathbf{X}'\tilde{\mathbf{R}}$, is distributed as $N(\mathbf{X}'\boldsymbol{\mu}, \mathbf{X}'\boldsymbol{\Sigma}\mathbf{X})$. Therefore, with $\tilde{z} \equiv (x'\mathbf{R}-\mu)/(X'\Sigma X)^{1/2}$ expected utility conditioned on μ and Σ is

$$E[U(P_{\bar{\mathbf{X}}})] = E_{\tilde{z}}[U(X_0\mu) + \mathbf{X}'\boldsymbol{\mu} + (\mathbf{X}'\boldsymbol{\Sigma}\mathbf{X})^{1/2}\cdot\tilde{z})].$$

11. Letting $\underline{\lambda}$ and $\bar{\lambda}$ denote the smallest and largest eigenvalue of $\boldsymbol{\Sigma}$, respectively,

$$\underline{\lambda}^m \leqslant |\boldsymbol{\Sigma}| \leqslant \bar{\lambda}^m.$$

$$P_{0\epsilon}(\mathbf{\Sigma})\ \alpha\ |\mathbf{\Sigma}|^{-(m+1)/2},\ \mathbf{\Sigma} \in \overline{\mathbf{A}}_\epsilon \equiv \{\mathbf{\Sigma}{:}\epsilon_1 < |\mathbf{\Sigma}| < \epsilon_2^{-1}\}, \qquad (7)$$

where $0 < \epsilon_1 < \epsilon_2^{-1}$. The parameters characterizing the boundary of $\overline{\mathbf{A}}_\epsilon$, $\boldsymbol{\epsilon} \equiv (\epsilon_1, \epsilon_2)$, measure the closeness of the proper prior for $\mathbf{\Sigma}$ in (7) with domain $\overline{\mathbf{A}}_\epsilon$ to the improper prior in (6) with domain $\overline{\mathbf{A}}$. As $\boldsymbol{\epsilon} \to \mathbf{O}$, the boundary of $\overline{\mathbf{A}}_\epsilon$ monotonically approaches that of $\overline{\mathbf{A}}$ (in Euclidean distance). Consequently, changes in prior information can be measured conveniently by changes in $\boldsymbol{\epsilon}$.

Since, as previously stated, $\mathbf{\Sigma}$ enters the portfolio problem as $\mathbf{X}'\mathbf{\Sigma}\mathbf{X}$, we now require the proper prior for $\mathbf{X}'\mathbf{\Sigma}\mathbf{X}$ induced by that for $\mathbf{\Sigma}$. This induced prior distribution is not mathematically tractable. However, it can be shown that the following will serve for our purposes as a satisfactory approximation:[12]

$$P_{0_\epsilon}(\mathbf{X}'\mathbf{\Sigma}\mathbf{X})\ \alpha\ (\mathbf{X}'\mathbf{\Sigma}\mathbf{X})^{-(3-m)/2},\ \mathbf{X}'\mathbf{\Sigma}\mathbf{X} \in A_\epsilon, \qquad (8)$$

where $A_\epsilon \equiv \{\mathbf{X}'\mathbf{\Sigma}\mathbf{X}{:}\epsilon_1\mathbf{X}'\mathbf{X} < \mathbf{X}'\mathbf{\Sigma}\mathbf{X} < \epsilon_2^{-1}\mathbf{X}'\mathbf{X}\}$ is the domain implied or induced by the restricted domain for $\mathbf{\Sigma}$ in (7) (see footnote 12).

The complete (induced) prior specification, employed in the remainder of this paper, is then given by

$$\begin{aligned} P_0(\boldsymbol{\mu}|\mathbf{\Sigma})\ &\alpha\ c,\ -\infty\cdot\boldsymbol{\iota} < \boldsymbol{\mu} < \infty\cdot\boldsymbol{\iota} \\ P_{0\epsilon}(\mathbf{X}'\mathbf{\Sigma}\mathbf{X})\ &\alpha\ (\mathbf{X}'\mathbf{\Sigma}\mathbf{X})^{-(3-m)/2},\ \mathbf{X}'\mathbf{\Sigma}\mathbf{X} \in A_\epsilon \end{aligned} \qquad (9)$$

We will refer to the entire specification in (9) as the induced $\boldsymbol{\epsilon}$-informative prior.

Although $T \ll m$, with the informative prior of (9), total information (prior plus sample) is sufficient. For this case, as in Theorem 2, we determine the effect of changes in information on investment in the riskless asset. Let $\tilde{\bar{R}}$ denote the return on any given investment in the risky assets. Then:

Theorem 3. Assume that the allocation constraint set is given by

$$\mathbf{C}_1 = \left[X_i{:}\sum_{i=0}^{m} X_i = 1,\ X_i \geqslant -B\right],$$

$B > 0$,[13] *that* $\tilde{\bar{R}}$ *is normally distributed with an induced* $\boldsymbol{\epsilon}$*-informative prior on its parameters. Then, for all* $U \in \mathbf{U}$, *the optimal investment in the riskless asset (which is assumed to be less than total initial wealth, where initial wealth is normalized at 1) is an increasing function of* ϵ_2^{-1}.

Therefore, appropriate bounds on $\underline{\lambda}$ and $\overline{\lambda}$ will restrict the domain of $\mathbf{\Sigma}$ as claimed.

12. The domain for $\mathbf{X}'\mathbf{\Sigma}\mathbf{X}$, $\mathbf{A}_\epsilon$, is implied by the domain for $\mathbf{\Sigma}$, $\overline{\mathbf{A}}_\epsilon$. This follows, because $\overline{\mathbf{A}}_\epsilon$ was derived by restricting the minimum and maximum eigenvalues of $\mathbf{\Sigma}$, $\underline{\lambda}$ and $\overline{\lambda}$ respectively, such that $\epsilon_1 \leqslant \underline{\lambda}$ and $\overline{\lambda} \leqslant \epsilon_2^{-1}$. From Graybill (1961, Theorem 11.8.4, p. 309),

$$\underline{\lambda} \cdot \mathbf{X}'\mathbf{X} \leqslant \mathbf{X}'\mathbf{\Sigma}\mathbf{X} \leqslant \overline{\lambda} \cdot \mathbf{X}'\mathbf{X},$$

from which the domain $\mathbf{A}_\epsilon$ now follows. As to the functional form of $p_{0\epsilon}(\mathbf{X}'\mathbf{\Sigma}\mathbf{X})$ in (8), note that we are mainly concerned with cases in which $\boldsymbol{\epsilon} \equiv (\epsilon_1, \epsilon_2) \to 0$. Let $p_0(\mathbf{X}'\mathbf{\Sigma}\mathbf{X})$ be the prior on $\mathbf{X}'\mathbf{\Sigma}\mathbf{X}$ induced by the "noninformative" prior on $\mathbf{\Sigma}$, $p_0(\mathbf{\Sigma})$. From Tiao and Zellner (1964, p. 278-280), $p_0(\mathbf{X}'\mathbf{\Sigma}\mathbf{X})\ \alpha\ (\mathbf{X}'\mathbf{\Sigma}\mathbf{X})^{-(3-m)/2}$, $\mathbf{X}'\mathbf{\Sigma}\mathbf{X} > 0$. Now, let $q_{0\epsilon}(\mathbf{X}'\mathbf{\Sigma}\mathbf{X})$ be the exact prior on $\mathbf{X}'\mathbf{\Sigma}\mathbf{X}$ induced by the $\boldsymbol{\epsilon}$-informative prior on $\mathbf{\Sigma}$, $p_{0\epsilon}(\mathbf{\Sigma})$. Then, as $\boldsymbol{\epsilon} \to \mathbf{O}$, $p_{0\epsilon}(\mathbf{\Sigma}) \to p_0(\mathbf{\Sigma})$, $q_{0\epsilon}(\mathbf{X}'\mathbf{\Sigma}\mathbf{X}) \to p_0(\mathbf{X}'\mathbf{\Sigma}\mathbf{X})$, and $p_{0\epsilon}(\mathbf{X}'\mathbf{\Sigma}\mathbf{X}) \to p_0(\mathbf{X}'\mathbf{\Sigma}\mathbf{X})$.

13. We are permitting short, but not infinitely short positions.

The interpretation of Theorem 3, which is proved in the appendix, is essentially the same as that for Theorem 2. As expected, as the degree of prior information decreases (through decreases in ϵ_2),[14] the risk-averse investor, with $U \in \mathbf{U}$, seeks to avoid the increased estimation risk by investing more in the riskless security.

In this section, we have examined cases of sufficient information. In each instance, we have assumed $T > m$ (sufficient sample information) or that the prior distribution was sufficiently informative. The following section considers several cases of insufficient (minimal information) in that $T < m$ (insufficient sample information) and the prior is as given in Theorem 3 with $\boldsymbol{\epsilon} \equiv (\epsilon_1, \epsilon_2) \to \mathbf{0}$ (a prior arbitrarily close to the "noninformative" prior, a situation of insufficient or minimal prior information). In this framework we will show that limited diversification is asymptotically optimal for risk-averse investors.

3. Optimal portfolio choice: Insufficient information and limited diversification

In this section, we consider two extreme, but realistic, cases of insufficient information and characterize the optimal portfolio choice under each one. In the first case, which is examined in Theorem 4, let $\partial E[U|\sigma_p]/\partial\sigma_p$ denote the derivative of conditional expected utility [conditioned on the portfolio standard deviation, $\sigma_p = (\mathbf{X}'\boldsymbol{\Sigma}\mathbf{X})^{1/2}$] with respect to the portfolio standard deviation. For the results that follow, we require essentially that individuals are risk-averse in that their utility is concave over a "wide" range. Formally, we assume that the utility function, U, belongs to either

(1) $\mathbf{U}_u$: $U(w)$ is continuous and unbounded from below, $U' \geqslant 0$, $U'' \leqslant 0$, $U'' < 0$ on a set of positive probability, and $\partial E[U|\sigma_p]/\partial\sigma_p$ is continuous in the portfolio allocation, $\mathbf{X}$.

or

(2) $\mathbf{U}_b$: $U(w)$ is constant and finite for $w \leqslant l$, continuous, non-decreasing, concave for $w \geqslant l$, and $\partial E[U(\cdot)|\sigma_p]/\partial\sigma_p$ is strictly negative (for any non-zero allocation to the risky securities) and continuous in the portfolio allocation, $\mathbf{X}$.[15]

We can now establish the following theorem:

Theorem 4. Let $R_0, \ldots, \tilde{R}_m$ be the returns to the $m+1$ available securities where $R_0 \equiv \mu_0$ is the known riskless return. Let the allocation constraint set be given by

14. This theorem would not hold if only ϵ_1 were decreased. In this case, we would only be increasing the probability of small variances, which effectively makes investment in the risky securities more attractive.

15. For $U \in \mathbf{U}_b$, since U's domain is the entire real line, U cannot be concave everywhere. Here, $U(w)$ is concave for $w \geqslant l$. If l is sufficiently small, then one can show that

$$\partial E[U|\sigma_p]/\partial\sigma_p < 0$$

(for any non-zero allocation to the risky securities).

$$\mathbf{C}_1 \equiv \left\{ X_i : \sum_{i=0}^{m} X_i = 1, \qquad X_i \geqslant -B \right\},$$

$B > 0$. *Assume that there are $T < m$ observations per security and that the prior is the induced ϵ-informative prior. Finally, assume that $U \in U_u$ or U_b. Then, for every $\delta > 0$, there exists $\epsilon_0(\delta) > 0$ such that if $0 < \epsilon \leqslant \epsilon_0(\delta)$, then $|X_i^*(\epsilon)| < \delta$ for all $i \neq 0$, where $X_i^*(\epsilon)$ denotes the optimum investment in risky security i.*

Theorem 4 is proved in the appendix.

The implication of this theorem is that asymptotically (as $\epsilon \rightarrow \mathbf{0}$) there will be no diversification into the risky assets. Before explaining this implication, it is necessary to dispose of an objection that might be raised. Namely, one can argue that an investor can always choose to consider only a subset of m_2+1 securities that include the riskless security and m_2 other risky securities. Clearly, m_2 can be chosen such that T, the number of observations per security, is much greater than m_2. Let $\boldsymbol{\mu}_2$ be the mean vector of these m_2 securities and $\boldsymbol{\Sigma}_2$ the variance-covariance matrix. Then, with the "noninformative" prior on m_2 securities,

$$p'_0(\boldsymbol{\mu}_2|\boldsymbol{\Sigma}_2) \ \alpha \ c, \qquad -\infty\boldsymbol{\iota} < \boldsymbol{\mu}_2 < \boldsymbol{\iota}\infty, \tag{10}$$

$$p'_0(\mathbf{X}_2\boldsymbol{\Sigma}'_2\mathbf{X}_2) \ \alpha \ (\mathbf{X}'_2\boldsymbol{\Sigma}_2\mathbf{X}_2)^{-(3-m)/2}, \qquad \mathbf{X}'_2\boldsymbol{\Sigma}_2\mathbf{X}_2 > 0,$$

the resulting predictive distribution [see Klein and Bawa (1976)], is a Student-t distribution with $T - m_2 >> 0$ degrees of freedom. In this instance, there may clearly be substantial diversification into the m_2 risky securities. Yet, Theorem 4 states that such diversification will be asymptotically zero!

This apparent contradiction can be resolved as follows: Theorem 4 assumed a joint prior arbitrarily close to the "noninformative" prior for the parameters of all m securities. If one chooses to consider only m_2 of the m securities, then one must derive, from the joint prior for all m securities, the marginal prior for the security subset. This marginal prior (derived either from the ϵ-informative prior with $\epsilon \rightarrow \mathbf{0}$ or from the "noninformative" prior) is not the prior shown in (11). The prior in (11) is inconsistent with the joint prior assumption in Theorem 4. Indeed, to avoid inconsistencies, whenever one considers various subsets, one must obtain the relevant marginal distributions from the joint distribution. With the marginal prior appropriately derived from the entire joint prior, Theorem 4 follows. Another way of understanding why there is no contradiction is to note that Theorem 4 is based on a "minimal" information prior for *all m* securities. The prior for m_2 securities in (11), p'_0, is non-informative only with respect to a specific set of m_2 securities. Even if one chooses, before optimizing, to consider all subsets of m_2 securities, one is implicitly assuming prior information that guarantees that one need only consider subsets of the alternatives. Theorem 4 presumes no such information.

To explain Theorem 4 intuitively, from Theorems 2-3 above, the impact of estimation risk can, as one might expect, cause a risk-averse investor to increase the proportion invested in the riskless security. Theorem 4 assumes that there is little information in the data ($T < m$) and that prior information is minimal. Consequently, estimation risk is extremely large, so large as to cause a risk-averse investor to minimize such risk by asymptotically investing only in the riskless security.

Theorem 4 explains why it may be optimal for some investors asymptotically to invest only in a safe security, a type of behavior that is observed. Theorem 4 is admittedly an extreme case, since some investors have more than minimal information on all of the m securities. At the very least, an investor may have more than minimal information about a security subset. Such information may come from the data or from the prior. Theorem 5 examines this differential information case by permitting there to be more observations on one subset of securities relative to all others. Though this additional information comes from the data, it should be interpreted as a proxy for additional information that is data or prior based.

Theorem 5. Let the set of feasible allocations be given by

$$\mathbf{C}_2 \equiv \left\{ X_i : \sum_{i=0}^{m} X_i = 1, \quad X_i \geqslant 0 \right\}.$$

Let $R_0, \ldots, \tilde{R}_m$ be the returns to the $m+1$ available securities, partitioned as

$$\tilde{R}' \equiv \left[\tilde{R}^{1'} \vdots \tilde{R}^{2'} \right] 1 \times m+1.$$

$\tilde{R}^1$ is a subset of $m_1 + 1$ security returns that includes the riskless return. For each of the m_1 risky securities with returns in $\tilde{R}^1$, assume that there are $T_1 > m$ observations per security. $\tilde{R}^2$ consists of the returns for the remaining $m - m_1$ securities, for which there are $T_2 < m$ observations per security. Further, assume that $U \in \mathbf{U}_b$ and in addition that, with $l \leqslant 0$, $U(w) = 0$, $w \leqslant l$.[16] *Denote X^*_{2i} as the optimal investment in security i of the second security subset. Then, for each $\delta > 0$, there exists $\epsilon_0(\delta) > 0$ such that if $0 < \epsilon \leqslant \epsilon_0(\delta)$, then $X^*_{2i} < \delta$ for all i.*[17]

Theorem 5 is proved in the appendix.

The intuitive explanation of Theorem 5 is similar to that for Theorem 4. Under the assumptions outlined in Theorem 5, there is minimal information on the securities with returns $\tilde{\mathbf{R}}^2$. Consequently, the estimation risk associated with these securities is very large. Here, this risk is so large as to cause the risk-averse investor asymptotically (as $\epsilon \rightarrow \mathbf{0}$) not to diversify into any of these $m - m_1$ securities.

4. Summary and conclusions

In this chapter, we have examined the portfolio choice problem when the joint probability distribution of security returns is multivariate normal with unknown parameter values. We have shown that both the admissible set of portfolios and

16. This restriction is consistent with limited liability. Rather than assuming $U(w) = 0$, $w \leqslant l$, it would be, for our purposes, equivalent to assume that $\{w : w \leqslant l\}$ is a set of probability measure zero.

17. The allocation set $\mathbf{C}_2$ precludes short sales. We have been unable to prove that if short sales are permitted (in $\tilde{\mathbf{R}}^2$) then X^*_{2i} would approach zero as $\epsilon \rightarrow 0$. We conjecture, however, that as in Theorem 4, $X^*_{2i} \rightarrow 0$ as $\epsilon \rightarrow \mathbf{0}$ even when short sales are permitted.

an investor's optimal portfolio choice (a member of the admissible set) are, in general, different under the UCS (that incorporates estimation risk) from that under the ECS (that ignores estimation risk). We have also analyzed the effect of changes in information (about the parameters whose values are unknown) on the optimal portfolio choice.

As a result of estimation risk, one would expect risk-averse investors to invest relatively more in those securities about which they have the most information. Theorems 1-3, which generalize Theorems 1 and 2 in Chapter 4, show that this is indeed the case. Theorems 4 and 5 can be viewed as extensions of Theorem 3 to the case in which there is a large informational difference between security subsets. In Theorem 4, we examined a situation in which a riskless security existed and there was minimal information on all risky securities. In this instance, we showed that estimation risk became so large as to cause the risk-averse investor asymptotically to invest only in the (nominally) safe security. Theorem 5 considered the situation in which there was insufficient sample information on one security subset. Here, estimation risk caused the risk-averse investor asymptotically not to diversify into this low information security subset.

These limited diversification results are consistent with observed behavior in two respects. First, from these results, one would expect to observe investors with different (perceived) information structures limiting their diversification to different security subsets. This theoretical implication corroborates casual empiricism of what one observes in practice. Second, in a portfolio choice problem (or in any choice problem for that matter), one can view the decision process in two stages. First, a set of alternatives (securities in the portfolio problem) are selected for consideration (e.g., all securities on the New York Stock Exchange). Second, a choice is made among these alternatives. It is common in many decision problems to take the set of alternatives as given and proceed directly to this second stage optimization. Theorem 5 can be viewed as stating the conditions under which this second stage optimization is (asymptotically) optimal. It is quite common to have information about some narrow set of alternatives and minimal information about others. In such situations, one typically proceeds to the second-stage problem of choosing among the members of this restricted set. Theorem 5 shows that this strategy is indeed optimal (asymptotically).

Appendix

The following lemmas will be used in proving Theorem 3.

Lemma 1. Assume the joint (induced ϵ-informative) prior specification,

$$p_0(\boldsymbol{\mu}|\boldsymbol{\Sigma}) \; \alpha \; c, \qquad -\infty\boldsymbol{\iota} < \boldsymbol{\mu} < \infty\boldsymbol{\iota},$$

$$p_{0\epsilon}(\mathbf{X'\Sigma X}) \; \alpha \; (\mathbf{X'\Sigma X})^{-(3-m)/2}, \qquad \mathbf{X'X}\cdot\epsilon_1 < \mathbf{X'\Sigma X} < \mathbf{X'X}\cdot\epsilon_2^{-1},$$

where ϵ_1 and ϵ_2 are real numbers satisfying $0 < \epsilon_1 < \epsilon_2^{-1}$. Let the likelihood for $\boldsymbol{\mu}$ and $\boldsymbol{\Sigma}$ be the multivariate normal distribution discussed in section 2. Then, the posterior distribution of $\tilde{\nu} \equiv (\mathbf{X'\Sigma X})$ is

$$g_{\mathbf{X}}(\tilde{\nu}) \; \alpha \; (\tilde{\nu})^{-(1/2)(T-m+2)}\exp(-\mathbf{X'SX}/2\nu).$$

Proof of Lemma 1. The posterior is proportional to the product of the likelihood function and the prior. Therefore, if two priors have the same functional form, differing only in their respective domains, the posteriors will be of the same functional form. Therefore, $g_{\mathbf{X}}(\nu)$ must have the same functional form as the distribution in (4), with $\mathbf{X'\Sigma X} \in (\mathbf{X'X}\cdot\epsilon_1, \mathbf{X'X}\cdot\epsilon_2^{-1})$.

Q.E.D.

Lemma 2. Under the assumptions on the conditional distribution of $\tilde{P}_{\mathrm{X}}$ (given $\boldsymbol{\mu}$, $\boldsymbol{\Sigma}$), the likelihood function, and the distribution of $\boldsymbol{\mu}$ given in section 2, expected utility given $\boldsymbol{\Sigma}$ is

$$E[U(\tilde{P}_{\mathrm{X}})|\boldsymbol{\Sigma}] = \int_z U[X_0\mu_0+X'\hat{\mu}+\delta_T(\mathbf{X'\Sigma X})^{\frac{1}{2}}\cdot z]\phi(z)\,dz,$$

where μ_0 is the certain return to the riskless asset with investment proportion X_0; $\hat{\boldsymbol{\mu}}$, a vector of sample means, is the posterior mean of $\boldsymbol{\mu}$ with investment proportions $\mathbf{X}$;$\delta_T \equiv (1+1/T)^{\frac{1}{2}}$*; and $\tilde{z}$ is a random variable with standard normal distribution $\phi(\tilde{z})$.*

Proof of Lemma 2. From Zellner (1971, example 2.8, pp. 29-30), one can show that the predictive distribution of $\mathbf{X'\tilde{R}}$, given $\boldsymbol{\Sigma}$, is $N(\mathbf{X'}\hat{\boldsymbol{\mu}}, \delta_T^2\cdot\mathbf{X'\Sigma X})$. Letting $\tilde{z} \equiv (\mathbf{X'}\tilde{R}-\mathbf{X'}\hat{\boldsymbol{\mu}})/[\delta_T(\mathbf{X'\Sigma X})^{\frac{1}{2}}]$, the lemma follows immediately.

Q.E.D.

Proof of Theorem 3. From Lemma 2, with X and $\Sigma = \sigma^2$ as scalars and $X_0 \equiv 1-X$, expected utility is given as

$$\int_{\epsilon_1}^{\epsilon_2^{-1}} \underset{\tilde{Z}}{E}\{U((1-X)\mu_0+X\hat{\mu}+\delta_T\cdot X\cdot\sigma\cdot\tilde{Z})\}g(\sigma)\,d\sigma, \tag{A.3.1}$$

where $\tilde{Z}$ is a standard normal random variable and $g(\sigma)$, from Lemma 1, has the form

$$g(\sigma) = h(\sigma)/K(\epsilon), \tag{A.3.2}$$

with $h(\sigma) > 0$ independent of ϵ and

$$K(\epsilon) \equiv \int_{\epsilon_1}^{\epsilon_2^{-1}} h(\sigma)\,d\sigma. \tag{A.3.3}$$

Differentiate (A.3.1) first with respect to X to yield the first-order condition (holding at $X \equiv X^* \neq 0$ by assumption):

$$\int_{\epsilon_1}^{\epsilon_2^{-1}} \underset{\tilde{Z}}{E}\Big[\{U'((1-X^*)\mu_0+X^*\hat{\mu}+\delta_T X^*\sigma\tilde{Z})(\hat{\mu}-\mu_0+\delta T\sigma\cdot\tilde{Z})\}$$

$$g(\sigma)\Big]d\sigma = 0. \tag{A.3.4}$$

Differentiating (A.3.4) with respect to ϵ_2^{-1} yields:

$$\underset{\tilde{Z}}{E}\{U'((1-X^*)\mu_0+X^*\hat{\mu}_1+\delta_T X_2^*\epsilon_2^{-1}\tilde{Z})(\hat{\mu}-\mu_0+\delta_T\epsilon_2^{-1}\cdot\tilde{Z})\}g(\epsilon_2^{-1})$$

$$+\int_{\epsilon_1}^{\epsilon_2^{-1}} \underset{\tilde{Z}}{E}\{U''(P^*)(\hat{\mu}_1-\mu_0+\delta_T\sigma\cdot\tilde{Z})^2\partial X^*/\partial\epsilon_2^{-1}\}g(\sigma)\,d\sigma$$

$$+\int_{\epsilon_1}^{\epsilon_2^{-1}} \underset{\tilde{Z}}{E}\{U'(P^*)(\hat{\mu}-\mu_0+\delta_T\sigma\cdot\tilde{Z})\}\partial g(\sigma)/\partial\epsilon_2^{-1}\,d\sigma = 0,$$

where

$$\tilde{P}^* = (1-X^*)\mu_0+X^*\hat{\mu}+\delta_T X^*\sigma\tilde{Z},$$

the optimal portfolio at $X = X^*$. Since, from (A.3.2) and (A.3.3),

$$\partial g(\sigma)/\partial\epsilon_2^{-1} = -[\partial K(\epsilon)/\partial\epsilon_2^{-1}]h(\sigma)/K^2(\epsilon)$$

$$= g(\sigma)[-\partial K(\epsilon)/\partial\epsilon_2^{-1}]/K(\epsilon),$$

the last term in (A.3.5) is zero from the first-order condition in (A.3.4). Since $U''(P^*) < 0$, the sign of the second term is $\gtreqless$ as $\partial X^*/\partial\epsilon_2^{-1} \gtreqless 0$. Turning to the first term, the following argument will show that it is negative under the assumptions of this theorem.

Consider

$$S \equiv \underset{\tilde{Z}}{E}\{U'((1-X^*)\mu_0+X^*\hat{\mu}+\delta_T X^*\sigma\cdot\tilde{Z})(\hat{\mu}-\mu_0+\delta_T\sigma\cdot\tilde{Z})\} \tag{A.3.6}$$

Differentiating S with respect to σ yields

$$\partial S/\partial\sigma = \underset{\tilde{Z}}{E}\{U''(\tilde{p}^*)\delta_T X^*\tilde{Z}[\hat{\mu}-\mu_0+X^*\hat{\mu}+\delta_T\sigma\cdot Z]\}+\underset{\tilde{Z}}{E}\{U'(P^*)\delta_T Z\}. \tag{A.3.7}$$

If $\partial S/\partial\sigma \leqslant 0$, then the first term if (A.3.5) will be negative and the theorem will follow. Now, note that in the proof to Lemma 2, $\tilde{Z}$ is implicitly defined by $\tilde{\bar{R}} = \hat{\mu} + \delta_T\sigma\tilde{Z}$ where the conditional distribution (predictive) of $\bar{R}$ given σ is $N(\hat{\mu},\ \sigma^2\delta_T^2)$. Then,

$$\delta_T X^*\tilde{Z}[\hat{\mu}-\mu_0+\delta_T\sigma\tilde{Z}] = (\tilde{R}-\hat{\mu})(\tilde{P}^*-\mu_0)/\sigma.$$

Therefore, the first term in (A.3.7) can be written as

$$\underset{\tilde{\bar{R}}|\sigma}{E}\{U''(\tilde{P}^*)(\tilde{\bar{R}}-\hat{\mu})(\tilde{P}^*-\mu_0)/\sigma\} < \underset{\tilde{\bar{R}}|\sigma}{E}\{U''(\tilde{P}^*)(\tilde{\bar{R}}-\hat{\mu})\tilde{P}^*/\sigma\}, \tag{A.3.8}$$

under decreasing absolute risk aversion. Now, rewrite $\tilde{P}^*$ as

$$\tilde{P}^* = (1-X^*)\mu_0 + X^*\hat{\mu} + X^*(\tilde{\bar{R}}-\hat{\mu}) \equiv E + X^*(\tilde{\bar{R}}-\hat{\mu}),$$

where $E \equiv (1-X^*)\mu_0 + X^*\hat{\mu}$ is non-random. Note that since investment in the riskless security was assumed to be less than total initial wealth, $1-X^* < 1$ and therefore $X^* > 0$. Let $RR(w) \equiv -wU''(w)/U'(w)$ denote the relative risk-aversion index, and, following a derivation in Arrow (1974a, p. 120), consider two cases. First, if $\bar{R} < \hat{\mu}$, then non-decreasing relative risk aversion implies

$$-U''(P^*)P^*/U'(P^*) \leqslant RR(E) \Rightarrow$$

$$U''(P^*)P^* \geqslant -U'(P^*)RR(E) \Rightarrow$$

$$U''(P^*)P^*(\bar{R}-\hat{\mu}) \leqslant -U'(P^*)(\bar{R}-\hat{\mu})RR(E). \tag{A.3.9}$$

Repeating this argument for $\bar{R} > \hat{\mu}$ shows that the last inequality in (A.3.9) again holds. Therefore,

$$\underset{\tilde{\bar{R}}|\sigma}{E}\{U''(\tilde{P}^*)(\tilde{\bar{R}}-\hat{\mu})/\sigma\} \leqslant -\underset{\tilde{\bar{R}}|\sigma}{E}\{U'(\tilde{P}^*)(\tilde{\bar{R}}-\hat{\mu})\}RR(E)/\sigma$$

$$= -\underset{\tilde{Z}}{E}\{U'(\tilde{P}^*)\delta_T\tilde{Z}\}RR(E). \tag{A.3.10}$$

Therefore, from (A.3.7), (A.3.8) and (A.3.10),

$$\partial S/\partial\sigma < \underset{\tilde{Z}}{E}\{U'(\tilde{P}^*)\delta_T\tilde{Z}\}-\underset{\tilde{Z}}{E}\{U'(\tilde{P}^*)\delta_T\tilde{Z}\}RR(E). \tag{A.3.11}$$

Since U is strictly concave, the first expectation in (A.3.11) is negative. Therefore, since $RR(E) \leqslant 1$ (by assumption), $\partial S/\partial\sigma < 0$. Therefore, from (A.3.4), the first term in (A.3.5) must be negative, which implies that $\partial X^*/\partial\epsilon_2^{-1} < 0$.

Q.E.D.

The following additional lemmas will be used in proving Theorem 4:

Lemma 3. Let $\gamma_1 > \gamma_2 > 1$, $B_1 > 0$, *and* $C \geqslant 0$. *Then, there exists* $a_0 = a_0(\gamma_1, \gamma_2, B_1, C)$ *such that* $0 < a \leqslant a_0$, $b \geqslant 1$, *and* $0 \leqslant \gamma_0 \leqslant B_1$ *implies*

$$\int_a^b y^{-\gamma_1} e^{-\gamma_3 y} dy \Big/ \int_a^b y^{-\gamma_2} e^{-\gamma_3 y} dy > C.$$

Proof of Lemma 3. The ratio of integrals in the conclusion is

$$\geqslant \int_a^1 {}^{-}y^{\gamma_1} e^{-\gamma_3 y} dy \Big/ \int_a^b y^{-\gamma_2} e^{-\gamma_3 y} dy$$

$$> e^{-B_1} \int_a^1 y^{-\gamma_1} dy \Big/ \int_a^b y^{-\gamma_2} dy$$

$$= e^{-B_1}[(\gamma_2 - 1)/(\gamma_1 - 1)][a^{1-\gamma_1} - 1]/[a^{1-\gamma_2} - b^{1-\gamma_2}]$$

$$> e^{-B_1}[(\gamma_2 - 1)/(\gamma_1 - 1)][a^{1-\gamma_1} - 1]/a^{1-\gamma_2}$$

$$= e^{-B_1}[(\gamma_2 - 1)/(\gamma_1 - 1)][a^{\gamma_2 - \gamma_1} - a^{\gamma_2 - 1}].$$

Clearly, there exists $a_0 > 0$ such that if $0 < a \leqslant a_0$, the above expression will exceed C.

Q.E.D.

Proof of Theorem 4. Let $\delta > 0$ and let $\mathbf{X}_\delta$ be any allocation vector for the risky securities, where, with $X_{\delta i}$ as the allocation to security i (an element of $\mathbf{X}_\delta$), $|X_{\delta i}| \geqslant \delta$ for some i. then, we show that there exists $\epsilon_o(\delta) \equiv (\epsilon_{01}(\delta), \epsilon_{02}(\delta))$ such that $0 < \boldsymbol{\epsilon} \equiv (\epsilon_1, \epsilon_2) < \epsilon_0(\delta)$ implies that there exists $I(\delta)$ satisfying

$$E[U(\tilde{P}_{\mathbf{X}_\delta})] \leqslant I(\delta) < U(\mu_0). \tag{A.4.1}$$

Therefore, when $\epsilon \leqslant \epsilon_0(\delta)$ and $|X_{i\delta}| \geqslant |\delta|$ for some i, $\mathbf{X}_\delta$ is not an optimal allocation. Thus, at the optimum, $\mathbf{X}^*$, $|X_i^*| < |\delta|$ for all $i \neq 0$. To find $I(\delta)$ satisfying the second inequality in (A.4.1), consider the integral

$$\int_{\delta^2\epsilon_1}^{\delta^2\epsilon_2^{-1}} (v)^{\frac{1}{2}} g_{\mathbf{X}}(v)\,dv. \tag{A.4.2}$$

Under the transformation $y \equiv (\mathbf{X}'\mathbf{\Sigma}\mathbf{X})^{-1}$ and with $g_{\mathbf{X}}$ defined as in Lemma 1, this integral will be of the form

$$\int_a^b y^{-\gamma_1} e^{-\gamma_3 y} dy \Big/ \int_a^b y^{-\gamma_2} e^{-\gamma_3 y} dy, \tag{A.4.3}$$

where $a = \epsilon_2/\delta^2$, $b = 1/(\epsilon_1\delta^2)$, $\gamma_1 > \gamma_2 > 1$, and $\gamma_3 = \mathbf{X}'\mathbf{S}\mathbf{X}/2$. Note that $\gamma_3 \geqslant 0$ (because $\mathbf{S}$ is positive semi-definite) and γ_3 is bounded above (since $\mathbf{C}_1$ is compact). Therefore, from Lemma 3, for each $C \geqslant 0$, there exists $\epsilon_{02}(\delta) > 0$ such that if $0 < \epsilon_2 \leqslant \epsilon_{02}(\delta)$, then the integral in (A.4.2) exceeds C. Therefore, since $\epsilon_2/(\mathbf{X}_\delta'\mathbf{X}_\delta) \leqslant \epsilon_2/\delta^2$, for $\epsilon_2 \leqslant \epsilon_{02}(\delta)$,

$$\int_{\mathbf{X}_\delta'\mathbf{X}_\delta\cdot\epsilon_1}^{\mathbf{X}_\delta'\mathbf{X}_\delta\cdot\epsilon_2^{-1}} (v)^{\frac{1}{2}} g_{\mathbf{X}_\delta}(v)\,dv > C, \tag{A.4.4}$$

as long as $1/(\epsilon_1\cdot\mathbf{X}_\delta'\mathbf{X}_\delta) \geqslant 1$. Since $\mathbf{X}'\mathbf{X}$ is bounded above ($\mathbf{C}_1$ is compact), there exists $\epsilon_{01}(\delta) > 0$ such that if $\epsilon_1 \leqslant \epsilon_{01}(\delta)$, $1/(\epsilon_1\cdot\mathbf{X}'\mathbf{X}) \geqslant 1$ for all $\mathbf{X} \in \mathbf{C}_1$.

We can now make a convenient choice of C in (A.4.4) that will permit us to derive $I(\delta)$ in (A.4.1). Define

$$H_X(v^{\frac{1}{2}}) = \int_z U[X_0\mu_0 + X'\hat{\mu} + \delta_T\cdot v^{\frac{1}{2}}\cdot z]\phi(z)\,dz, \tag{A.4.5}$$

where $v \geqslant 0$ and $X \in \mathbf{C}_2$.

It will be useful to note that

$$H_{\mathbf{X}}'(1) < 0 \quad \text{and} \quad \sup_{\mathbf{X}\in\mathbf{C}_2} H_{\mathbf{X}}'(1) < 0.^{18}$$

18. From (A.4.5),

$$H_{\mathbf{X}}'[v^{1/2}] = \int_z U'[X_0\mu_0 + X\hat{\mu} + \delta_T\cdot v^{1/2}\cdot z]\delta_T\cdot z\phi(z)\,dz.$$

For $U \in U_b$, $H_X'(1) < 0$ by assumption. For $U \in U_u$, since $U'' \leqslant 0$, $H_X'(v^{1/2}) \leqslant 0$ for all X and all $v \geqslant 0$. Moreover, for $U \in U_u$, $U'' < 0$ on a set of positive probability, which implies that $H_X''(v^{1/2}) < 0$ for all X and all $v \geqslant 0$. Consequently, for $U \in U_u$, since

Now, let

$$C \equiv \sup_{\mathbf{X}\in \mathbf{C}_2}\left[\frac{U(\mu_0)-H_{\mathbf{X}}(1)+H_{\mathbf{X}}'(1)}{H_{\mathbf{X}}'(1)}\right], \tag{A.4.6}$$

which is bounded above.[19] Therefore, for $\epsilon \leqslant \epsilon_0(\delta)$,

$$\int_{\mathbf{X}_\delta'\mathbf{X}_\delta\epsilon_1}^{\mathbf{X}_\delta'\mathbf{X}_\delta\epsilon_2^{-1}} v^{\frac{1}{2}} g_{\mathbf{X}_\delta}(v)\,dv > \frac{U(\mu_0)-H_{\mathbf{X}_\delta}(1)+H_{\mathbf{X}_\delta}'(1)}{H_{\mathbf{X}_\delta}'(1)}. \tag{A.4.7}$$

From (A.4.7), since $H_{\mathbf{X}_\delta}'(1) < 0$ (see footnote 19), for $\epsilon \leqslant \epsilon_0(\delta)$,

$$I(\delta) \equiv H_{\mathbf{X}_\delta}(1)+H_{\mathbf{X}_\delta}'(1)\int_{\mathbf{X}_\delta'\mathbf{X}_\delta\epsilon_1}^{\mathbf{X}_\delta'\mathbf{X}_\delta\epsilon_2^{-1}} [v^{1/2}-1]g_{\mathbf{X}_\delta}(v)dv$$

$$< U(\mu_0). \tag{A.4.8}$$

To complete the proof, from (A.4.1) we must show that $E[U(\tilde{P}_{\mathbf{X}_\delta})] \leqslant I(\delta)$. Expanding $H_{\mathbf{X}}[v^{\frac{1}{2}}]$ in a Taylor series about 1 yields [see Apostle (1975, Theorem 5.19, p. 113)]

$$H_{\mathbf{X}_\delta}[v^{\frac{1}{2}}] = H_{\mathbf{X}_\delta}(1)+H_{\mathbf{X}_\delta}'(c)[v^{\frac{1}{2}}-1], \tag{A.4.9}$$

where c is between 1 and $v^{\frac{1}{2}}$. From Lemma 2 and the definition of $H_{\mathbf{X}}$ in (A.4.5), expected utility (unconditioned on $\mathbf{\Sigma}$) is the expectation of the expression

---

$H_{\mathbf{X}}'(0) = 0$ for all $\mathbf{X}$, $H_{\mathbf{X}}'(1) < 0$ for all $\mathbf{X}$. Therefore, for $U \in U_u$ or U_b, since $H_X'(1)$ is continuous in $\mathbf{X}$ (by assumption) and since $\mathbf{X} \in \mathbf{C}_1$, a compact set, $sup_{\mathbf{X}\in \mathbf{C}_1} H_{\mathbf{X}}'(1) < 0$.

19 Let sup denote $sup_{\mathbf{X}\in \mathbf{C}_2}$ and recall that $sup H_{\mathbf{X}}'(1) < 0$. From (A.4.6),

$$C \leqslant 1+sup[U(\mu_0)/H_{\mathbf{X}}'(1)]+sup[H_{\mathbf{X}}(1)/-H_{\mathbf{X}}'(1)].$$

Proceeding term by term, we need only consider the case where the second and third terms are positive. Beginning with the second term, for $U(\mu_0) < 0$, it is bounded above by $U(\mu_0)/sup H_X'(1)$ (which is finite because the numerator is finite and the denominator is strictly negative). Turning to the third term, and assuming that it is positive, since $\mathbf{C}_1$ is compact, there exists $\hat{\mathbf{X}} \in \mathbf{C}_1$ such that

$$0 < sup[H_{\mathbf{X}}(1)/-H_{\mathbf{X}}'(1)] = H_{\hat{\mathbf{X}}}(1)/-H_{\hat{\mathbf{X}}}'(1)$$

$$\leqslant sup H_{\mathbf{X}}(1)/-sup H_{\mathbf{X}}'(1).$$

To complete the argument, we now need only show that $sup H_X(1)$ is finite, which follows from

in (A.4.9) over ($\boldsymbol{\Sigma}$ or $\mathbf{X}_\delta'\boldsymbol{\Sigma}\mathbf{X}_\delta$):

$$E[U(\tilde{P}_{\mathbf{X}_\delta})] = H_{\mathbf{X}_\delta}(1) + \int_{\mathbf{X}_\delta'\mathbf{X}_\delta\epsilon_1}^{\mathbf{X}_\delta'\mathbf{X}_\delta\epsilon_2^{-1}} H_{\mathbf{X}_\delta}'(c)[v^{\frac{1}{2}}-1]g_{\mathbf{X}_\delta}(v)\,dv. \qquad \text{(A.4.10)}$$

$$= H_{\mathbf{X}_\delta}(1) + \int_{\mathbf{X}_\delta'\mathbf{X}_\delta\epsilon_1}^{1} H_{\mathbf{X}_\delta}'(c)[v^{\frac{1}{2}}-1]g_{\mathbf{X}_\delta}(v)\,dv$$

$$+ \int_{1}^{\mathbf{X}_\delta'\mathbf{X}_\delta\epsilon_2^{-1}} H_{\mathbf{X}_\delta}'(c)[v^{\frac{1}{2}}-1]g_{\mathbf{X}_\delta}(v)\,dv.$$

In the first integral of (A.4.10) above, $[v^{\frac{1}{2}}-1] \leqslant 0$. Since $H_{X_\delta}' \leqslant 0$, $H_{\mathbf{X}_\delta}'' < 0$, and $c \in (v^{\frac{1}{2}}, 1)$, this integral is bounded above by

$$H_{\mathbf{X}_\delta}'(1) \int_{\mathbf{X}_\delta'\mathbf{X}_\delta\epsilon_1}^{1} [v^{\frac{1}{2}}-1]g_{\mathbf{X}_\delta}(v)\,dv. \qquad \text{(A.4.11)}$$

In the second integral of (A.4.10), $[v^{\frac{1}{2}}-1] \geqslant 0$. Since $H_{\mathbf{X}_\delta}' \leqslant 0$, $H_{\mathbf{X}_\delta}'' < 0$, and $c \in [1, v^{\frac{1}{2}}]$, this second integral is bounded above by

$$H_{\mathbf{X}_\delta}'(1) \int_{1}^{\mathbf{X}_\delta'\mathbf{X}_\delta\epsilon_2^{-1}} [v^{\frac{1}{2}}-1]g_{\mathbf{X}_\delta}(v)\,dv. \qquad \text{(A.4.12)}$$

From (A.4.10)-(A.4.12) and the definition of $I(\delta)$ in (A.4.8), the theorem follows directly.

Q.E.D.

The following additional lemma will be useful in proving Theorem 5:

Lemma 4. With $l \leqslant 0$, let

$$U(w) = V(w), \quad w \geqslant l,$$
$$= 0, \quad w \leqslant l,$$

Where $V(w)$ is non-decreasing, non-negative, and concave. Then,

$$U(a+b) \leqslant U(a)+U(b).^{20}$$

---

an extension of a method of proof given by Arrow (1974b, p. 138).

Proof of Lemma 4. If $a = 0$ or $b = 0$, then the lemma clearly holds. If $a < 0$ and $b > 0$, then since U is non-decreasing,

$$U(a+b) \leqslant U(b) \leqslant U(a) + U(b)$$

If $a > 0$ and $b > 0$ and, without loss of generality, if $b > a$, then[21]

$$[U(a)-U(0)]/a-[U(b)-U(0)]/b \geqslant 0,$$
$$\Rightarrow \quad U(a)/a-U(b)/b \geqslant U(0)[1/a-1/b] \geqslant 0.$$

Therefore,

$$U(a)/a-U(a+b)/(a+b) \geqslant 0 \Rightarrow \quad aU(a+b) \leqslant (a+b)U(a),$$
$$U(b)/b-U(a+b)/(a+b) \geqslant 0 \Rightarrow \quad bU(a+b) \leqslant (a+b)U(b).$$

Summing these inequalities yields the desired result.

Q.E.D.

Proof of Theorem 5. Expected utility is given as

$$E[U(\tilde{P}_{\mathbf{X}})] \equiv E[U(\mathbf{X}'\tilde{R})]$$
$$\equiv E[U(\mathbf{X}'(1)\tilde{R}^1 + \mathbf{X}'(2)\tilde{R}^2)],$$

where $\mathbf{X}(i)$, $i = 1, 2$, denotes investment allocations to security set i. Let $\mathbf{X}_\delta' \equiv [\mathbf{X}'(1), \ \mathbf{X}'(2\delta)]$ be any portfolio allocation such that with $\delta > 0$, more than δ is allocated to at least one of the securities in the second subset. From (A.5.1) and Lemma 4,

$$E[U(\tilde{P}_{\mathbf{X}_\delta})] \leqslant E[U(\mathbf{X}'(1)\tilde{R}^1)] + E[U(\mathbf{X}'(2\delta)\tilde{R}^2)]. \qquad \text{(A.5.2)}$$

Let m_1 be the dimension of the column vector $X(1)$ and let 1 be an $m_1 \times 1$ vector of l's. Then, since $\mathbf{X}_\delta \in \mathbf{C}_2$ and given the definition of $\mathbf{X}(2\delta)$,

$$\mathbf{X}(1) \in \mathbf{C}_3 = \{\mathbf{X}(1) \leqslant 1-\delta\}. \qquad \text{(A.5.3)}$$

Now, let $\mathbf{X}^*(1)$ denote the optimal allocation to the first subset when there is no investment in the second subset ($\mathbf{X}(2) = 0$).

Given the definitions of $\mathbf{X}^*(1)$ and $\mathbf{C}_3$,

$$D \equiv E[U(\mathbf{X}^{*\prime}(1)\tilde{R}^1)] - \sup_{\mathbf{X}(1)\in \mathbf{C}_3} \{E[U(\mathbf{X}'(1)\tilde{R}^1)]\} > 0. \qquad \text{(A.5.4)}$$

---

20. We are grateful to our colleague, John Panzar for this proof.

21. This inequality follows from an inequality for convex functions given in Katzner (1970, Lemma B2-3, p. 286).

Employing the same method of proof as in Theorem 4, for each $\delta > 0$, there exists $\epsilon_o(\delta) > 0$ such that if $\epsilon \leqslant \epsilon_0(\delta)$,[22]

$$E[U(\mathbf{X}'(2\delta)\tilde{R}^2)] < D \leqslant E[U(\mathbf{X}^{*\prime}(1)\tilde{R}^1)] - E[U(\mathbf{X}'(1)\tilde{R}^1)]. \quad \text{(A.5.5)}$$

Combining (A.5.2) and (A.5.5),

$$E[U(\tilde{P}_{\mathbf{X}_\delta})] < E[U(\mathbf{X}^{*\prime}(1)\tilde{R}^1)]. \quad \text{(A.5.6)}$$

Therefore, for each $\delta > 0$, when $\epsilon \leqslant \epsilon_0(\delta)$, it is suboptimal to invest more than δ in any of the securities in the second subset.

Q.E.D.

---

22. In the proof of Theorem 4, redefine C in (A.4.6) by replacing $U(\mu_0)$ with D [defined in (A.5.4)] and take the sup over the appropriate set. Then, employing the same method of proof as in that to Theorem 4, for each $\delta > 0$, there exists $\epsilon_0(\delta)$ and $I(\delta)$ such that if $0 < \epsilon \leqslant \epsilon_o(\delta)$,

$$E[U(\mathbf{X}'(2\delta)\tilde{R}^2)] \leqslant I(\delta) < D.$$

CHAPTER 6

CAPITAL MARKET EQUILIBRIUM: DOES ESTIMATION RISK REALLY MATTER?

Vijay S. BAWA and Stephen J. BROWN

1. Introduction

Klein and Bawa [(1976, 1977); also appearing as Chapters 4 and 5 in this book] and Brown (1976) analyze the effect of estimation risk on optimal portfolio choices of individual decision-makers. They relax the standard, but unrealistic, assumption made in most theoretical portfolio analyses that the parameters of the probability distribution of security returns are known to individual investors. The uncertainty about the unknown parameters, termed "estimation risk", can be properly taken into account under the von Neumann-Morgenstern-Savage axioms. Estimation risk is part of the risk or uncertainty faced by the individual decision maker and is, under the axiomatic framework, properly taken into account by using the predictive distribution of returns.

Using the common assumption of a normal distribution of security returns, but with unknown parameter values, it was shown by Klein and Bawa in Chapters 4 and 5 and Brown (1976) that for the family of conjugate priors, the predictive distribution of returns is a Student-*t* distribution, where the parameters depend upon both the prior and sample information. For the special case of diffuse or noninformative priors considered in Chapter 4, it was shown that the set of admissible portfolios for all investors is the same as that obtained under the traditional analysis where the estimated values of the unknown parameters are treated as the "true" values, thereby ignoring estimation risk. However, when estimation risk is properly taken into account, while the admissible set is the same, the optimal portfolio choice, a point in that set, is different. Since each portfolio is associated with a higher level of risk when estimation risk is explicitly considered, for most risk-averse investors, the optimal portfolio choice involves investing in a lower mean, less risky portfolio (Chapter 4, Theorem 2)). In the presence of a riskless asset, this implies investing less in the "market" portfolio of risky assets and more in the riskless asset. For a given informative prior, it was shown in Chapter 5 in this book that the admissible set of portfolios and the optimal portfolio choices can be very different when estimation risk is explicitly considered. However, it still follows that in the presence of a riskless asset, and under certain distributional assumptions, risk averse investors will invest more in the riskless asset and less in the "market" portfolio of risky assets.

When the effect of estimation risk on optimal portfolio choices of individual investors can be characterized as a shift in the demand from the "market" portfolio of risky assets to the riskless asset, it is natural to ask the following questions:

(i) How do the equilibrium prices of these financial assets change when all investors account for estimation risk? and (ii) What are the observable implications of a market equilibrium derived when there is explicit recognition of estimation risk?

We analyze the first question using the following two scenarios to describe the alternative situations being compared. In the first scenario, capital market equilibrium is determined using the traditional mode of analysis under the assumption that all investors replace unknown parameters by their estimated values. For the assumption of a normal distribution of security returns, the equilibrium prices are thus given by the well-known Sharpe (1964), Lintner (1965), Mossin (1966) Capital Asset Pricing Model (CAPM). The alternative scenario considered is one where all investors, explicitly recognizing that the parameters of the returns distribution are unknown, take proper account of estimation risk. Under the assumption that all investors have access to the same amount of information (analogous to the homogeneous expectations assumption in the traditional CAPM), equilibrium prices are derived using results provided in Chapter 4 of this book and in Brown (1979). We show that holding the risk free rate of interest fixed, the equilibrium prices of all risky assets change and under the assumptions outlined in Theorem 2 in Chapter 4), equilibrium prices of all risky assets fall when estimation risk is taken into account. Intuitively, estimation risk increases the uncertainty facing the investor. Consequently, in a market dominated by risk averse investors, the demand for all risky assets falls, thereby causing a fall in their equilibrium prices relative to the riskless asset. Perhaps more important, however, is the result that the relative price of a risky asset in terms of another is invariant to estimation risk. This result conforms to economic intuition in that we will show under both scenarios that investors hold the same indistinguishable "market" portfolio of risky assets.

The answer to the second question raised is intimately linked to the result on the invariance of the prices of risky assets relative to each other. Given the assumption that all investors have the same information under the two scenarios, we show that the composition of the market portfolio, expected return on the market, and beta, the measure of systematic risk, for any security or any portfolio is the same under the two scenarios. Thus, on the basis of an observed set of sample data that corresponds to market equilibrium quantities, one cannot distinguish between the two alternative equilibrium models.[1] Indeed, in empirical testing of equilibrium pricing models, one should not necessarily be concerned with the problem of estimation risk -- or expect estimation risk to be a factor explaining any possible deviations between CAPM and observed market rates of return!

In Section 2, we formulate the problem, define the notation used and recall some results from the literature that we later use. The effect of estimation risk on capital market equilibrium is analyzed in Section 3.

2. Some Preliminaries

Let $\tilde{\mathbf{R}}_i$ denote the return on security i and X_i denote the amount invested in security i, $i = 1,2,...,m$. Let R_F denote the (known) return on the riskless asset and X_0 denote the amount invested in the riskless asset. Then, with $\mathbf{X}' \equiv (X_1,X_2,...,X_m)$ and $\tilde{\mathbf{R}}' \equiv (\tilde{R}_1,\tilde{R}_2, \ldots, \tilde{R}_m)$, the return on portfolio $\overline{\mathbf{X}}$, with

1. They are "observationally equivalent" in the sense of Goldberger (1964, p. 306).

$\overline{\mathbf{X}}' \equiv (X_0, \mathbf{X}')$, is $X_0 R_F + \mathbf{X}'\tilde{R}$. It is assumed that $\tilde{R}$ has a multivariate normal distribution with mean vector $\boldsymbol{\mu}$ and covariance matrix $\boldsymbol{\Sigma}$, where $\boldsymbol{\mu}' \equiv (\mu_1, \mu_2, \ldots, \mu_m)$ and $\boldsymbol{\Sigma} = (\sigma_{ij})$ with $\mu_i = E(\tilde{R}_i)$ and $\sigma_{ij} = Cov\ (\tilde{R}_i, \tilde{R}_j)$, $i,j = 1,2,\ldots,m$. Thus, the return on a portfolio $\overline{\mathbf{X}}$ has a normal distribution with mean $X_0 R_F + \mathbf{X}'\boldsymbol{\mu}$ and variance $\mathbf{X}'\boldsymbol{\Sigma}\mathbf{X}$. Values of the parameters $\boldsymbol{\theta} \equiv (\boldsymbol{\mu}, \boldsymbol{\Sigma})$ are assumed unknown to the investors.

Let R_{it} denote the (observed) return on security i, $i = 1,2,\ldots,m$ at time t, $t = 1,2,\ldots,T$. Assume that the data, $(R_{11}, R_{12}, \ldots, R_{1T}; R_{21}, \ldots, R_{2T}; \ldots; R_{m1}, \ldots, R_{mT})$; $1 \times mT$ consist of observations drawn from a multivariate normal distribution with mean vector $(\mu_{11}, \ldots, \mu_{1T}; \mu_{21}, \ldots, \mu_{2T}; \ldots; \mu_{m1}, \ldots, \mu_{mT})$: $1 \times mT$ and covariance matrix $\boldsymbol{\Sigma} \otimes \mathbf{I}$, where I is a $T \times T$ identity matrix and $\otimes$ the Kronecker product operator.

Let $\hat{\mu}_i = \sum_{t=1}^{T} R_{it}/T$, $i = 1,2,\ldots,m$ and $\hat{\boldsymbol{\mu}}' \equiv (\hat{\mu}_1, \hat{\mu}_2, \ldots, \hat{\mu}_m)$ the vector of sample means. Finally, let $\mathbf{S}$ be defined as the matrix, with $S_{ij} = \sum_{t=1}^{T} (R_{it} - \hat{\mu}_i)(R_{jt} - \hat{\mu}_j)$, $i,j = 1,2,\ldots,m$, a matrix proportional to the sample covariance matrix, $\hat{\boldsymbol{\Sigma}} = \mathbf{S}/(T-1)$.

The traditional mode of analysis uses the estimated values of the parameters, $\hat{\boldsymbol{\theta}} \equiv (\hat{\boldsymbol{\mu}}, \hat{\boldsymbol{\Sigma}})$, as if they were the true parameter values, $\boldsymbol{\theta} = (\boldsymbol{\mu}, \boldsymbol{\Sigma})$. Thus, the return on portfolio $\overline{\mathbf{X}}$ is assumed to be normal with parameters $(\hat{\mu}_{\overline{X}}, \hat{\sigma}_{\overline{X}})$, where

$$\hat{\mu}_{\overline{X}} = X_o R_F + \mathbf{X}'\hat{\boldsymbol{\mu}} \tag{1}$$

$$\hat{\sigma}^2_{\overline{X}} = \mathbf{X}'\hat{\boldsymbol{\Sigma}}\mathbf{X}\,.$$

The Bayesian method of analysis takes account of estimation risk by using the predictive distribution of returns. This distribution does not involve any parameters with unknown values and depends upon the sample and prior information. For the case of the "noninformative" or Jeffreys' "invariant" prior:

$$p_o(\boldsymbol{\theta})\ \alpha\ |\boldsymbol{\Sigma}|^{-\frac{m+1}{2}}, \tag{2}$$

it is shown in Chapter 4 that the predictive distribution of returns in portfolio $\overline{\mathbf{X}}$ is a Student-t distribution with $(T-m)$ degrees of freedom. The mean and variance parameters are respectively:[2]

---

2. The parameter $\sigma^{*2}_{\overline{X}}$, which is the variance of the predictive distribution, is not identical to the scale parameter reported in Klein and Bawa (1976). In their paper, expected utility is taken with respect to a *standardized* Student-t distribution. A random variable, t, has a standardized (central) Student-t distribution with r degrees of freedom if and only if

$$\tilde{t} = \tilde{Z}/(\tilde{V}/r)^{1/2},$$

where $\tilde{Z}$ is a normal random variable with mean zero and variance one. The random variable $\tilde{V}$ is independent of $\tilde{Z}$ and distributed as chi-square with r degrees of freedom. As a result of this standardization, the scale parameter in Klein-Bawa (1976, 1977) differs from the variance in (3). These parameters differ by a constant of proportionality, which depends only on the sample size

$$\mu^*_{\bar{X}} = X_o R_F + \mathbf{X}'\hat{\boldsymbol{\mu}}$$

$$\sigma^{*2}_{\bar{X}} = \mathbf{X}'\boldsymbol{\Sigma}^*\mathbf{X},\ \boldsymbol{\Sigma}^* = \hat{\boldsymbol{\Sigma}}(1+\frac{1}{T})\left[\frac{T-1}{T-m-2}\right] \tag{3}$$

As noted earlier, the admissible and hence optimal, portfolios are still obtained using a mean-variance analysis done in terms of $(\mu^*_{\bar{X}}, \sigma^*_X)$ rather than in terms of $(\hat{\mu}_{\bar{X}}, \hat{\sigma}_{\bar{X}})$ as in the traditional analysis. It should be noted from (1) and (3) that for all portfolios $\bar{\mathbf{X}}$:

$$\mu^*_{\bar{X}} = \hat{\mu}_{\bar{X}}$$

$$\sigma^*_{\bar{X}} = C(T,m)\hat{\sigma}_{\bar{X}}, \tag{4}$$

with $C(T,m)^2 \equiv (1+1/T)[(T-1)/(T-m-2)] > 1$. Thus, in this case with the same set of information available under the two modes of analyses, the effect of estimation risk may be observed as a proportional increase in the scale parameter of the distribution.

For the case of an informative prior this result does not necessarily follow. In the simple case considered by Klein and Bawa in Chapter 5 of a diffuse prior for the mean and an informative prior for the covariance matrix:

$$p_o(\boldsymbol{\theta}) = p_o(\boldsymbol{\mu}|\boldsymbol{\Sigma})p_o(\boldsymbol{\Sigma})$$

$$p_o(\boldsymbol{\mu}|\boldsymbol{\Sigma})\ \alpha\ c \quad -\infty\boldsymbol{\iota} < \boldsymbol{\mu} < \infty\boldsymbol{\iota} \tag{5}$$

$$p_o(\boldsymbol{\Sigma})\ \alpha\ |\boldsymbol{\Sigma}|^{-(m+1+d)/2}\exp\{-\frac{1}{2}tr[d_0\boldsymbol{\Omega}.\boldsymbol{\Sigma}^{-1}]\}, |\boldsymbol{\Sigma}| > 0.$$

Klein and Bawa show in Chapter 5 that the predictive distribution for the return on portfolio $\bar{\mathbf{X}}$ is a Student-t distribution with $d \equiv d_o + T-m$ degrees of freedom. The mean and variance parameters are respectively:[3]

$$\mu^*_{\bar{X}} = X_o R_F + \mathbf{X}'\hat{\boldsymbol{\mu}}$$

$$\sigma^{*2}_{\bar{X}} = \mathbf{X}'\boldsymbol{\Sigma}^*\mathbf{X},\ \boldsymbol{\Sigma}^* = (1+\frac{1}{T}) \cdot \frac{1}{d}\left\{(T-1)\hat{\boldsymbol{\Sigma}} + d_o\boldsymbol{\Omega}\right\} \tag{6}$$

We note that in this case, $\mu^*_{\bar{X}} = \hat{\mu}_{\bar{X}}$ but $\sigma^*_{\bar{X}}$ is not proportional to $\hat{\sigma}_{\bar{X}}$. This is to be expected since $\sigma^*_{\bar{X}}$ and $\hat{\sigma}_{\bar{X}}$ are obtained using different sets of information with $\sigma^*_{\bar{X}}$ using both sample and prior information. For the more general case of Ando and Kaufmann (1965) with conjugate priors for the mean and covariance matrix, not only are the standard deviations not proportional but also $\mu^*_{\bar{X}}$ does not equal $\hat{\mu}_{\bar{X}}$ in this case.

---

and the total number of risky securities.

3. As in (4), the variance in (6) differs, because of a standardization, from the scale parameter

However, in the context of informative priors it might be more reasonable to reinterpret the traditional analysis to permit a comparison on the basis of the same set of information available to each procedure. In the traditional analysis, a Bayesian would derive estimates of the parameters from the posterior distribution. For a quadratic loss function these would be given by the expectation of the marginal posterior distribution for $\boldsymbol{\mu}$ and $\boldsymbol{\Sigma}$, which we shall denote $\hat{\boldsymbol{\mu}}$ and $\hat{\boldsymbol{\Sigma}}$ respectively. For either the Ando and Kaufman conjugate prior, or the informative prior in (5), it can be shown that the mean of the predictive distribution of security returns is given by $\boldsymbol{\mu}^* = \hat{\boldsymbol{\mu}}$. The covariance matrix of the predictive distribution is given by $\boldsymbol{\Sigma}^* = C(T,d)^2\, \hat{\boldsymbol{\Sigma}}$, where

$$C(T,d)^2 = (1+1/T)d/(d-2). \tag{7}$$

Therefore, with

$$\begin{aligned} \hat{\mu}_{\mathbf{X}} &\equiv X_0 R_f + E(\mathbf{X}'\boldsymbol{\mu}) = X_0 R_f + \mathbf{X}'\hat{\boldsymbol{\mu}} \\ \hat{\sigma}^2_{\mathbf{X}} &\equiv \mathbf{X}'\hat{\boldsymbol{\Sigma}}\mathbf{X}, \end{aligned} \tag{8}$$

from (6)-(8) we have $\mu^*_{\mathbf{X}} = \hat{\mu}_{\mathbf{X}}$ and $\sigma^*_{\mathbf{X}} = C(T,d)\hat{\sigma}_{\mathbf{X}}$. Hence for this reinterpretation of the traditional analysis, for both noninformative and informative priors considered, estimation risk results in a proportional increase in the scale parameter of the distribution.

3. Effect of Estimation Risk on Capital Market Equilibrium

We derive the equilibrium prices using the technique of Sharpe (1964).[4] For the traditional (Parameter Certainty Equivalent) mode of analysis, it is well known that for a normal distribution of returns, the admissible or "efficient" portfolios of all risky assets are obtained as parametric solutions to the following optimization problem:

$$\min_{\mathbf{X}} \ \mathbf{X}'\hat{\boldsymbol{\Sigma}}\,\mathbf{X}$$

$$s.t \ \mathbf{X}'\hat{\boldsymbol{\mu}} = \mu$$

$$\mathbf{X}'\boldsymbol{\iota} = 1$$

where $\boldsymbol{\iota}$ denotes a vector of ones. With $\mu_{\mathbf{X}} \equiv \mathbf{X}'\boldsymbol{\mu}$, the portfolio mean, we let $\hat{\sigma}^2(\mu)$ denote the minimum variance for the portfolio mean μ. The locus $\hat{\sigma}(\mu)$ is plotted in Figure 6.1, where the increasing portion of $\hat{\sigma}(\mu)$ is the well known Markowitz-Tobin mean, standard deviation efficient boundary. Also by familiar separation theorem arguments, in the presence of a riskless asset all investors allocate their wealth between the riskless asset and the mutual fund of risky assets, denoted by $\hat{M}$ in Figure 6.1. In equilibrium, $\hat{M}$ is then the market portfolio of risky assets, and as given in Sharpe (1964), one obtains in equilibrium that for any portfolio $\mathbf{X}$, with $\mathbf{X}_{\hat{M}}$ denoting the market portfolio and $R_{\hat{M}} \equiv \mathbf{X}'_{\hat{M}}\tilde{\mathbf{R}}$,

reported in Klein and Bawa (1977).

4. Our results can be as easily derived using the total returns framework of Mossin (1966).

MINIMUM STANDARD DEVIATION LOCI FOR BAYES (σ^*) AND CERTAINTY EQUIVALENT ($\hat{\sigma}$) ANALYSES.

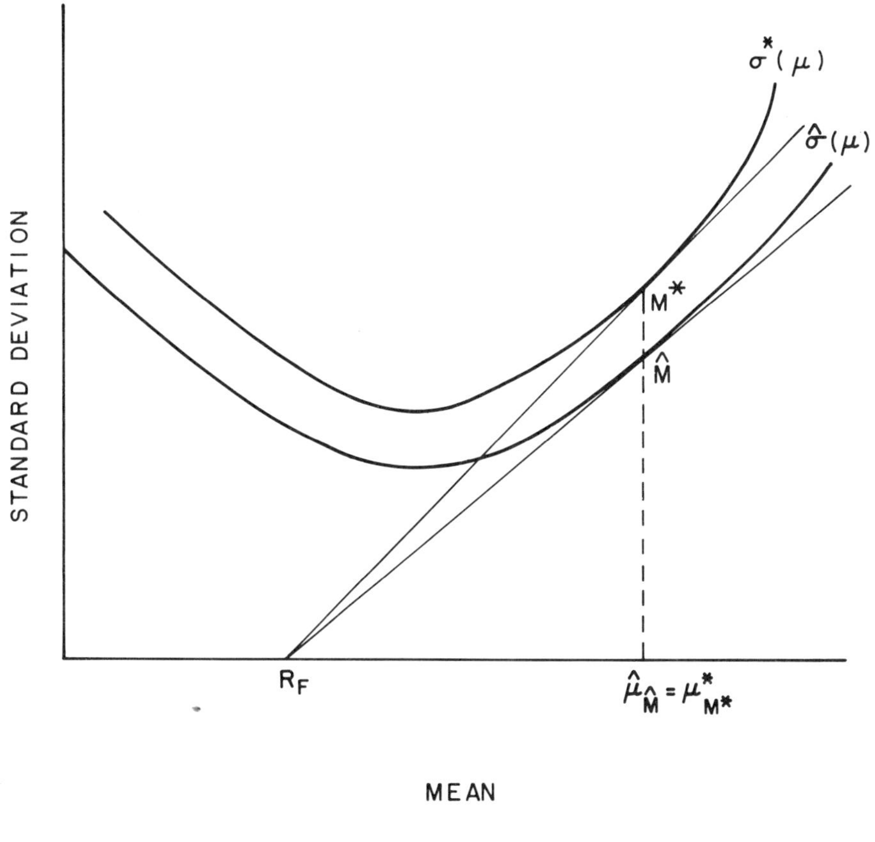

Figure 6.1

$$\mathbf{X}'\hat{\boldsymbol{\mu}} \equiv E(\overline{\mathbf{X}}'\tilde{\mathbf{R}}) = R_F + \hat{\beta}_{\mathbf{X}}(E(\tilde{R}_{\hat{M}}) - R_F), \tag{9}$$

where

$$\hat{\beta}_{\mathbf{X}} = Cov\ (\mathbf{X}'\tilde{\mathbf{R}}, \tilde{R}_M)/\ Var(\tilde{R}_M)$$
$$= \mathbf{X}'\hat{\boldsymbol{\Sigma}}\mathbf{X}_{\hat{M}}/\mathbf{X}_{\hat{M}}'\hat{\boldsymbol{\Sigma}}\mathbf{X}_{\hat{M}}. \tag{10}$$

In the Bayesian analysis, the predictive distribution of the portfolio **X** of risky assets is Student-t with mean $\mu_{\mathbf{X}}^*$, variance $\sigma_{\mathbf{X}}^{*2}$, and degrees of freedom that depend on the prior and sample information. As noted in previous chapters, the admissible portfolio of risky assets is still obtained using a mean-variance analysis and is given by the parametric solution to the following optimization problem:

$$\min_{\mathbf{X}} \quad \mathbf{X}'\boldsymbol{\Sigma}^*\mathbf{X}$$
$$s.t. \quad \mathbf{X}'\boldsymbol{\mu}^* = \mu$$
$$\mathbf{X}'\boldsymbol{\iota} = 1$$

We let $\sigma^{*2}(\mu)$ denote the minimum variance for portfolio mean μ. The locus $\sigma^*(\mu)$ is plotted in Figure 6.1, where the increasing portion of $\sigma^*(\mu)$ represents the admissible portfolio set under the Bayesian analysis.

Following exactly the reasoning of the previous case, it follows that M^* represents the market portfolio of risky assets, where all investors allocate their wealth between M^* and the riskless asset. In equilibrium,

$$\mathbf{X}'\boldsymbol{\mu}^* \equiv E(\mathbf{X}'\tilde{\mathbf{R}}) = R_F + \beta_{\mathbf{X}}^*(E(\tilde{R}_{M^*}) - R_F), \tag{11}$$

where,

$$\beta_{\mathbf{X}}^* = Cov\ (\mathbf{X}'\mathbf{R}, R_{M^*})/\ Var(R_{M^*}) \tag{12}$$
$$= \mathbf{X}'\boldsymbol{\Sigma}^*\mathbf{X}_{M^*}/\mathbf{X}_{M^*}'\boldsymbol{\Sigma}^*\mathbf{X}_{M^*}.$$

If we let $\hat{\mathbf{X}}(\mu)$ and $\mathbf{X}^*(\mu)$ denote the optimal solutions to I and II respectively for portfolio mean μ, then it directly follows that from results in Section 2 that for all μ,

$$\hat{\mathbf{X}}(\mu) = \mathbf{X}^*(\mu). \tag{13}$$

Also, as demonstrated in Brown (1979), since the point of tangency of lines drawn from R_F to curves $\hat{\sigma}(\mu)$ and $\sigma^*(\mu)$ occurs at the same mean as in Figure 6.1, it follows that the market portfolios are identical in both cases, i.e.,

$$\mathbf{X}_{\hat{M}} = \mathbf{X}_{M^*} \equiv \mathbf{X}_M \tag{14}$$

Therefore,

$$E(\tilde{R}_M) = E(\tilde{R}_{M^*}) \equiv E(\tilde{R}_M). \tag{15}$$

It also follows from (10), (12) and the fact that $\hat{\boldsymbol{\Sigma}}$ is proportional to $\boldsymbol{\Sigma}^*$, that for all portfolios **X**,

$$\hat{\beta}_{\mathbf{X}} = \beta^*_{\mathbf{X}} \tag{16}$$

Equations (14)-(16) imply that the equilibrium under the two models is observationally equivalent and that one cannot discern any effect of estimation risk on equilibrium determined market data. They also imply that the relative prices of all risky assets do not change when estimation risk is explicitly considered.

Finally, we note that it follows from Theorem 2 of Chapter 5 that when investors have the same set of information in both cases, all investors invest less in the market portfolio of risky assets, if their utility functions belong to the following class $\bar{U}$ of utility functions:

$$\bar{U} = \{U \mid U' > 0,\ U'' < 0,\ AR' \leqslant 0,\ RR' \geqslant 0,\ RR \leqslant 1\}. \tag{17}$$

In (17), the primes denote derivatives and AR and RR denote respectively the Arrow-Pratt absolute and relative risk aversion indices (Arrow (1965), Pratt (1964)), which are given by:

$$AR \equiv -U''(w)/U'(w), \quad RR = -wU''(w)/U'(w), \tag{18}$$

where w denotes the level of wealth. Thus, in equilibrium, it follows that the price of the market portfolio M, and hence of all risky assets, must fall relative to the riskless rate when estimation risk is explicitly considered and the utility function of all investors belongs to $\bar{U}$.

Our results are summarized by the following:[5]

Theorem 1: *If the investors have the same set of information under either noninformative or conjugate informative priors, then in equilibrium*

i. Relative prices of all risky assets remain unchanged when estimation risk is explicitly considered;

ii. The composition of the market portfolio expected return on the market and beta, the measure of systematic risk for any security or portfolio is invariant to estimation risk; and

iii. Prices of all risky assets fall when estimation risk is explicitly considered if the utility functions of all investors belong to the class $\bar{U}$.

5. It is shown in Bawa (1977b) that this result holds even when we relax the class of utility functions to include some non risk-averse investors.

CHAPTER 7

PORTFOLIO CHOICE AND CAPITAL MARKET EQUILIBRIUM WITH UNKNOWN DISTRIBUTIONS

Vijay S. BAWA

1. Introduction

Optimal portfolio choice involves selecting an optimal portfolio from among the given set of investment alternatives. This set includes the securities available in the market as well as all portfolios (i.e., feasible convex linear combinations) of these basic securities. Portfolio choice under uncertainty has traditionally been viewed as a choice among known probability distributions of the return on these investment alternatives. Then, under the well known von Neumann-Morgenstern (1943) paradigm, an individual should choose a portfolio (of available investment choices) that maximizes the expected utility of return. This utility function is determined uniquely, up to a positive linear transformation by the individual's preferences.

The determination of an optimal portfolio may be viewed as a two-stage process: In the first stage, one obtains the admissible set of portfolios under restrictions on the utility function that follow from prevalent types of economic behavior. This admissible set is thus useful for a large group of individuals. The optimal portfolio choice for an individual can then be determined in the second stage from among the smaller set of admissible portfolios.

It is well known that for the portfolio selection problem, as for the general problem of choice under uncertainty, the admissible choices are given by the Stochastic Dominance (SD) rules [see, for example, Bawa (1975) for a detailed discussion of, and references to, the Stochastic Dominance literature]. These SD rules are complex, requiring pairwise comparisons of Lower Partial Moment functionals of the distribution functions.[1] Thus, for the portfolio problem with an infinite choice set, these rules would appear to be intractable for arbitrary probability distributions.

The traditional way of circumventing this problem is to assume that the probability distributions of security and portfolio returns belong to a certain parametric family, e.g., normal or stable distributions.[2] In the case of normal distributions, the SD rule reduces to the well known Markowitz-Tobin (1952, 1965) mean-minimum variance selection rule for all risk averse investors, while the admissible set for all investors is as given in Bawa (1976). These mean-variance selection rules have been shown by Klein and Bawa in Chapter 4 to be invariant to estimation risk

1 The SD rules are generally stated in the literature in terms of integrals of distribution functions. The lower partial moment representation of the SD rules was introduced in Bawa (1978a).

2 Alternatively, one could further restrict attention to a narrower and frequently unacceptable class of utility functions (e.g., quadratic or in general power utility functions) for which the expected utility leads to analytic solutions for arbitrary probability distributions. In the case of quadratic utility, the well known mean-variance analysis applies.

under certain conditions. Similarly, for other two parameter families of stable distributions with constant characteristic exponent and constant skewness index, not necessarily zero, the SD rules reduce to a two parameter mean-scale parameter rule [see Bawa (1976, 1978b) for details]. However, empirical studies of security prices (e.g., Lintner (1972)) reveal that the probability distribution of returns is more likely to be lognormal than normal. For lognormal distributions, the admissible set of portfolios is, as shown in Bawa and Chakrin (1977), given by the use of the two parameter mean-logarithmic variance rule. In short, under various distributional assumptions commonly employed, admissible portfolios and hence optimal portfolio choice are provided by the use of two parameter selection rules, where portfolio mean may be viewed as the return measure and the scale parameter as the risk measure.

In all of these cases, it has been shown that if short sales are permitted, the admissible portfolios admit separation between the riskless asset (if one is assumed to exist) and a mutual fund of risky assets; where by separation we mean that the admissible portfolio choices and hence optimal choices of all individuals can be represented as linear combinations of two funds, the riskless asset and the 'market' fund of all risky assets. The admissible portfolios of only the risky assets has been shown to admit separation between two mutual funds of risky assets. These separation properties have been essential in the analysis of capital market equilibrium wherein the optimal portfolio choices of all investor's are aggregated to derive equilibrium prices of risky assets. For a multivariate normal distribution of returns and with riskless borrowing and lending, this leads to the well-known Sharpe-Lintner-Mossin Capital Asset Pricing Model, CAPM [Sharpe (1964), Lintner (1965), Mossin (1966)] with the expected excess return on any security or portfolio, where the excess is over the riskless rate, is in equilibrium equal to the (nondiversifiable) systematic risk of the security, called beta, times the expected excess return on the market. Black (1972) has shown that a zero beta version of this model holds if no riskless asset exists or with restricted borrowing and lending. Brown (1979) has shown that these equilibrium results are invariant to estimation risk in case of diffuse priors and as demonstrated in Chapter 6, this invariance to estimation risk holds even under a class of informative priors. Fama (1971) has derived a CAPM when the probability distribution of portfolio return is a symmetric nonnormal two parameter stable distributions. Bawa (1977b) has shown that all of these CAPM's hold under much weaker conditions than those postulated in the aforementioned papers. Bawa and Chakrin (1977) have derived a CAPM in the case of lognormal distributions of portfolio returns, wherein the linear risk/return relationship of the other CAPM's is replaced by a nonlinear relationship.

There is an alternative way of reducing the dimensionality of the SD rules to that of two parameter rules, without making the assumption that portfolio returns belong to a certain parametric family of distributions. For arbitrary probability distributions, the SD rules are mean-lower partial moment functional rules. The mean may be viewed as the return measure, and the lower partial moment functional (computed at every point in the domain of the underlying random variable) may be viewed as the risk measure. Thus, a "mean-risk" selection rule, which employs the mean as the return measure and the lower partial moment evaluated at a single point only as a scalar risk measure, is a two parameter rule which theory suggests may be a reasonable approximation for arbitrary probability distributions. Bawa (1978a) and Bawa and Lindenberg (1977) have shown that optimal portfolio choice and capital market equilibrium can be analyzed in the mean-lower partial moment (MLPM) framework just as easily as in the traditional mean-variance, or more generally mean-scale frameworks. More importantly, as shown in Bawa and Lindenberg (1977), the usefulness of the two parameter mean-lower partial moment framework is that it includes the mean-variance as well as the mean-scale parameter frameworks as special cases under appropriate distributional assumptions. Bawa, Goroff and Whitt (1978) have shown that the two parameter MLPM portfolio selection rules are good approximations to the full blown SD rules if the probability distribution of portfolio returns is close to any of the two parameter location-scale families of distributions. Thus, the lower partial moment may be viewed as a risk measure which reduces to the appropriate risk measure (variance or scale parameter) whenever the appropriate distributional assumptions hold.

Perhaps, the most appealing quality of the MLPM framework is that it generates an empirical hypothesis of the equilibrium valuation formula that can be tested using available market data without unduly restrictive distributional assumptions. Moreover, it reduces to the traditional models when the data supports the distributional assumptions of those models.

In all of the papers referenced above, as in most of the literature on portfolio theory and capital market equilibrium, it is assumed that the probability distribution of security and portfolio returns are known. In addition, except in the new MLPM framework, it is also assumed explicitly (or certainly implicitly) that the probability distributions of portfolio returns belong to a certain parametric family of distributions with the values of the parameters that completely characterize these distributions as being known.

But is the joint probability distribution of the (random) returns on the basic securities, and hence the return on all portfolios, ever completely known? The answer appears to be negative, certainly for realistic portfolio selection problems. One may, for example, know from past experience that the distribution function belongs to a certain parametric family of distributions (e.g., normal or lognormal). However, due to inherent nonstationarity, the values of the parameters that completely characterize the distribution within the assumed parametric family are unknown (e.g., mean and variance for the normal or logarithmic mean and logarithmic variance for the lognormal). These parameter values are generally estimated using relevant past data. For example, Markowitz (1952) uses historical data to estimate the mean vector and the covariance matrix for use in determining the admissible/efficient portfolios; Miller and Scholes (1972) point out that even though theoretical development of mean-variance CAPM assumes that the underlying parameter values are known, they have to be estimated and are used as if they were the true parameter values during the empirical testing of the equilibrium models. Thus, traditional analysis neglects estimation risk in determining optimal portfolio choice under uncertainty by treating the estimated parameter values as if they were the true parameter values. However, since estimation risk is part of the uncertainty faced by the individual decision-maker, it should be explicitly considered.

In a Bayesian framework, estimation risk can be explicitly considered. Optimal portfolio choice under uncertainty is obtained in the von Neumann-Morgenstern-

Savage paradigm ((1943),(1954)) by using the predictive distribution of returns under each alternative in lieu of the unknown probability distribution of returns. This predictive distribution, as argued in Chapter 1, does not condition on parameter estimates being equal to the true parameter values. Rather, this distribution depends on prior and sample (data) information in a way that reflects estimation risk.

The Bayesian method of analysis has been employed in other contexts, for example, by Zellner and Tiao (1964), Zellner and Geisel (1968), Prescott (1972) and Chow (1973) for non portfolio selection problems. More recently, Klein and Bawa in Chapters 4 and 5 of this book and Brown (1976) have considered the effect of estimation risk on the portfolio choice problem when the underlying probability distribution of returns is normal with unknown parameter (means and variance-covariance matrix) values, making use of the results on the predictive distributions of portfolio returns as derived in Zellner and Chetty (1965) and Ando and Kaufman (1966).

In all of the aforementioned papers, the analysis assumes that the probability distribution of returns belongs to a known parametric family of distributions and that the values of the (finitely many) parameters that completely characterize the distribution are unknown. For example, the joint distribution of security returns is usually assumed to be normal with unknown means and variance-covariance matrix. It should be noted that the assumption of a parametric family may be viewed as an extremely informative prior on the space of all probability measures (i.e., assuming the distribution function to be normal in the class of all positive nondecreasing bounded functions is indeed assuming an informative prior). For the portfolio selection problem, for example, due to nonstationarity over time in the underlying stochastic process and/or limited past empirical analysis that undoubtedly affects subjective beliefs, one may not have enough prior information to assume a functional form for the distribution function. Thus, it is important to consider the optimal portfolio choice under uncertainty with unknown probability distributions in a nonparametric context.

Such an analysis has perhaps been hindered by the analytical difficulties in deriving the posterior and predictive distribution of returns for a sufficiently general family of prior distributions. Recently, in fundamental papers on nonparametric Bayesian inference, Ferguson [(1973), (1974)] has shown that under certain plausible conditions, the family of Dirichlet processes is the conjugate prior family on the space of all probability measures; i.e., the posterior distribution also belongs to the family of Dirichlet processes. From this basic result, it will be seen below that the predictive distribution of returns takes on a simple analytic form and that for the important special case of the noninformative (on the space of all probability measures) Dirichlet prior, the predictive distribution is the well known, and traditionally used, empirical distribution function. This result points out the invariance of Stochastic Dominance rules to estimation risk [as in the parametric context in Klein and Bawa (1976)]. It also points out that the optimal choices of all individuals do not change when estimation risk is considered explicitly for the important special case of the noninformative Dirichlet prior. This result also provides the theoretical rationale for empirical economic analysis wherein the empirical distribution function is used in lieu of the true but unknown distribution function. From this invariance result, the traditional method of using the empirical distribution function (when the underlying distribution function is completely unknown)[3] is the correct procedure; estimation risk is indeed present but is properly incorporated directly in the empirical distribution function.

In Section 2, it is shown that the joint predictive distribution of security returns, when the underlying distribution function characterizing alternative choice is unknown and Dirichlet priors are used, is the joint empirical distribution function for the noninformative prior case. In addition for the informative prior case, the predictive distributions are shown to be weighed averages of the empirical distributions and the priors. This result, under the von Neumann-Morgenstern-Savage axioms implies that the admissible portfolio choice under uncertainty problems with unknown distributions is given by the use of Stochastic Dominance (SD) rules now applied to the empirical distribution functions or the appropriate predictive distributions under informative priors. In Section 3, we formulate the portfolio choice problem when the underlying probability distributions are unknown, note the computational infeasibility of the problem and show that it can be (approximately) solved using the two parameter (mean, lower partial moment) selection rules.[4,5] We show that in the presence of a riskless asset, market equilibrium results are obtained using the methodology developed in Bawa and Lindenberg (1977). In particular, with no restrictions on the predictive distributions, and with a riskless asset available as an investment opportunity, investors' optimal portfolios admit the well known mutual fund separation property: wealth is optimally allocated between the riskless asset and the market portfolio of risky assets. This is shown to directly imply that the CAPM in the MLPM framework also provides a linear risk/return relationship. We discuss the methodology for empirical testing of this new capital asset pricing model under alternate specifications of prior information. The relationship to results in parametric models is also noted in Section 3.

2. Predictive Distribution of Returns in a Nonparametric Context: Invariance of Stochastic Dominance to Estimation Risk

For portfolio choice under uncertainty when the distribution function characterizing each alternative is unknown, one needs to obtain the predictive distribution of returns for each alternative. To do this, one needs to obtain the joint predictive distribution of security returns; the predictive distribution for each portfolio is directly obtained from this joint distribution.

Let F denote the true, but unknown, joint distribution of security returns, $\tilde{\mathbf{R}}$, with $\tilde{\mathbf{R}}' = (\tilde{R}_1, \tilde{R}_2, \ldots, \tilde{R}_m)$. We note that

$$F_{Pred}(t) \equiv E_p F(t), \tag{1}$$

where p denotes the posterior distribution of returns. In a nonparametric context,

3 See footnote 4 in Bawa (1979a) for detailed discussion of this issue.

4 One could restrict the utility function to a form that leads to an analytically tractable form for expected utility and thus solve the problem. This approach is obviously of limited usefulness.

5 One could check to see if the predictive distributions satisfy the necessary and sufficient conditions for mutual fund separation given by Ross (1978). For the nonparametric case of interest here, this appears not to be a fruitful approach.

it is important that the class of prior distributions be defined in such a way as to have the following desirable properties: i) the class of priors is rich enough to incorporate varying degrees of prior information, (i.e., that the support of the prior with respect to some suitable topology on the space of all probability measures be large); ii) the posterior distribution is manageable analytically; and iii) the class of priors is parameterized in a manner that allows for direct incorporation and interpretation of prior information.

Ferguson ((1973), (1974)) has shown that the Dirichlet process prior achieves the above desirable properties and that the resulting posterior distribution also belongs to the class of Dirichlet processes. Thus, in the nonparametric context, Dirichlet priors may be viewed as the conjugate family. This is the only known conjugate prior that provides the needed analytic tractability.

To define this prior, let $\mathbf{R}_1, \mathbf{R}_2, \ldots, \mathbf{R}_n$ denote a random sample of size n drawn from F, with $\mathbf{R}_i' = (R_{i1}, R_{i2}, \ldots, R_{im})$. Let

$$\mathbf{F} = \{\text{F:F is a probability measure on } (\mathbf{R}^m, \mathbf{B})\},$$

where $\mathbf{R}^m$ is the m-dimensional Eucleadian space and $\mathbf{B}$ is the σ-algebra of Borel subsets of $\mathbf{R}^m$. The Dirichlet process can now be defined by the following:

Definition 1: [Ferguson (1973), (1974)] Let $\tilde{Z}_1, \ldots, \tilde{Z}_k$, be independent random variables with $\tilde{Z}_j$ having a gamma distribution with shape parameter $\alpha_j \geqslant 0$ and scale parameter 1, for $j = 1, 2, \ldots, k$.[6] Let $\alpha_j > 0$ for some j. The Dirichlet distribution with parameter $(\alpha_1, \alpha_2, \ldots, \alpha_k)$, denoted by $D(\alpha_1, \alpha_2, \ldots, \alpha_k)$, is defined as the distribution of $(\tilde{\theta}_1, \tilde{\theta}_2, \ldots, \tilde{\theta}_k)$, where $\tilde{\theta}_j = \tilde{Z}_j / \sum_{i=1}^{k} \tilde{Z}_i$, $J = 1, 2, \ldots, k$.

Definition 2: [Ferguson (1973), 1974)] Let α be a finite nonnull measure (nonnegative and finitely additive) on $(\mathbf{R}^m, \mathbf{B})$. P is a Dirichlet process with parameter α, denoted by $P \epsilon D(\alpha)$, if for every finite measurable partition $\{B_1, \ldots, B_n\}$ of $\mathbf{R}^m \left(\text{i.e., the } B_i \text{ are measurable, disjoint and } \bigcup_{i=1}^{n} B_i = \mathbf{R}^m\right)$, the random vector $(P(B_1), P(B_2), \ldots, P(B_n))$ has a Dirichlet distribution with parameter $(\alpha(B_1), \alpha(B_2), \ldots \alpha(B_n))$.

The analytical tractability of the Dirichlet process is exhibited by the following:

Lemma 1: [Ferguson (1973)] If $F \epsilon D(\alpha)$ and if $R_1, R_2, \ldots, R_n$ is a random sample from F, then the posterior distribution of F given $R_1, R_2, \ldots, R_n$ is $D\left(\alpha + \sum_{i=1}^{n} \delta_{R_i}\right)$, where δ_R is the measure giving mass one to R.

6 A gamma distribution with shape parameter α and scale parameter β has the pdf

$$g(x|\alpha,\beta) = \begin{cases} \dfrac{x^{\alpha-1} e^{-x/\beta}}{\beta^{\alpha}\Gamma(\alpha)} & x \geqslant 0, \\ 0 & \text{otherwise} \end{cases}$$

The explicit form of the predictive distribution function now follows from Lemma 1. Let $\tilde{\mathbf{R}}$ be a vector of random variables with unknown distribution function F. Then, with $\alpha(t) \equiv \alpha[(-\infty,t)]$ and $t' = (t_1,t_2,...,t_m)$, the form of the predictive distribution is stated as Theorem 1 below:[7]

Theorem 1. If the prior distribution of F is $p_0 \in D(\alpha)$ and a random sample $R_1,...,R_n$ is drawn from F, then the predictive distribution function is given as:

$$\hat{F}_n(t) = p_n F_o(t) + (1-p_n) F_n(t), \tag{2}$$

where

$$F_o(t) \equiv \alpha(t)/\alpha(\mathbf{R}^m),$$
$$p_n = \alpha(\mathbf{R}^m)/[\alpha(\mathbf{R}^m) + n],$$

and F_n is the empirical distribution function

$$F_n(t) = \{\# \text{ of } R_i \leqslant t\}/n \tag{3}$$

From (2), the predictive distribution function has a very simple form. It is a weighted average of F_o, the prior guess, and F_n, the empirical distribution function. The weights $(p_n, 1-p_n)$ as intuitively expected, depend on the relative strength of belief in prior information ($\boldsymbol{\alpha}$) and sample information (the sample size, n). For example, for very small sample sizes, the prior receives, as expected, most of the weight.

As an important special case of (2), suppose that there is minimal prior information so that $\alpha \to 0$ (the "noninformative" Dirichlet prior). Then, the weighting factor $p_n \to 0$. Consequently, as noted by Ferguson (1973, p. 223), the distribution function in (2) becomes the empirical distribution function. This is summarized by the following:

Corollary 1: For the case of the noninformative Dirichlet prior and a random sample $R_1,R_2, \ldots, R_n$ drawn from the true distribution F, the predictive distribution of returns $\hat{F}_n(t)$ is the empirical distribution function $F_n(t)$ given by (3).

It is also important to note that as the sample size $n \to \infty$, the predictive distribution $\hat{F}_n$ (for informative and noninformative Dirichlet priors) converges almost surely to the true distribution F [see Ferguson (1973, p. 223)]. Thus, the effect of estimation risk, directly incorporated in the predictive distribution, decreases, as intuitively expected, as the sample size increases.

We also note that for any feasible portfolio $\mathbf{X}$, $\mathbf{X}' \equiv (X_1,X_2, \ldots, X_n)$, with X_i denoting the fractional allocation of initial wealth in security i, $i = 1,2,...,m$, the

7 Ferguson (1973; p. 222) shows that $E(F) = p_n F_o(R) + (1-p_n) F_n(R)$ in an estimation context, where the expectation is taken over the posterior distribution. Bawa (1977a, 1979a) notes that $E(F)$ is indeed the predictive distribution function required in decision-making.

predictive distribution of return $R_{\mathbf{X}} = \mathbf{X}'\mathbf{R}$ on portfolio $\mathbf{X}$, $\hat{F}_{\mathbf{X}}$,

$$\hat{F}_X(t) = P_r\{R_x \leqslant t\} \tag{4}$$

$$= \underset{X'R \leqslant t}{\int \dots \int} d\hat{F}_n(\mathbf{X}'\mathbf{R}),$$

is known for any $\mathbf{X}$ once the joint predictive distribution of security returns $(\hat{F}_n)$ is known. Thus, under the von Neumann-Morgenstern-Savage paradigm ((1943), (1954)), an individual decision-maker should choose a portfolio $\mathbf{X}(1)$ over a portfolio $\mathbf{X}(2)$ if and only if

$$\Delta E_{Pred} U \equiv E_{\hat{F}_{\mathbf{X}(1)}} U(\mathbf{X}'(1)\mathbf{R}) - E_{\hat{F}_{\mathbf{X}(2)}} U(\mathbf{X}'(2)\mathbf{R}) > 0. \tag{5}$$

(i.e., the expected utility under the predictive distribution of $\mathbf{X}'(1)\mathbf{R}$ is greater than that under the predictive distribution of $\mathbf{X}'(2)\mathbf{R}$, where U denotes the von Neumann-Morgenstern utility function.

Consequently, once the predictive distribution of portfolio returns is obtained, all of the results obtained in the literature for the case of known distribution directly carry over. It should be noted that this result holds in general and is not restricted to the use of Dirichlet priors. In particular, Theorem 1 enables us to extend the applicability of the well known Stochastic Dominance rules in obtaining the admissible set of portfolios for commonly accepted classes of utility functions. Let $\mathbf{Y} = [a,b)$, $a < b$, denote the range of possible outcomes. Let U' denote the first derivative of U, U'' the second derivative, and U''' the third derivative. Then, let the classes of utility functions commonly considered in economics be defined as follows:

$$\mathbf{U}_1 = \{U(y) \mid U'(y) > 0, \ \forall y \epsilon \mathbf{Y}\} \tag{6}$$

$$\mathbf{U}_2 = \{U(y) \epsilon \mathbf{U}_1 \mid U''(y) < 0, \ \forall y \epsilon \mathbf{Y}\}$$

$$\mathbf{U}_3 = \{U(y) \epsilon \mathbf{U}_2 \mid U'''(y) > 0, \ \forall y \epsilon \mathbf{Y}\}$$

$$\mathbf{U}_{DARA} = \left\{U(y) \epsilon \mathbf{U}_2 \mid \frac{d}{dy}(-U''(y)/U'(y)) < 0, \ \forall y \epsilon \mathbf{Y}\right\}.$$

For a distribution function F, define, for $i \geqslant 0$, the ith order lower partial moment, computed at point t, as

$$LPM_i(t;F) \equiv \int_a^t (t-y)^i dF(y) \ , \tag{7}$$

and

$$\mu_F \equiv E_F X. \tag{8}$$

Our result is summarized by the following:

Theorem 2: Under the von Neumann-Morgenstern-Savage Axioms, with Dirichlet prior about the unknown distribution F of security returns, and a random sample of size n drawn from F, a portfolio $\mathbf{X}(1)$ *is preferred to a portfolio* $\mathbf{X}(2)$*:*

i. *for all utility functions in* $\mathbf{U}_i$, $i = 1,2$, *if and only if*

$$LPM_{i-1}(t;\hat{F}_{X(1)}) - LPM_{i-1}(t;\hat{F}_{X(2)}) \leqslant 0, \quad \forall t \in \mathbf{Y}$$

and < 0 *for some* t

ii. *for all utility functions in* $\mathbf{U}_3$ *if and only if*

$$\mu_{\hat{F}_{X(1)}} \geqslant \mu_{\hat{F}_{X(2)}}$$

and $LPM_2(t;\hat{F}_{X(1)}) - LPM_2(t;\hat{F}_{X(2)}) \leqslant 0, \forall t \in \mathbf{Y}$ *and* < 0 *for some* t

iii. *if* $\mu_{\hat{F}(1)} = \mu_{\hat{F}(2)}$, *for all utility functions in* U_{DARA} *if and only if*

$$LPM_2(t;\hat{F}_{X_1}) - LPM_2(t;\hat{F}_{X_2}) \leqslant 0, \quad \forall t \in \mathbf{Y}$$

and < 0 *for some* t,

where $\hat{F}_{X(1)}$ *and* $\hat{F}_{X(2)}$, *the predictive distribution of portfolio returns* $X'(1)R$ *and* $X'(2)R$ *are given by (4).*

The proof of Theorem 2 follows directly when one notes that using Theorem 1, the predictive distributions are given by (4), and it follows directly from (5) that the Stochastic Dominance rules hold. The statement of the Stochastic Dominance rules in Theorem 2 in terms of the lower partial moments is exactly as in Bawa (1978a). Again it should be noted that Theorem 2 holds in general, once the predictive distribution has been determined.

Finally, since the empirical distribution function is traditionally used (with no explicit consideration of estimation risk) our invariance result is summarized by the following:

Theorem 3: For the general choice under uncertainty problem with unknown distributions, the admissible set of alternatives as well as the optimal choice for all individual decision makers is the same for the Bayesian method and the traditional method for the case of noninformative Dirichlet priors and the same sample (data) information available in both cases.

3. Portfolio Selection and Capital Market Equilibrium With Unknown Distributions

The results in the last section show that with the simple substitution of the unknown distribution function by the predictive distribution of returns, Stochastic Dominance rules provide the admissible set of portfolio choices. Thus, for the portfolio choice problem with an infinite number of alternatives and an arbitrary predictive distribution, the pairwise comparisons mandated by Theorem 2 cannot be carried out. Hence, the need for approximation is paramount in this case.

In earlier papers (Bawa (1978a), Bawa and Lindenberg (1977), we have proposed as an approximation for arbitrary but known distributions, the use of the two parameter MLPM (mean, lower partial moment) rule suggested by the Stochastic Dominance rules as stated in Theorem 2. In view of the results in Section 2, the two parameter mean, lower partial moment (MLPM) portfolio selection rule can be used for the problem at hand as well. The result in Bawa, Goroff and Whitt (1978) on the "goodness" of the two parameter MLPM approximation holds in this case too: The quality of the approximation is determined by testing how close the predictive distribution is to a member of any of the two parameter location-scale families of distributions.

If we let, for $n = 1, 2$,

$$LPM_n(t;X) \equiv \int_a^t (t-y)^n d\hat{F}_X(y); \tag{9}$$

then as given in Bawa (1978a) and can be seen from Theorem 2, an investor's optimal portfolio has the characteristic that it lies in the admissible set of portfolios generated by the parametric solutions, over μ, to the following optimization problems (with $n = 1, 2$) for any fixed value of t:[8]

$$\min_{x} LPM_n(t;\mathbf{X}) \tag{I}$$

$$\text{s.t.} \sum_{i=1}^{m} X_i E_i = \mu$$

$$\mathbf{X} \in \mathbf{C} = \{X \mid \Sigma X_i = 1 \text{ } or \text{ } \Sigma X_i = 1 \text{ and } X \geqslant 0\}.$$

For any fixed value of t and $n \geqslant 1$ $LPM_n(t;\mathbf{X})$ is a convex function of $\mathbf{X}$ [see Bawa (1978a, Theorem 4)]. Hence (I) is a standard optimization problem, with a convex function being minimized over a convex set, that can be parametrically solved by using any one of several available algorithms. Indeed, since the predictive distribution is a discrete distribution, special algorithms used in Ang (1975) and Hogan and Warren (1972) can be used to obtain the MLPM admissible portfolios for $n = 1$ and 2 respectively.

Note that t may be an arbitrary constant. In particular, for the market equilibrium analysis, we set t equal to r_F, the riskless rate, which may be viewed as the opportunity cost of investing in a risky portfolio and thus has intuitive appeal (see Bawa and Lindenberg (1977, p. 192).

As noted in Bawa (1978a), the optimal value of $LPM_n(r_F;\mathbf{X})$, as a function of μ (denoted as $LPM_n(\mu)$), is increasing and convex over all μ greater than the mean, $\mu(n,r_F)$, of the portfolio that yields the minimum lower partial moment over the

8 Our results apply equally well to any feasible portfolio set which is a compact convex subset of $\mathbf{C}$.

feasible set **C**. This is the same property exhibited by the admissible boundary in mean-variance space under the distributional approximations of traditional portfolio theory. Thus, the admissible boundary in the MLPM framework, represented by curve AB in Figure 7.1, is the solution to (I) for $\mu \geqslant \mu(n, r_F)$.[9]

Suppose that a riskless asset is also available and that X_0 is the proportion of initial wealth that the investor places into that asset. Let $\mathbf{X}' = (X_1, \ldots, X_m)$ now represent the proportions of his risky portfolio held in each risky asset. Then if $\overline{\mathbf{X}}' = (X_0, \mathbf{X}')$, the investor's problem I reduces to

(I')

$$\min_{\overline{\mathbf{X}}} LPM_n(r_F; \overline{\mathbf{X}})$$

subject to

$$\sum_{i=1}^{m} (1-X_0) X_i E_i + X_0 r_F = \mu$$

and

$$X \in \mathbf{C}.$$

We note that as can be directly inferred from Bawa and Lindenberg (1977),

$$LPM_n^{1/n}(r_F; \overline{\mathbf{X}}) = \left[\int_a^{r_F} (r_F - X_0 r_F - (1-X_0) y)^n d\hat{F}_X(y) \right]^{1/n} \tag{10}$$

$$= (1-X_0) LPM_n^{1/n}(r_F; X).$$

Thus, for $n = 1, 2$ in the mean-$LPM_n^{1/n}$ space, linear combinations of a portfolio X of risky assets and the riskless asset lie along a straight line. Because of the convexity of the $LPM_n(\mu)$ function, this implies that the portfolio with minimum lower partial moment is found by drawing a tangent to the admissible boundary (AB in Figure 7.2) from the point r_F.[10] Thus, the separation property of the traditional portfolio theory developed in the parametric context still obtains and M, the point of tangency in Figure 7.2, may be termed the "market" portfolio of risky assets. We note that Figure 7.2 is identical to Sharpe's graphical solution to the optimal portfolio choice problem with $(LPM_n)^{1/n}(n=1, 2)$ replacing standard deviation as the relevant risk measure.

The separation property obtained above directly implies, using, for example, Sharpe's graphical cum analytical methodology, that one obtains a CAPM in the

9 Figure 7.1 is reproduced from Figure 1 in Bawa and Lindenberg (1977).

10 See footnote 5 in Bawa and Lindenberg (1977) regarding the existence of unique tangency point. Figure 7.2 is reproduced from Figure 7 in Bawa and Lindenberg (1977).

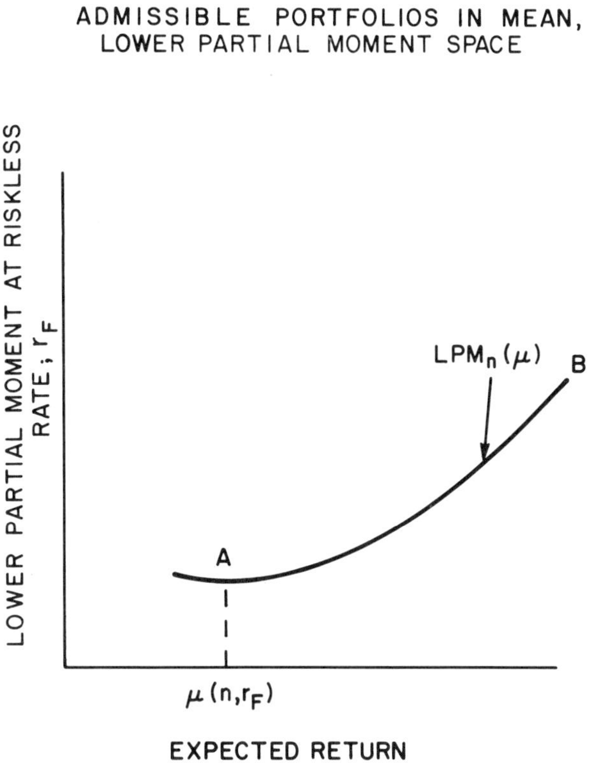
ADMISSIBLE PORTFOLIOS IN MEAN, LOWER PARTIAL MOMENT SPACE
LOWER PARTIAL MOMENT AT RISKLESS RATE; r_F
$LPM_n(\mu)$
B
A
$\mu(n,r_F)$
EXPECTED RETURN

Figure 7.1

MLPM framework just as the CAPM is the parametric context analyzed in the finance literature. Figure 7.2 represents the essence of this methodology. This result, initially proved in a somewhat different context by Bawa and Lindenberg (1977), is summarized by the following.

Theorem 4: Under the standard assumptions employed in analysis of capital market equilibrium, and with all investors having access to the same sample information and same Dirichlet prior, if all investors evaluate portfolios in a mean, lower partial moment of order 1 ($MLPM_1$) *framework, or evaluate portfolios in a mean, lower partial moment of order 2* ($MLPM_2$) *framework, then the market equilibrium prices satisfy the following relationship, with* $n = 1$ *or 2 appropriately,*

$$E(R_j) = r_F + \beta_j^{MLPM_n}(E(R_M) - r_F) \quad j = 1,2,\ldots, \,. \tag{11}$$

where

$$\beta_j^{MLPM_n} = \frac{CLPM_n(r_F;M,j)}{LPM_n(r_F;M)}, \tag{12}$$

$CLPM_n(r_F;M,j)$, *the colower partial moment of order n between the returns* R_j *on security j and* R_M *on the market portfolio M, is given by*

$$CLPM_n(r_F;M,j) = \int_{r_M=-\infty}^{r_F} \int_{r_j=-\infty}^{\infty} (r_F - r_M)^{n-1}(r_F - r_j)\, d\hat{F}(r_M, r_j), \tag{13}$$

where $LPM_n(r_F;M)$ *is defined by (7) and where in* $E(R_j)$ *and* $E(R_M)$ *the expectation is over the predictive distribution* $\hat{F}$ *of security returns.*

We note that in (11), the security market line in the mean-lower partial moment framework using the predictive distribution is identical to the one obtained in Bawa and Lindenberg (1977) when distributions were assumed known. It is also identical in form to the traditional Capital Asset Pricing Model obtained in the mean-variance (MV) framework except that $\beta_j^{MV} = Cov(R_M,R_j)/Var(R_M)$ is replaced by $\beta_j^{MLPM_n}$.

As discussed in Bawa and Lindenberg (1977, p. 197), in the mean-lower partial moment framework, the market portfolio, M, has positive risk ($LPM_n(r_F;M) > 0$) only when there is a positive probability of the return of that portfolio falling below r_F. By the definition of $\beta_j^{MLPM_n}$, a particular security contributes to the market's risk when its return, as well as the market's return, are below r_F. When $R_j > r_F$ and $R_M < r_F$ security j reduces the risk of M. Thus the premium paid for risk in (4) is positive whenever $\beta_j^{MLPM_n} > 0$ and negative when $\beta_j^{MLPM_n} < 0$. If the market's return exceeds the risk free rate, it is not considered to be risky and, thus, individual security returns contribute nothing to it,

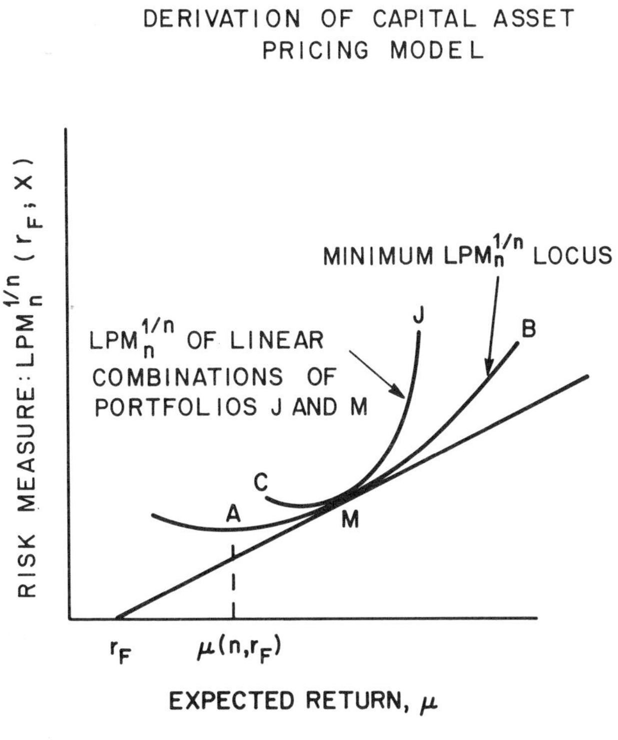
DERIVATION OF CAPITAL ASSET PRICING MODEL
RISK MEASURE: $LPM_n^{1/n}(r_F; X)$
MINIMUM $LPM_n^{1/n}$ LOCUS
$LPM_n^{1/n}$ OF LINEAR COMBINATIONS OF PORTFOLIOS J AND M
J
B
C
A
M
r_F
$\mu(n, r_F)$
EXPECTED RETURN, μ

Figure 7.2

regardless of whether $R_j \gtreqless r_F$.

In the nonparametric case of interest here, the predictive distribution is discrete for the noninformative case, and discrete for the informative Dirichlet prior case as well if the prior is assumed to be discrete. Let R_{jt}, r_{Ft}, and R_{Mt}, $t = 1, 2, \dots, T$, $j = 1, 2, \dots, m$, denote T observations[11] on the security j's return, the risk free rate, and the return on the market. Let $S \equiv \{t \mid 1 \leqslant t \leqslant T,\ R_M \leqslant r_{Ft}\}$. Their $\beta_j^{MLPM_n}$, the measure of systematic risk, is for discrete predictive distribution,

$$\beta_j^{MLPM_n} = \frac{\sum_{t \in S} (r_{Ft} - R_{Mt})^{n-1} (r_{Ft} - R_{jt})}{\sum_{t \in S} (r_{Ft} - R_{Mt})^n} \tag{14}$$

Equation (14) provides a convenient expression for $\beta_j^{MPLM_n}$ that can be used in the empirical testing of the CAPM in the MLPM framework under the usual assumptions of homogeneous expectations across investors.

In conclusion we note that it is clear that Theorem 4 holds for arbitrary predictive distribution of security returns obtained either in parametric or nonparametric contexts. It is interesting to note that Theorem 4 contains as special cases, the well known mean-variance and mean-scale CAPM's if the predictive distribution belongs to a location and scale family of distributions. Thus, for example, the CAPM's in Brown (1979), Bawa (1977b) and as given by Bawa and Brown in Chapter 6 of this book, may all be viewed as special cases of Theorem 4 with the predictive distribution being a Student-t distribution. This provides a link to the parametric models and points out the strength of the results in the MLPM framework.

---

11 For the noninformative prior case, T denotes the number of samples. For the informative prior case, T denotes some of the number of sample points and the number of data points implied by the prior. Thus, (14) holds for both cases with appropriate interpretation of T.

CHAPTER 8

OPTIMAL PORTFOLIO CHOICE UNDER UNCERTAINTY: A BAYESIAN APPROACH*

Stephen J. BROWN

1. Introduction

As pointed out in Chapter 3 of this book, it is generally assumed that individuals know the values of parameters that characterize the distribution of security returns. Models of optimal portfolio choice so derived are important not only for their own sake, but also because they provide testable implications for equilibrium in the capital markets. Yet in applying these models, it is often assumed that true parameter values are unknown, and that sample estimates can represent them not only in the portfolio problem but also in testing the market equilibrium implications of the models.

A number of *ad hoc* suggestions have been made to correct for the estimation risk that arises from the difference between the estimates and the true parameter values, ranging from aggregation (Blume, 1970) to adjustment of estimates (Vasicek, 1973). However, as indicated in previous chapters, there is a superior way of handling this particular problem through the use of the "predictive" distribution of returns. This predictive distribution is found by averaging the returns distribution over the unknown parameter values. Zellner and Chetty (1965), Mao and Särndal (1966) and Barry (1974) show how to apply this suggestion in the portfolio choice context, but it was not until the papers of Klein and Bawa (1976) reproduced as Chapter 4 of this book and Brown (1976) that attention was given to comparing in a quite general setting this Bayesian approach with the other portfolio selection procedures that have appeared in the literature.

In this chapter we define a measure of the differences between alternative portfolio choices and derive for the first time some quantitative orders of magnitude for this difference. We consider the relative performance of the optimal Bayes portfolio in repeated samples, and find that the Bayesian approach uniformly dominates the alternative strategies across all sample sizes considered, sometimes by quite significant amounts. This was true for different parameters that were assumed to generate observed returns, and held even where the returns distribution was severely misspecified.

In Section 2 we use a single risky asset example to illustrate the comparison of the methods and to introduce the statistical risk function as an appropriate measure

* This chapter is based in part on results contained in my doctoral dissertation. I wish to thank my chairman Professor Nicholas Gonedes, and Arnold Zellner who helped and encouraged me throughout the project. I am also indebted to Professor Robert Hamada and to the other members of my committee, Jonathan Ingersoll, Uday Karmarkar, and Myron Scholes, for many helpful comments and suggestions.

of relative portfolio performances in repeated samples. Section 3 analyzes a many risky asset example. In this context we consider the performance of the methods, and present results of the comparison in Section 4. In Section 5, we investigate an informative prior example. Section 6 assesses the sensitivity of the results to misspecifications of the returns distribution, and in Section 7 we conclude with a summary of our major findings.

2. The Single Risky Asset Example

In this section we define the conventional or (parameter) "Certainty Equivalent" and Bayesian approaches to the problem of optimal portfolio choice in the context of estimation risk, and compare them on the basis of a single risky asset example. Not only is the optimal Bayes portfolio different, but, in addition, it has superior relative performance in repeated samples. It can be shown that optimal portfolio choice in the context of estimation risk can be characterized by an optimal choice between a risk-free security and an optimal portfolio of risky securities. Thus the simple example is very important, and characterizes the problem of an investor deciding what proportion of his assets to hold in the form of a "market fund" (Black and Scholes, 1974).[1]

Suppose there are two assets: a risk-free security with known return R_f and a risky security with return $\tilde{R}_t$ in period t where $\tilde{R}_t$ is distributed independently across time as normal, with mean μ and variance σ^2. The values of these parameters are not known to the individual investor, as we assume for this example that his information set is limited to a sample of size T.[2]

The conventional approach to this problem is to estimate the parameters μ and σ^2 and to assume those estimates are the relevant true values for the purpose of portfolio selection. This approach is well known in a stochastic control framework, and is termed a Certainty Equivalent rule (Theil, 1964). The resulting portfolio is the solution to the problem

$$\underset{X}{Max}\, EU\left[W_1(1+\tilde{R}_p)\,|\,\mu = \hat{\mu},\ \sigma^2 = \hat{\sigma}^2\right].$$

where $\tilde{R}_p = (1-X)R_f + X\tilde{R}$. Since the distribution of returns is normal, the mean-variance optimal portfolio characterization applies, and the portfolio opportunity set can be represented in terms of the line zb in Figure 8.1, with an optimal portfolio choice at B.

The Bayes rule portfolio choice involves choosing a portfolio to maximize the expected utility of wealth where the expectation is taken with respect to the *predictive* distribution, given by averaging the returns distribution over the posterior distribution of the unknown parameter values. Provided certain conditions are met,[3] this Bayes portfolio choice is a solution to the problem

1. In the many risky asset examples, if the relevant predictive distribution is multivariate Student-t (see next section) one can demonstrate this proposition using standard separation theorem arguments.

2. Alternatively, we could assume that his information set is equivalent to a hypothetical sample of size T.

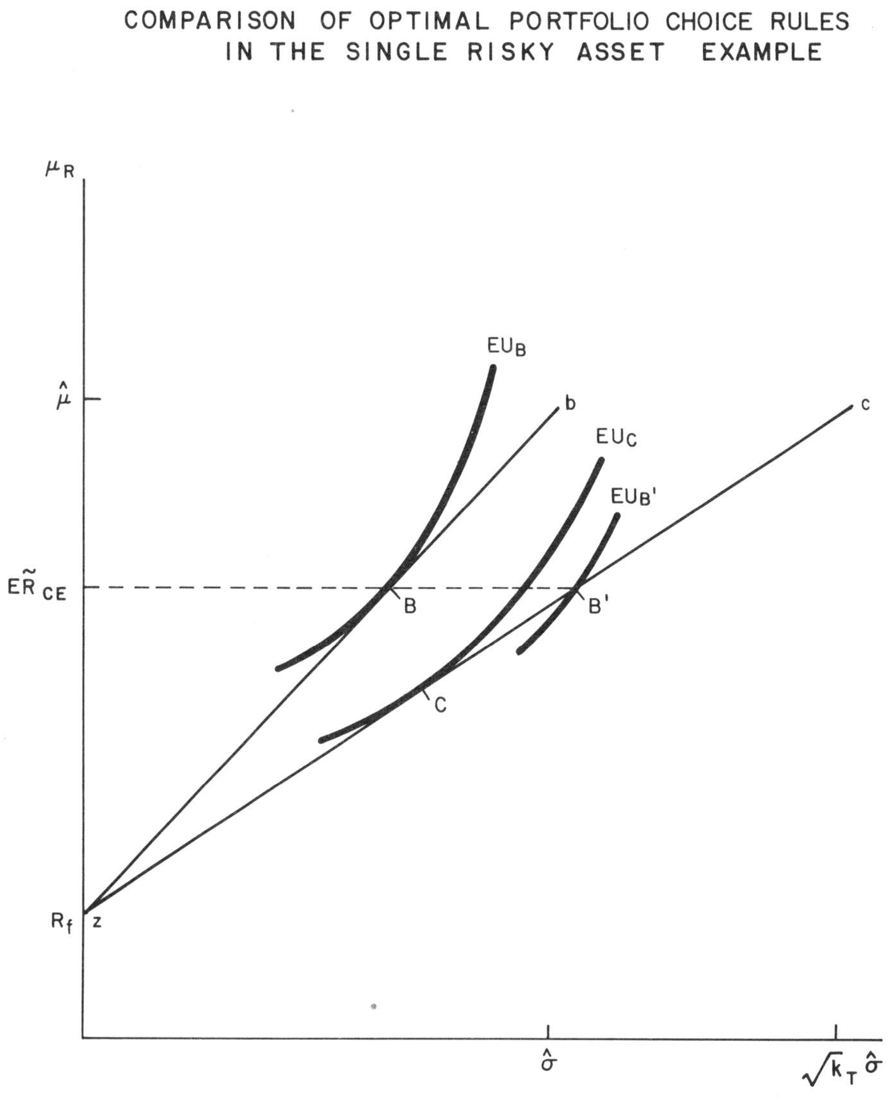
COMPARISON OF OPTIMAL PORTFOLIO CHOICE RULES
IN THE SINGLE RISKY ASSET EXAMPLE
μ_R
$\hat{\mu}$
$E\tilde{R}_{CE}$
R_f
z
EU_B
b
EU_C
$EU_{B'}$
c
B
B'
C
$\hat{\sigma}$
$\sqrt{k_T}\,\hat{\sigma}$
STANDARD DEVIATION

Figure 8.1

DERIVATION OF THE RISK FUNCTION

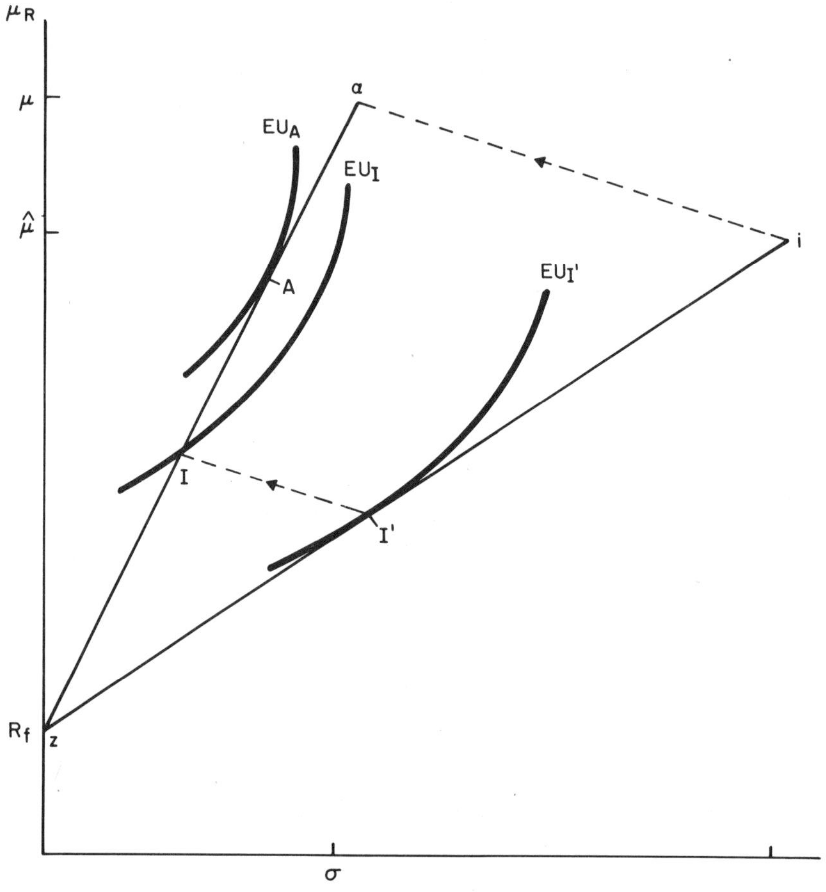

Figure 8.2

$$\underset{X}{Max} \underset{\mu,\sigma^2}{E}\left\{EU\left[W_1(1+\tilde{R}_p)\right]\mu,\sigma^2\right\}$$

where as before $\tilde{R}_p = (1-X)R_f + XR$.

In general, the predictive distribution will not be normal. If we assume that a noninformative, or "diffuse" prior characterizes the state of knowledge prior to observing data, then conditional on a sample of size T, the predictive distribution of returns is Student-t with mean

$$\mu^* = \hat{\mu} = 1/T \sum_{l=1}^{T} R_l$$

and variance

$$\sigma^{*2} = k_T\hat{\sigma}^2 = \frac{k_T}{T-1}\sum_{l=1}^{T}(R_l-\hat{\mu})^2 ,$$

$$k_T = (1+1/T)(T-1)/(T-3)$$

with $(T-1)$ degrees of freedom.[4]

Given the degrees of freedom the Student-t distribution is a member of the location scale family of distribution functions (Bawa 1975). Hence we can represent the portfolio opportunity set in terms of the line zc of Figure 8.1. The curve EU_C represents the locus of combinations of portfolio means and standard deviations yielding the same expected utility as the optimal Bayes portfolio choice at C.

In terms of the predictive mean and standard deviation opportunity set, the Certainty Equivalent portfolio choice is represented by the point B'. Clearly EU_C must be at least greater than $EU_{B'}$ and as indicated in Chapter 4 of this book it can be proved under fairly general conditions[5] that the point C lies below B' which implies that the Bayes rule invests less in the risky asset than would the Certainty Equivalent rule.

How much less? Since k_T approaches one for large T, the point C approaches B and the rules will converge. In finite samples the rules will differ and the magnitude of this difference will clearly depend on the form of the utility function. For a quadratic utility example

$$U[W] = a_0 + a_1W - a_2W^2,\ a_o,a_1,a_2 > 0,$$

it is easy to show that the amount of wealth invested in the risky asset by the

3. A sufficient condition is that the posterior distribution integrates to unity.

4. Assuming a diffuse prior of the form $p(\mu,\sigma)\ \alpha\ 1/\sigma$, use Zellner (1971) p. 22 to show the posterior distribution is of normal-inverted gamma form, and apply the result in Raiffa and Schlaifer (1961) p. 304.

5. These sufficient conditions are that the utility function $U(W)$ display decreasing absolute risk aversion $\partial\{-U''(W)/U'(W)\}/\partial W \leqslant 0$, and relative risk aversion less than unity: $-WU''(W)/U'(W) < 1$, where this measure of relative risk aversion is nondecreasing in W.

Bayes rule relative to the Certainty Equivalent rule is given by

$$X_B/X_{CE} = (1+\hat{\eta}^2)/(k_T+\hat{\eta}^2)$$

where k_T is as defined before and

$$\hat{\eta} = (\hat{\mu}-R_f)/\hat{\sigma}$$

represents the slope of the line *zb* in Figure 8.1.

For a negative exponential utility example:

$$U[W] = d(h - exp(-gW)) \quad d,g,h > 0,$$

we can derive the ratio

$$X_B/X_{CE} = 1/k_T$$

provided that we are willing to approximate the Student-*t* predictive distribution in terms of a normal distribution with the same mean and variance.[6]

For both specifications of the utility function, the ratio of wealth invested in the risky asset by the two rules does not depend on the utility function parameters. For the negative exponential case, it depends on the sample evidence *only* through the sample size, *T*. On Table 8.1 we record the value of this ratio for various values of *T* and across a range of values of $\hat{\eta}$. For both specifications of the utility function, there is a measurable difference between the rules. However, in the quadratic utility case the difference is sensitive to the particular value of $\hat{\eta}$.

To gain some idea of what might be a reasonable value for $\hat{\eta}$, we investigated a market fund example where the fund comprising all securities traded on the New York Stock Exchange yielded a rate of return equal to that of the Fisher (1966) index of the market. The risk-free asset was represented by holdings of one month to maturity Treasury bills. The ratio of the sample mean excess return (return on the fund less the risk-free rate) to the standard deviation was computed for the data covering the period January 1935 to December 1970 and for different subsets of that data, with the results reported on Table 8.2. While there is considerable variation in these estimates for different subsamples, the maximum value of $\hat{\eta}$ observed was $\hat{\eta} = .455$. Even for a value of $\hat{\eta}$ this high, there is substantial difference between the Bayes and Certainty Equivalent rules for the sample sizes considered (as can be seen from Table 8.1).

For a simple example we have shown a measurable difference between the Bayes and Certainty Equivalent rules. We have not demonstrated their relative performance in repeated samples. Of course, a portfolio manager is confronted with only *one* set of data, and as a consequence portfolio performance criteria that have appeared in the past (e.g., Fama 1972) have been limited to analyzing performance in terms of that set of data. Fortunately the structure of our problem is such that we can control for the distribution of returns and derive a criterion of portfolio performance that does not depend on the accidentals of a given set of sample data.

6. Otherwise expected utility over the predictive distribution is not defined for this utility function.

TABLE 8.1--Ratio of Wealth Invested in the Risky Security
Bayesian/Certainty Equivalence

	T				
$(\hat{\mu}-R_f)/\hat{\sigma}$	10	16	20	30	50
			a. Quadratic Utility		
0.1	0.709127	0.817178	0.853380	0.901885	0.940932
0.2	0.715128	0.821510	0.857004	0.904445	0.942538
0.3	0.724596	0.828292	0.862663	0.908427	0.945029
0.5	0.751073	0.846906	0.878099	0.919201	0.951725
0.8	0.798331	0.878904	0.904314	0.937209	0.962778
1.0	0.828402	0.898488	0.920162	0.947923	0.969272
2.0	0.923483	0.956762	0.966458	0.978497	0.987478
3.0	0.960220	0.977903	0.982943	0.989132	0.993700
5.0	0.984316	0.991384	0.993370	0.995792	0.997567
8.0	0.993667	0.996536	0.997338	0.998312	0.999026
	b. Negative Exponential Utility				
	0.707071	0.815686	0.852130	0.901001	0.940376

This criterion is familiar in the statistics literature as a "risk function" (e.g., Mood, Graybill and Boes 1974, pp. 297-99).

Both the Bayes and Certainty Equivalent rules can be viewed as alternative ways of processing a given set of sample data. Suppose we sample from a distribution with mean μ and variance σ^2. Based on this sample, in terms of Figure 8.2 the investor perceives an opportunity set *zi*, the position of which depends on the particular decision rule chosen. The optimal choice at I' has expected utility EU_I measured in terms of the true distribution, which is less than EU_A, the expected utility of the optimal choice at A given knowledge of μ and σ. If we measure EU_I relative to EU_A, and average this out over all possible samples generating the point i we have the risk function referred to before.[7] It is a measure of performance in the following sense. Suppose an investor constructs a series of portfolios based on hypothetical samples from a given distribution of returns according to a particular decision rule. The investor would prefer the alternative that yields the highest expected utility on average. If one alternative is rejected for every value of μ and σ, it is said to be "inadmissible" (Lehmann 1959 p. 16).

In this context it is a little more convenient to work with a loss function for returns than a utility function for wealth. This loss function is a negative linear function of utility defined in such a way that minimizing expected loss $EL(\tilde{R}_p)$ is equivalent to maximizing expected utility $EU(\tilde{W})$:

7. That is, define risk as $(EU_A-\overline{EU}_I)/EU_A$, where $\overline{EU}_I$ represents the average in repeated samples of expected utility for decision rule I given μ and σ.

TABLE 2.--Ratio of the Sample Mean Excess Return to the Standard Deviation of Return: Return on Fisher Index Market Fund and One Month Treasury Bill Rate--January, 1935-December, 1970

Subperiod	$(\hat{\mu}-\bar{R}_f)/\hat{\sigma}$		$(\hat{\mu}-\bar{R}_f)/\hat{\sigma}$
1935/1-1938/12	0.168526	1935/1-1941/12	0.102718
1939/1-1942/12	0.082510	1942/1-1948/12	0.324458
1943/1-1946/12	0.434145	1949/1-1955/12	0.455029
1947/1-1950/12	0.222373	1956/1-1962/12	0.157816
1951/1-1954/12	0.381703	1963/1-1969/12	0.210698
1955/1-1958/12	0.323411		
1959/1-1962/12	0.094786	1935/1-1943/12	0.166213
1963/1-1966/12	0.253262	1944/1-1952/12	0.292361
1967/1-1970/12	0.101601	1953/1-1961/12	0.349493
		1962/1-1970/12	0.101881
1935/1-1939/12	0.145438		
1940/1-1944/12	0.274302		
1945/1-1949/12	0.186159	1935/1-1946/12	0.198013
1950/1-1954/12	0.440694	1947/1-1958/12	0.298254
1955/1-1959/12	0.338278	1959/1-1970/12	0.133426
1960/1-1964/12	0.148260		
1965/1-1969/12	0.161510	1935/1-1952/12	0.197583
		1953/1-1970/12	0.198173
1935/1-1940/12	0.122118		
1941/1-1946/12	0.354180	1935/1-1970/12	0.190611
1947/1-1952/12	0.236673		
1953/1-1958/12	0.376525		
1959/1-1964/12	0.175214		
1965/1-1970/12	0.105547		

$$EU(\tilde{W}) = k_0 - k_1 EL(\tilde{R}_p)$$

where k_0 and k_1 do not depend on alternate portfolio choices. If we define EL_A as the expected loss of the optimal portfolio given μ and σ^2, we can parameterize the risk function as

$$\text{Risk}_I(\mu,\sigma) = (\overline{EL}_I - EL_A)/EL_A$$

$$\text{for } I = \begin{cases} \text{Bayes} \\ \text{Certainty Equivalent} \end{cases}$$

where $\overline{EL}_I$ represents expected loss averaged over samples drawn from a population with mean μ and variance σ^2, which is proportional to the risk function defined in terms of expected utility.

We have shown elsewhere (Brown 1978) that this measure is defined for both Bayes and Certainty Equivalent rules in the simple quadratic utility example, and that one can derive an analytic expression for the risk function, as a function of sample size. Surprisingly, in the quadratic case this risk function does not depend on the utility function parameters. Further, it depends on μ, σ^2 and R_f *only* through the slope of the line *za* in Figure 8.2:

$$\eta = (\mu - R_f)/\sigma \ .$$

In Table 8.3 we have computed values of the risk functions for different sample sizes. Risk varies with sample size and with η. For each value of η considered, the Bayes rule uniformly dominates the Certainty Equivalent strategy. Thus we have shown that not only is the Bayes rule different, but that it has superior performance in repeated samples for the quadratic utility example.

3. Many Risky Assets

In the previous section, we studied a case where there was a single risky asset and one asset yielding a risk free rate of return. In this section, we relax these assumptions, and consider a case where there are many risky assets, no one of which has a constant, known rate of return.[8]

We assume initially that returns have a multivariate normal distribution with mean $\boldsymbol{\mu}$ and covariance matrix $\boldsymbol{\Sigma}$. These parameters have values that are not known to the investor. We are thus led to consider the Certainty Equivalence and Bayes rules of the previous section.

As before, the optimal Certainty Equivalent portfolio maximizes expected utility for some estimate of the parameters. Use of minimum variance unbiased estimates in this context will yield the familiar Markowitz (1952, 1959) algorithm which we shall term a Markowitz Certainty Equivalent (CE) rule.

Sharpe (1963) suggests imposing a particular structure on the distribution of returns. This structure is given by the familiar "market model":

$$R_{it} = \alpha_i + \beta_i R_{Mt} + \epsilon_{it} \quad i = 1,\ldots,m$$

$$R_{Mt} = \alpha + \epsilon_{Mt},$$

where the ϵ_{it} and ϵ_{Mt} are zero mean stochastic terms that are independent across securities and time. In the simplest case they each have a normal distribution with mean zero and variance σ_i^2.[9] If we replace the unknown parameters of the Sharpe model by Ordinary Least-Squares estimates, and derive a mean and covariance matrix of returns, we have for the purposes of portfolio selection a Sharpe

8. The intermediate case of many risky assets and a risk-free asset can be subsumed within these two examples since an optimal portfolio choice in this case is given by an optimal combination of the risk-free security with a portfolio that is optimal for some utility function ignoring the risk-free rate.

9. This assumption can be relaxed. We shall not deal with the inconsistency that follows if R_{Mt} is considered a linear combination of *all* security returns.

TABLE 8.3--Risk Function Evaluation: Single Risky Asset, Quadratic Utility

	t				
$(\mu-R_f)/\sigma$	10	16	20	30	50
			$(\bar{E}L_{BAYES}-EL_A)/EL_A$		
0.1	0.065493	0.047298	0.039898	0.028679	0.018355
0.2	0.075447	0.052961	0.044232	0.031353	0.019827
0.3	0.091405	0.061983	0.051134	0.035619	0.022190
0.5	0.137504	0.087739	0.070826	0.047854	0.029050
0.8	0.223080	0.135065	0.107111	0.070668	0.042088
1.0	0.277008	0.165307	0.130500	0.085606	0.050764
2.0	0.420713	0.254005	0.201097	0.132368	0.078758
3.0	0.462177	0.283680	0.225792	0.148934	0.089439
5.0	0.486071	0.302469	0.239333	0.152487	0.087668
8.0	0.494497	0.272460	0.258815	0.168389	0.066371
			$(\bar{E}L_{CE}-EL_A)/EL_A$		
0.1	0.109563	0.065748	0.052079	0.034361	0.020496
0.2	0.118404	0.070602	0.055789	0.036680	0.021812
0.3	0.132952	0.078559	0.061867	0.040481	0.023972
0.5	0.177335	0.102614	0.080214	0.051951	0.030504
0.8	0.266632	0.150468	0.116667	0.074752	0.043516
1.0	0.324847	0.182090	0.140903	0.090053	0.052320
2.0	0.460965	0.268748	0.210338	0.136370	0.080167
3.0	0.485934	0.292745	0.231532	0.151434	0.090325
5.0	0.495964	0.306371	0.241829	0.153563	0.088047
8.0	0.498510	0.274018	0.259908	0.168892	0.066642
			$(\bar{E}L_{CE}-\bar{E}L_{BAYES})/EL_A$		
0.1	0.044070	0.018450	0.012181	0.005683	0.002140
0.2	0.042957	0.017642	0.011556	0.005327	0.001984
0.3	0.041547	0.016576	0.010733	0.004862	0.001782
0.5	0.039831	0.014875	0.009389	0.004097	0.001453
0.8	0.043551	0.015403	0.009556	0.004084	0.001428
1.0	0.047839	0.016783	0.010403	0.004447	0.001556
2.0	0.040252	0.014743	0.009241	0.004002	0.001409
3.0	0.023757	0.009065	0.005740	0.002500	0.000886
5.0	0.009893	0.003902	0.002495	0.001076	0.000378
8.0	0.004014	0.001557	0.001093	0.000504	0.000271

Certainty Equivalent (CE) rule. Of course, this procedure would require some modification in the case where the investor regarded the Sharpe model as only a first approximation (King 1966) or as useful, although not literally true (Fama, 1968).

Blume (1968) argues that one should aggregate individual securities into different equally weighted portfolio assets prior to using a Certainty Equivalent rule for portfolio selection. This procedure was advocated by Blume as a means for reducing estimation uncertainty. However, any improvement in precision of the estimates of the different parameters of the returns distribution may come at the expense of ignoring relevant differences. His procedure could be interpreted as a way of incorporating the information that the securities comprising each portfolio asset represent a homogeneous group.

Other variants of the simple Certainty Equivalent rule are possible. Elton and Gruber (1973) suggest a few alternatives to the Sharpe covariance restriction, while Vasicek (1973) and Fisher (1971) suggest ways to adjust the Sharpe model coefficient estimates to incorporate additional information. All of these modifications to the Markowitz Certainty Equivalence rule attempt to improve the precision of the different estimates by introducing additional information. The Bayes rule on the other hand incorporates all available information into the predictive distribution and defines expected utility with respect to that distribution.

In general, this predictive distribution is both difficult to derive and to work with.[10] The distribution will have a tractable form, if prior to observing the data available information can be represented in one of the following ways:

1. *Diffuse Prior* - Prior to any observations the portfolio manager is "ignorant" of the values of the relevant parameters.

2. *Informative Conjugate Prior; Covariance Known* - Uncertainty relates to the mean; the covariance matrix is known and could be given, for example, by a covariance matrix implied by the Sharpe model.

3. *Informative Conjugate Prior; Covariance Known Only to a Factor of Proportionality* - This model could represent, for example, the case where the portfolio manager knows the true parameters of the Sharpe model and the true coefficient of multiple determination for each asset but is uncertain of the market variance σ_M^2.

4. *Informative Conjugate Prior; Covariance Not Known* - Conditional on the covariance matrix, the individual has an informative conjugate prior as in (2); however, the covariance matrix itself has a prior distribution.

The intuition behind these "conjugate priors" is that the decision maker is assumed able to process information about the unknown parameters in such a way that it becomes equivalent to hypothetical sample data drawn from a distribution with those parameters.

We shall concentrate attention on Assumptions 1 and 4. For these assumptions, with T observations on m risky securities, the predictive distribution of portfolio returns is Student-t with $t-m$ degrees of freedom, and we can proceed as in the

10. If the Sharpe model generates security returns, with estimation risk a two parameter mean/variance rule no longer characterizes optimal portfolio choices (Brown 1977).

previous section. In particular for the diffuse prior example (Assumption 1) the mean and covariance matrix of the predictive distribution of returns will be given by (Brown 1976)

$$\boldsymbol{\mu}^* = \hat{\boldsymbol{\mu}}, \ \boldsymbol{\Sigma}^* = k_T\hat{\boldsymbol{\Sigma}}, \ k_T = (1+1/T)(T-1)/(T-m-2)$$

where $\hat{\boldsymbol{\mu}}$ and $\hat{\boldsymbol{\Sigma}}$ are the usual sample estimates of the mean and covariance matrix of returns for a given sample of size T where m is the number of risky assets.

Clearly, any portfolio $\mathbf{X}$ that minimizes estimated portfolio variance,

$$\hat{\sigma}_p^2 = \mathbf{X}'\hat{\boldsymbol{\Sigma}}\mathbf{X},$$

will also minimize the predictive variance,

$$\hat{\sigma}^{*2} = \mathbf{X}'\boldsymbol{\Sigma}^*\mathbf{X} = k_T\mathbf{X}'\hat{\boldsymbol{\Sigma}}\mathbf{X} \equiv k_T\hat{\sigma}_p^2,$$

for a given mean return

$$\mathbf{X}'\mu^* = \mathbf{X}'\hat{\mu} \ .$$

Thus we can represent the Bayes and Certainty Equivalent choices in terms of Figure 8.3, where point C represents the predictive mean and standard deviation of the optimal Bayes choice. Point B would represent the Bayes choice if the estimates $\hat{\boldsymbol{\mu}}$ and $\hat{\boldsymbol{\Sigma}}$ were based on an infinite sample (k_T=1). This point defines the Certainty Equivalent portfolio which yields B' in terms of its predictive mean and standard deviation. In general B' will differ from C. The magnitude and importance of this difference will depend on the utility function of the individual investor.

For the quadratic and negative exponential utility examples it happens that the optimal portfolios have simple closed form representations that facilitate comparison of the rules.[11] It is possible to show that point C must lie below B' for these specifications of the utility function (Brown 1976). How much less depends on the utility function parameters and on the sample data available to the investor. However, note that here as before, for the negative exponential utility function we are forced to approximate the Student-t predictive distribution by a normal with the same mean and covariance matrix. To illustrate this difference we estimated a covariance matrix and a vector of means and then compared the rules on the assumption that these estimates were based on hypothetical samples of different sizes.

Fifteen equally weighted portfolios were formed from the set of all New York Stock Exchange listed securities that were continuously traded from July 1953 to June 1968. The rules for selection of these portfolios correspond to those outlined by Fama and MacBeth (1973). The returns on each portfolio were computed on a monthly basis from January 1961 to June 1968 inclusive. These data were used to compute the minimum variance unbiased estimates of the covariance matrix and the vector of means, which appear in Table 8.4.

TABLE 8.4--Covariance Matrix and Vector of Means Used for the Purpose of Comparing Different Portfolio Strategies*

Covariance Matrix

	1	2	3	4	5
1	0.0005527				
2	0.0005695	0.0007091			
3	0.0005856	0.0007034	0.0008243		
4	0.0005955	0.0007258	0.0007942	0.0009102	
5	0.0005384	0.0006937	0.0007893	0.0008552	0.0009419
6	0.0005859	0.0007653	0.0008876	0.0009559	0.0010116
7	0.0005827	0.0007943	0.0009228	0.0010230	0.0010833
8	0.0005866	0.0008150	0.0009417	0.0010562	0.0011431
9	0.0006004	0.0008312	0.0009785	0.0011043	0.0011931
10	0.0006160	0.0008907	0.0010357	0.0011989	0.0012886
11	0.0006755	0.0009479	0.0010970	0.0012654	0.0013756
12	0.0006872	0.0009956	0.0011799	0.0013336	0.0014645
13	0.0006715	0.0010024	0.0011683	0.0013776	0.0015155
14	0.0007548	0.0011087	0.0013313	0.0015501	0.0016929
15	0.0008266	0.0012598	0.0015293	0.0018053	0.0020095

	6	7	8	9	10
6	0.0012131				
7	0.0012153	0.0014033			
8	0.0012888	0.0014316	0.0016099		
9	0.0013347	0.0014740	0.0015885	0.0016919	
10	0.0014709	0.0016073	0.0017123	0.0017762	0.0020631
11	0.0015571	0.0017011	0.0018348	0.0018857	0.0020914
12	0.0016927	0.0018280	0.0019756	0.0020298	0.0022811
13	0.0017143	0.0019126	0.0020776	0.0021032	0.0023936
14	0.0018955	0.0021451	0.0023299	0.0023589	0.0026702
15	0.0022604	0.0025375	0.0027433	0.0028157	0.0031874

11	12	13	14	15	
11	0.0023647				
12	0.0024212	0.0027615			
13	0.0025534	0.0027462	0.0030511		
14	0.0029094	0.0031309	0.0032947	0.0039718	
15	0.0034605	0.0037361	0.0039301	0.0045886	0.0055939

Vector of Means

1	0.008341	6	0.011524	11	0.015327
2	0.009487	7	0.011741	12	0.015244
3	0.010101	8	0.013092	13	0.018752
4	0.011327	9	0.011529	14	0.017808
5	0.011900	10	0.015104	15	0.019110

*See text.

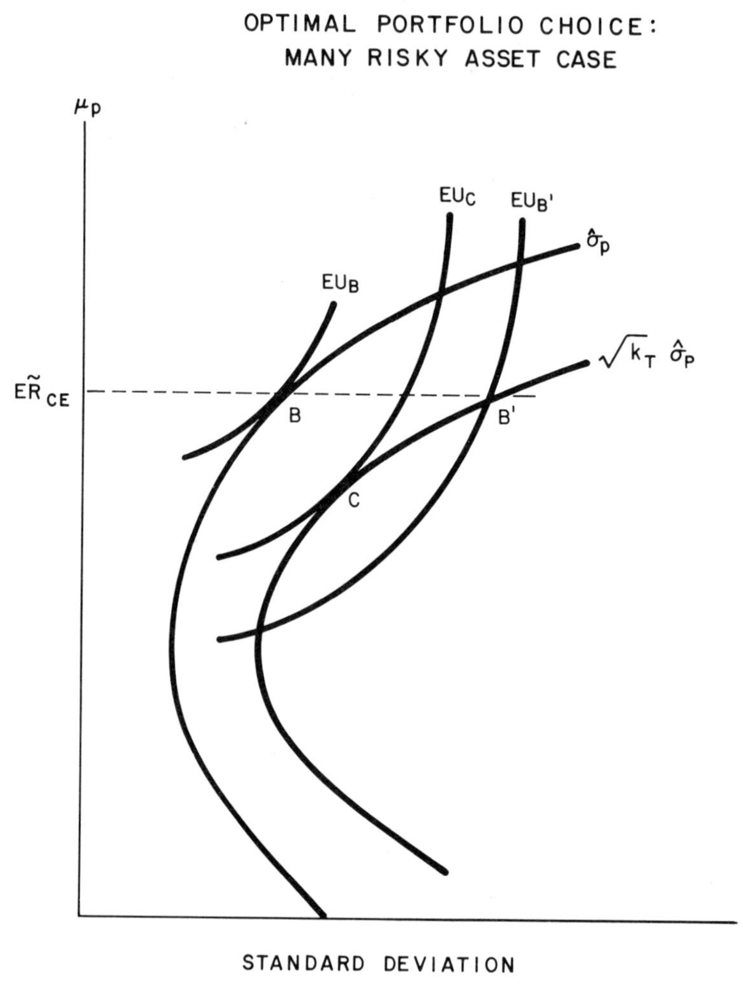
OPTIMAL PORTFOLIO CHOICE:
MANY RISKY ASSET CASE
μ_p
EU_C
$EU_{B'}$
$\hat{\sigma}_p$
EU_B
$\sqrt{k_T}\ \hat{\sigma}_p$
$E\tilde{R}_{CE}$
B
B'
C
STANDARD DEVIATION

Figure 8.3

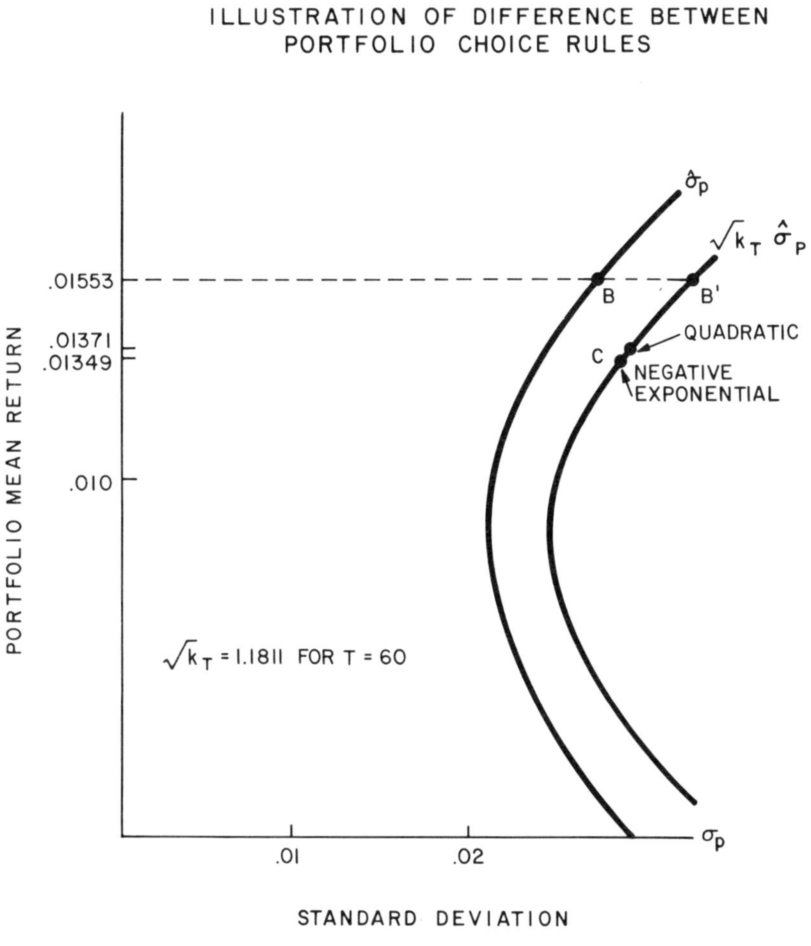
ILLUSTRATION OF DIFFERENCE BETWEEN
PORTFOLIO CHOICE RULES
PORTFOLIO MEAN RETURN
.01553
.01371
.01349
.010
B
B'
C
QUADRATIC
NEGATIVE
EXPONENTIAL
$\hat{\sigma}_P$
$\sqrt{k_T}\ \hat{\sigma}_P$
$\sqrt{k_T}$ = 1.1811 FOR T = 60
.01
.02
σ_P
STANDARD DEVIATION

Figure 8.4

We estimated the sample mean of the monthly return on a value weighted index (CRSP, 1974) for the period of July 1967 to June 1968 to be 1.552 percent per month. We then chose the utility function parameters so as to make that market rate of return the mean return on the optimal portfolio *if* the minimum variance unbiased estimates *were* the true parameters.[12]

In Figure 8.4 we compare the optimal solutions *if* the estimates were based on an infinite sample size (point B) with those *if* the estimates were based on a sample of 60 months' data (point C) for the two utility functions. Point B' represents the Markowitz Certainty Equivalent solution. In this situation, the optimal diffuse prior Bayesian solution would yield an expected rate of return between .18 percent and .20 percent less than the Markowitz CE solution.

Tables 8.5 and 8.6 demonstrate how the portfolios change as the hypothetical sample size increases. Recall that we are not restraining portfolio weights to be positive in this example. From inspection of the dispersion of portfolio weights the Bayes rule appears far more conservative than the Certainty Equivalent alternative. The deficiency of the Certainty Equivalence rule is clear: it would have prescribed the *same* portfolio for a given set of sample estimates *regardless* of the number of observations used to construct the estimates. For this reason we would expect the Certainty Equivalence rule to perform poorly in repeated samples, and this is indeed the case. To demonstrate this result we must use simulation methods to derive an empirical measure of the risk function introduced in the previous section, since it appears that this function has no convenient analytic representation in this more complex many risky asset case.

The simulation procedure took the following form. In each case two hundred drawings were made from a specified distribution of returns. These data can be

---

11. The optimal portfolio $\mathbf{X}$ is given by

$$\mathbf{X} = \frac{cER_p - b}{ac - b^2}\boldsymbol{\Sigma}^{*-1}\boldsymbol{\mu}^* + \frac{a - bER_p}{ac - b^2}\boldsymbol{\Sigma}^{*-1}\boldsymbol{\iota}$$

$$a = \boldsymbol{\mu}^{*\prime}\boldsymbol{\Sigma}^{*-1}\boldsymbol{\mu}^*,\ b = \boldsymbol{\mu}^{*\prime}\boldsymbol{\Sigma}^{*-1}\boldsymbol{\iota},\ c = \boldsymbol{\iota}'\boldsymbol{\Sigma}^{*-1}\boldsymbol{\iota}.$$

$$\boldsymbol{\iota}' = (1, \ldots, 1) \quad \text{(c.f., Merton 1972)},$$

where ER_p is determined such that

$$R^* = ER_p + \frac{cER_p - b}{ac - b^2}$$

in the quadratic utility case for $R^* = (a_1 - 2a_2W_1)/2a_2W_1$, where R^* is the rate of return at which risk aversion becomes infinite. In the negative exponential case ER_p is determined such that

$$1/g_1 = \frac{cER_p - b}{ac - b^2}$$

for $g_1 = gW$ where g is the measure of risk aversion (Brown 1976).

12. In the quadratic utility case $R^* = .059013$ and for the negative exponential utility example $1/g_1 = .043486$. Note that $R^* >> ER_p$.

viewed as a time series of returns from which we can estimate sample means and covariance matrices. For different sample sizes, the rules were used to compute optimal portfolios on the basis of the observed data.

TABLE 8.5.--Optimal Bayesian and Certainty Equivalent Portfolio Weights

	a: Quadratic Utility														
T	1	2	3	4	5	6	7	8	9	10	11	12	13	14	15
20	+0.56	-0.22	-0.24	+0.06	+1.11	-0.04	+0.11	+0.30	-0.43	+0.20	-0.08	-0.08	+0.03	+0.05	-0.34
25	+0.43	-0.30	-0.15	+0.20	+1.27	-0.13	-0.00	+0.37	-0.66	-0.26	-0.02	-0.07	+0.14	+0.04	-0.39
30	+0.34	-0.34	-0.08	+0.30	+1.37	-0.19	-0.07	+0.41	-0.08	+0.29	+0.01	-0.06	+0.21	+0.03	-0.42
35	+0.29	-0.38	-0.04	+0.37	+1.45	-0.23	-0.12	+0.44	-0.90	+0.31	+0.04	-0.06	+0.25	+0.03	-0.44
40	+0.24	-0.40	-0.01	+0.41	+1.50	-0.27	-0.16	+0.45	-0.97	+0.33	+0.05	-0.05	+0.29	+0.02	-0.45
45	+0.21	-0.42	+0.01	+0.45	+1.54	-0.29	-0.19	+0.48	-1.03	+0.34	+0.07	-0.05	+0.31	+0.02	-0.46
50	+0.18	-0.43	+0.03	+0.48	+1.57	-0.31	-0.21	+0.49	-1.07	+0.35	+0.08	-0.04	+0.33	+0.02	-0.47
55	+0.16	-0.44	+0.05	+0.50	+1.59	-0.32	-0.23	+0.50	-1.11	+0.36	+0.09	-0.04	+0.35	+0.02	-0.48
60	+0.15	-0.45	+0.06	+0.52	+1.61	-0.34	-0.24	+0.51	-1.14	+0.37	+0.09	-0.04	+0.37	+0.01	-0.49
65	+0.13	-0.46	+0.07	+0.54	+1.63	-0.35	-0.26	+0.52	-1.16	+0.37	+0.10	-0.04	+0.38	+0.01	-0.49
70	+0.12	-0.47	+0.08	+0.55	+1.65	-0.35	-0.27	+0.53	-1.18	+0.38	+0.10	-0.04	+0.39	+0.01	-0.50
80	+0.10	-0.48	+0.09	+0.57	+1.67	-0.37	-0.28	+0.54	-1.22	+0.39	+0.11	-0.03	+0.40	+0.01	-0.50
90	+0.08	-0.49	+1.10	+0.59	+1.69	-0.38	-0.30	+0.55	-1.24	+0.39	+0.12	-0.03	+0.41	+0.01	-0.41
100	+0.07	-0.50	+0.11	+0.61	+1.71	-0.39	-0.31	+0.55	-1.26	+0.40	+0.12	-0.03	+0.42	+0.01	-0.51
120	+0.05	-0.51	+0.13	+0.63	+1.73	-0.40	-0.32	+0.56	-1.29	+0.40	+0.13	-0.03	+0.44	+0.01	-0.52
140	+0.04	-0.51	+0.14	+0.64	+1.74	-0.41	-0.33	+0.57	-1.32	+0.41	+0.14	-0.03	+0.45	+0.01	-0.52
160	+0.03	-0.52	+0.14	+0.65	+1.76	-0.42	-0.34	+0.57	-1.33	+0.41	+0.14	-0.03	+0.46	+0.00	-0.53
180	+0.02	-0.52	+0.15	+0.66	+1.76	-0.42	-0.35	+0.58	-1.35	+0.42	+0.14	-0.03	+0.46	+0.00	-0.53
200	+0.02	-0.53	+0.15	+0.67	+1.77	-0.43	-0.35	+0.58	-1.36	+0.42	+0.14	-0.03	+0.47	+0.00	-0.53
Certainty Equiva-lent	-0.04	-0.56	+0.19	+0.73	+1.84	-0.47	-0.40	+0.61	-1.45	+0.44	+0.17	-0.02	+0.51	-0.00	-0.55

TABLE 8.6.--Optimal Bayesian and Certainty Equivalent Portfolio Weights

	b: Negative Exponential Utility														
T	1	2	3	4	5	6	7	8	9	10	11	12	13	14	15
20	+0.58	-0.22	-0.25	+0.04	+1.09	-0.02	+1.13	+0.29	-0.41	+0.20	-0.08	-0.08	+0.02	+0.05	-0.33
25	+0.45	-0.28	-0.16	+0.18	+1.24	-0.11	+0.02	+0.35	-0.62	+0.25	-0.03	-0.07	+0.12	+0.04	-0.38
30	+0.37	-0.33	-0.10	+0.27	+1.34	-0.17	-0.05	+0.40	-0.76	+0.28	+0.00	-0.06	+0.18	+0.03	-0.41
35	+0.31	-0.36	-0.06	+0.33	+1.41	-0.21	-0.10	+0.43	-0.85	+0.30	+0.02	-0.06	+0.23	+0.03	-0.43
40	+0.27	-0.39	-0.03	+0.38	+1.47	-0.25	-0.14	+0.45	-0.93	+0.32	+0.04	-0.05	+0.27	+0.03	-0.44
45	+0.24	-0.40	-0.01	+0.42	+1.51	-0.27	-0.17	+0.47	-0.99	+0.33	+0.06	-0.05	+0.29	+0.02	-0.45
50	+0.21	-0.42	+0.01	+0.45	+1.54	-0.29	-0.19	+0.48	-1.03	+0.34	+0.07	-0.05	+0.32	+0.02	-0.46
55	+0.19	-0.43	+0.03	+0.48	+1.57	-0.31	-0.21	+0.49	-1.07	+0.35	+0.08	-0.04	+0.33	+0.02	-0.47
60	+0.17	-0.44	+0.04	+0.50	+1.59	-0.32	-0.22	+0.50	-1.20	+0.36	+0.08	-0.04	+0.35	+0.02	-0.48
65	+0.15	-0.45	+0.05	+0.52	+1.61	-0.33	-0.24	+0.51	-1.13	+0.37	+0.09	-0.04	+0.36	+0.02	-0.48
70	+0.14	-0.46	+0.06	+0.53	+1.62	-0.34	-0.25	+0.52	-1.15	+0.37	+0.10	-0.04	+0.37	+0.01	-0.49
80	+0.12	-0.47	+0.08	+0.56	+1.65	-0.36	-0.27	+0.53	-1.19	+0.38	+0.10	-0.04	+0.39	+0.01	-0.50
90	+0.10	-0.48	+0.09	+0.57	+1.67	-0.37	-0.28	+0.54	-1.22	+0.39	+0.11	-0.03	+0.40	+0.01	-0.50
100	+0.09	-0.49	+0.10	+0.59	+1.69	-0.38	-0.29	+0.54	-1.24	+0.39	+0.12	-0.03	+0.41	+0.01	-0.51
120	+0.07	-0.50	+0.12	+0.61	+1.71	-0.39	-0.31	+0.56	-1.27	+0.40	+0.13	-0.03	+0.43	+0.01	-0.52
140	+0.05	-0.51	+0.13	+0.63	+1.73	-0.40	-0.32	+0.56	-1.30	+0.40	+0.13	-0.03	+0.44	+0.01	-0.52
160	+0.04	-0.51	+0.14	+0.64	+1.74	-0.41	-0.33	+0.57	-1.32	+0.41	+0.14	-0.03	+0.45	+0.01	-0.52
180	+0.03	-0.52	+0.14	+0.65	+1.75	-0.42	-0.34	+0.57	-1.33	+0.41	+0.14	-0.03	+0.46	+0.00	-0.53
200	+0.03	-0.52	+0.15	+0.66	+1.76	-0.42	-0.35	+0.58	-1.34	+0.42	+0.14	-0.03	+0.46	+0.00	-0.53
Certainty Equiva-lent	+0.03	-0.52	+0.15	+0.66	+1.76	-0.42	-0.35	+0.58	-1.34	+0.42	+0.14	-0.03	+0.46	+0.00	-0.53

These portfolios were compared on the basis of the expected loss of each, defined in terms of the *true* distribution from which the data were drawn. This was recorded for each sample size, and the experiment replicated 50 times. A measure of the empirical risk function is then defined by comparing the mean expected loss with the expected loss of a portfolio optimal for the true distribution of returns.

These empirical risk functions assess the sampling performance of the different modifications to the Certainty Equivalent and Bayes rules incorporating different forms of prior information. As we show in the next section, they provide strong evidence that the results for the single risky asset case reported in the previous section carry through to this more complicated many risky asset case.

4. Comparison of Rules

Initially we assume that all relevant information relating to the parameters of the returns distribution is contained within the sample data. Thus, we compare in this context the relative performance of the diffuse prior Bayes rule with the Markowtiz Certainty Equivalent rule. We also evaluate the suggestion of Blume that aggregation will of itself improve the performance of this Certainty Equivalence strategy.

Our findings indicate that the results of Section 2 carry over to the many risky asset case. In repeated samples the diffuse Bayes rule dominates the Markowitz Certainty Equivalent rule. In Section 6, we show that this result holds even where the probability distribution of returns is severely misspecified.

In the next section, we assess the performance in repeated samples of several informative prior models, comparing them with a Sharpe model Certainty Equivalent (CE) rule. This CE rule would select the same portfolio for a given set of sample estimates regardless of the number of observations upon which those estimates are based, and so it is not surprising that the rule is dominated by the Bayes rules even in the case where a Sharpe model actually generates the observed data.

Returns were initially simulated from a multivariate normal distribution with mean and covariance matrix given in Table 8.4.[13] For the two utility functions referred to above, optimal portfolios were computed for various sample sizes[14] under each of the following rules:

1. Diffuse prior Bayes rule
2. Markowitz CE
3. Aggregation CE
4. Equal weight rule

The first and second portfolio selection rules were as described in the previous section, with the Markowitz Certainty Equivalent rule defined in terms of the usual sample estimates of the mean and covariance matrix of returns. Blume's (1968) suggestion is incorporated into the third portfolio strategy: aggregate the individual securities into distinct equally weighted portfolios ranked by estimates of the Sharpe model coefficients β_i and apply a Certainty Equivalent rule on the basis of the aggregated data. The securities reported on Table 8.4 have already been ranked according to estimates of β_i defined in terms of an equally weighted market index.[15] Hence, to implement Blume's suggestion in this context, it is sufficient to

13. A full discussion of the simulation procedures used can be found in Brown (1976).

14. $T = 20(5)65,\ 70(10)100,\ 120(20)200.$

15. for $\boldsymbol{\beta} = m\boldsymbol{\Sigma}\iota/\iota'\boldsymbol{\Sigma}\iota$; $\beta_l < \beta_j$ for $l < j$ given the covariance matrix $\boldsymbol{\Sigma}$ of Table 4.

aggregate adjacent assets into seven equally weighted portfolios of (2,2,2,2,2,2,3) securities each prior to determining an optimal portfolio consisting of these securities. It is possible to combine Blume's suggestion with other modifications to the Markowitz CE rule, such as implied by the use of the Sharpe model. We will not do so here. Our interest is merely to determine the effect of the aggregation on the performance of one of the Certainty Equivalent rules.

The equal weight rule serves as a useful benchmark for comparison of the different rules. It simply assigned an equal weight to each asset in the portfolio. It did not use any sample evidence and did not involve any optimization.

For each optimal portfolio we computed the expected loss in terms of the true underlying distribution. This quantity was recorded, and the experiment replicated 50 times. Figure 8.5 gives the empirical risk function for the various strategies as the sample size increases. Displayed there are the results for the quadratic utility case; use of the negative exponential utility function did not affect the relative performance of the various rules.

As before, the diffuse Bayesian rule uniformly dominates the Certainty Equivalent rule in repeated samples. The aggregation strategy is only marginally superior to the Bayesian solution for small sample sizes. As the sample size increases, the loss of information from aggregation clearly outweigh any advantage this strategy has in reducing estimation risk.[16]

The equal weight rule yields a convenient upper bound on the acceptable risk of the different portfolio rules. For very small sample sizes this naive strategy outperforms the optimization rules, thus suggesting that rule may be useful where, for example, the number of securities exceeds the number of usable observations.

As mentioned in the previous section, the Aggregation rule need not be interpreted as merely a device to reduce estimation risk at whatever cost: It could be justified from a Bayesian point of view as a tractable means of introducing the information that securities are essentially identical within certain groups. A Diffuse Bayesian rule can be formulated on the basis of the aggregated securities; the risk function of this rule appears in Figure 8.6. Where the Aggregation CE rule dominates the Diffuse Bayes rule, the aggregated Bayes rule *also* dominates it. In addition, it dominates its Certainty Equivalent alternative for all sample sizes considered, although the difference is slight for greater than 60 observations.

To assess how sensitive these results are to the particular values used to represent the true parameters, we estimated a covariance matrix and vector of means corresponding to Table 8.4 using data from July 1951 to December 1958. Optimal portfolios were computed on the basis of simulated returns from this distribution for the utility function parameters given above. The empirical risk functions are displayed in Figure 8.7. These results conform to the conclusions drawn on the basis of parameters estimated on the basis of 1961-1968 data, although the magnitude of the difference between the Diffuse prior and Markowitz CE models has declined.

In addition, we conducted some simulations assuming that a Sharpe model

---

16. The standard errors of the differences were all small relative to the mean differences between the rules, except for the case of the aggregation strategy. While this strategy was superior to the Bayes solution, the standard error was large relative to the mean difference. An Hotelling T^2 statistic for testing the hypothesis that the mean difference was in fact zero at the sample sizes 35, 100 and 200, was significant at the 1 percent level for both the Diffuse Prior-Markowitz CE and

actually generated the data for 1961-1968. The coefficients α_1, β_i, σ_i^2 were estimated using Ordinary Least-Squares for a market index defined by an equally weighted Fisher (1966) index of the market; these estimates were substituted into the covariance matrix implied by the Sharpe model, where the variance of the market was given by a minimum variance unbiased estimate of this parameter. The means were given by the relevant sample means.[17] The utility function parameters were adjusted in such a way as to make the expected return 1.552 percent per month optimal for this new distribution of returns.[18]

The performance of the Bayesian rule relative to the CE strategy is unchanged, as shown in Figure 8.8. There is, however, a slight improvement in the relative performance of the Aggregation CE and Equal Weight rules. As shown in Figure 8.9, the relative performance of the diffuse prior applied to aggregated data remains unchanged in this example.

5. An Informative Prior Example

To this point, we have assumed that the individual has no information beyond the observed sample data to guide his portfolio choice. He may, for example, believe that something resembling a Sharpe model generates observed returns. A Bayesian believing the process generating returns to be *exactly* described by such a model may be tempted to use a Sharpe Certainty Equivalent (CE) model on the grounds that the Bayesian portfolio solution may not be tractable given this restriction (Brown, 1979), except in cases where the parameters of the Sharpe model are known to the investor. However, this is an extreme case--the investor may regard the Sharpe model as a valuable practical device even if not strictly true (e.g., Fama, 1968). Such an individual presumably would be persuaded away from the model if it was in conflict with observed data.

It is interesting in this context to compare the performance in repeated samples of a Sharpe CE model with two informative prior Bayesian rules conforming to Assumption 4 of the previous section. Toward this end, we repeated the previous simulations defining a "market index" at each point of time as an arithmetic mean of the individual asset returns, in the spirit of Fisher (1966).

For the Sharpe CE model we derived an estimate of the covariance matrix implied by the model, by substituting in OLS estimates of the parameters of the model and using the minimum variance unbiased estimate of the market variance. The vector of means was given by the sample mean of the simulated data. These parameters were reestimated for each point at which an optimal portfolio was required.

Diffuse Prior-Aggregation comparisons.

17. Note that $\bar{R}_i = \hat{\alpha}_i + \hat{\beta}_i \bar{R}_M$, where $\hat{\alpha}_i$ and $\hat{\beta}_i$ are the OLS estimates of the parameters of the Sharpe index model.

18. $R^* = .089292$, $1/g_1 = .0737653$.

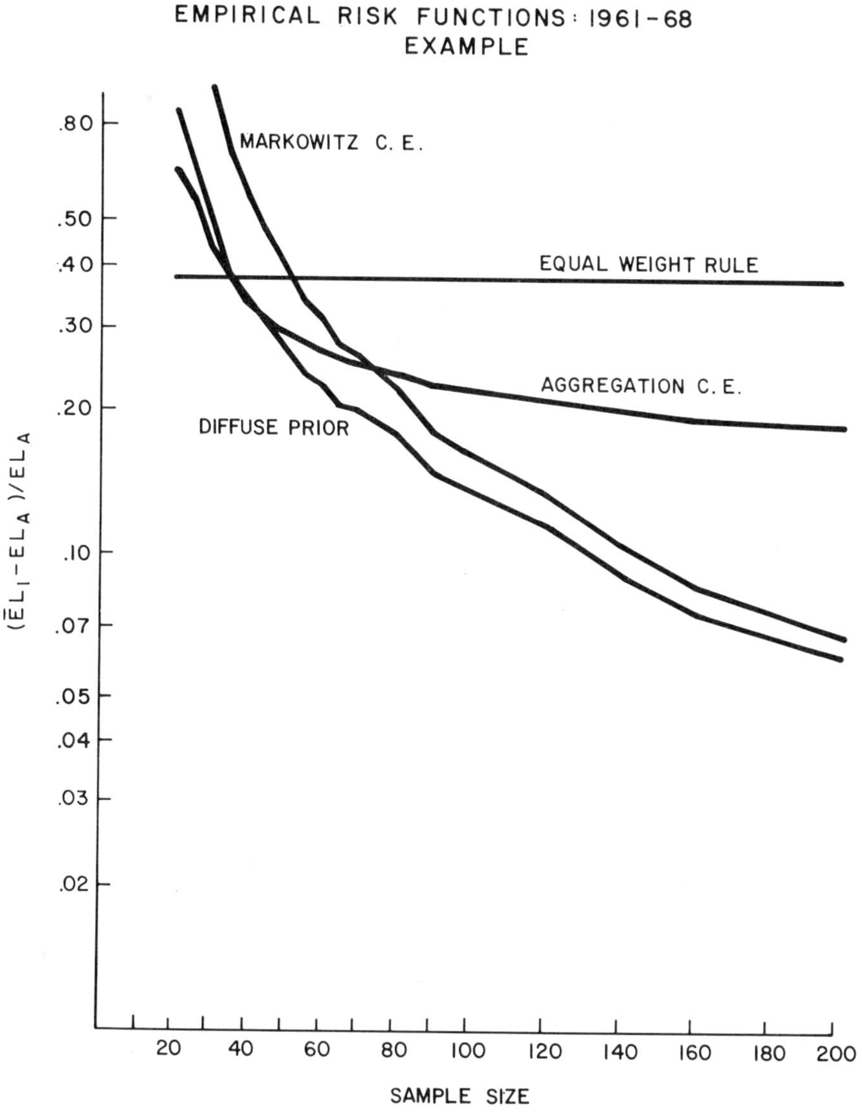
EMPIRICAL RISK FUNCTIONS: 1961-68
EXAMPLE
MARKOWITZ C. E.
EQUAL WEIGHT RULE
AGGREGATION C. E.
DIFFUSE PRIOR
$(\bar{E}L_I - EL_A)/EL_A$
.80
.50
.40
.30
.20
.10
.07
.05
.04
.03
.02
20
40
60
80
100
120
140
160
180
200
SAMPLE SIZE

Figure 8.5

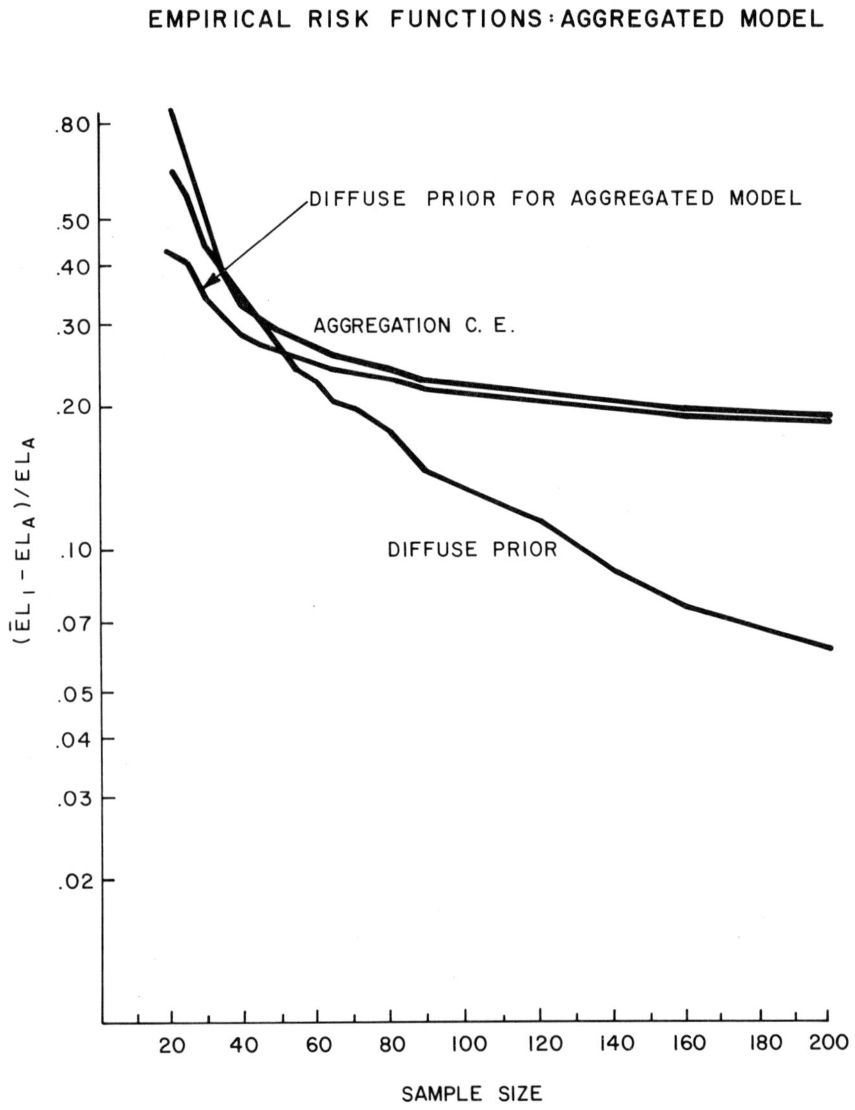
EMPIRICAL RISK FUNCTIONS: AGGREGATED MODEL
DIFFUSE PRIOR FOR AGGREGATED MODEL
AGGREGATION C. E.
DIFFUSE PRIOR
.80
.50
.40
.30
.20
.10
.07
.05
.04
.03
.02
(ĒL I - EL A)/EL A
20
40
60
80
100
120
140
160
180
200
SAMPLE SIZE

Figure 8.6

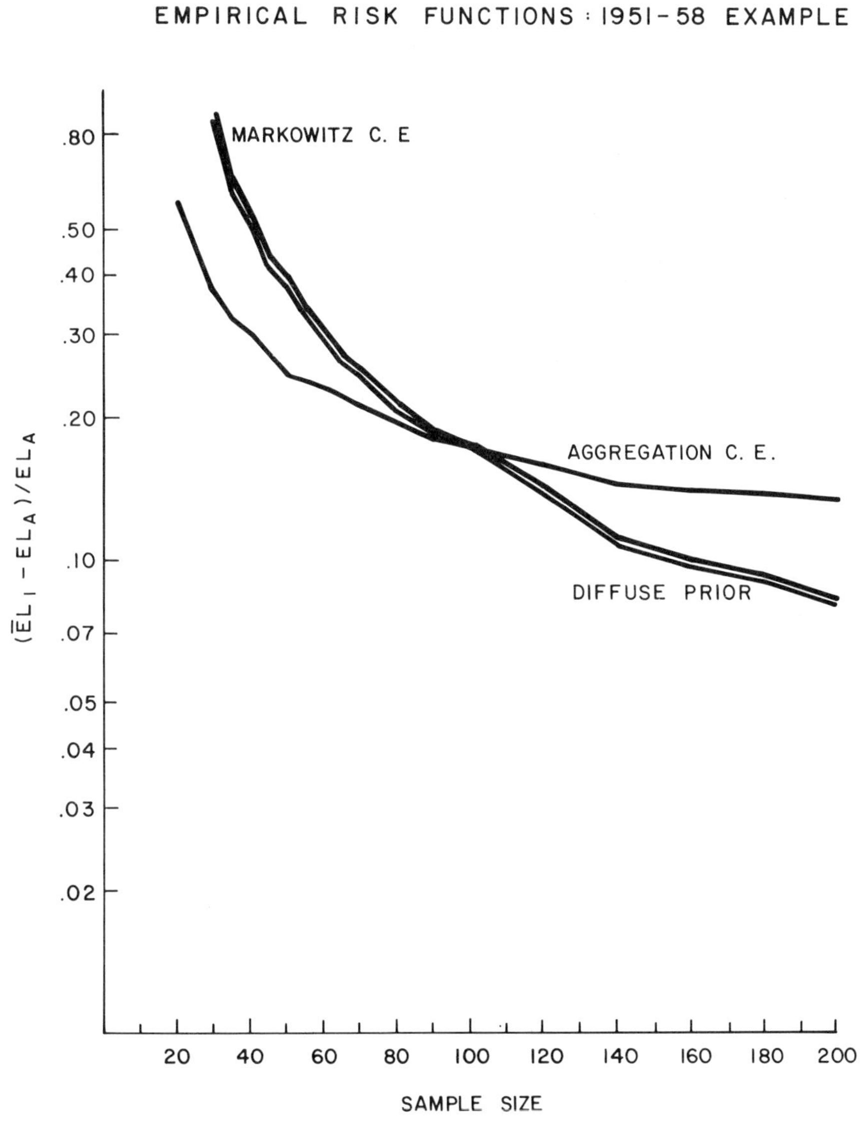
EMPIRICAL RISK FUNCTIONS : 1951-58 EXAMPLE
MARKOWITZ C. E
AGGREGATION C. E.
DIFFUSE PRIOR
.80
.50
.40
.30
.20
.10
.07
.05
.04
.03
.02
$(\bar{E}L_I - EL_A)/EL_A$
20
40
60
80
100
120
140
160
180
200
SAMPLE SIZE

Figure 8.7

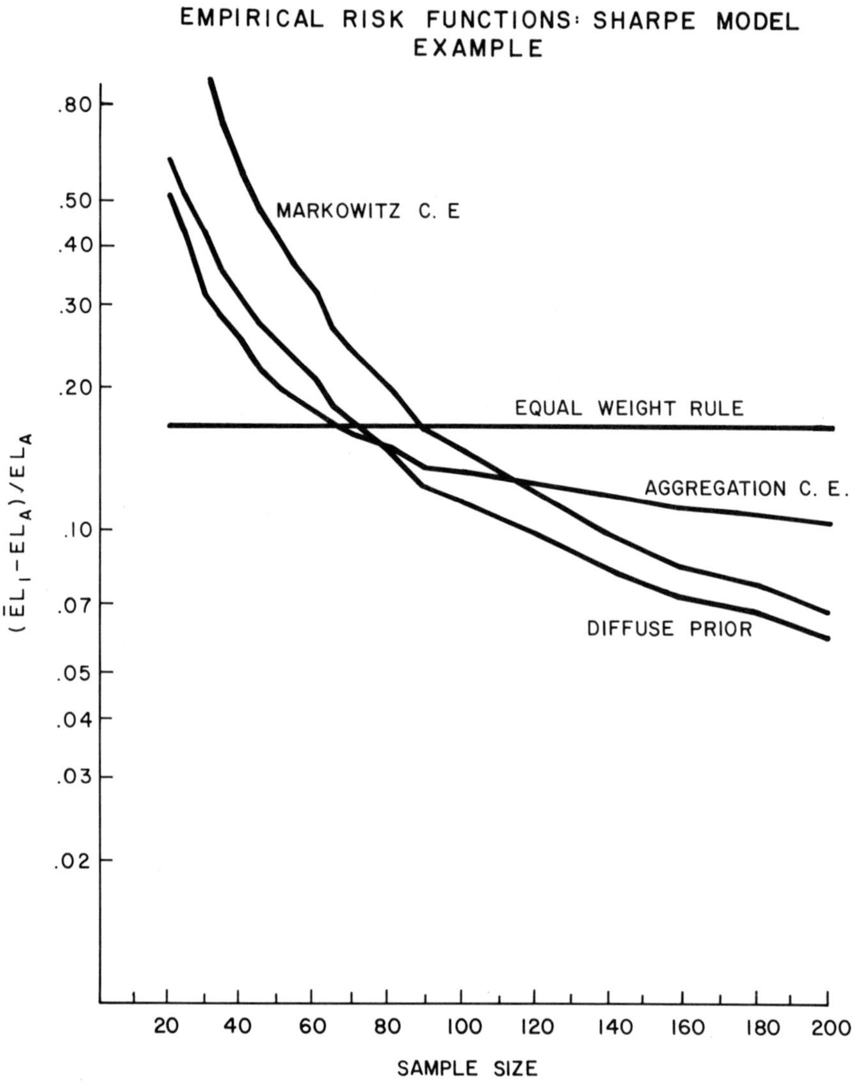
EMPIRICAL RISK FUNCTIONS: SHARPE MODEL EXAMPLE
MARKOWITZ C. E
EQUAL WEIGHT RULE
AGGREGATION C. E.
DIFFUSE PRIOR
.80
.50
.40
.30
.20
.10
.07
.05
.04
.03
.02
$(\bar{E}L_I - EL_A)/EL_A$
20
40
60
80
100
120
140
160
180
200
SAMPLE SIZE

Figure 8.8

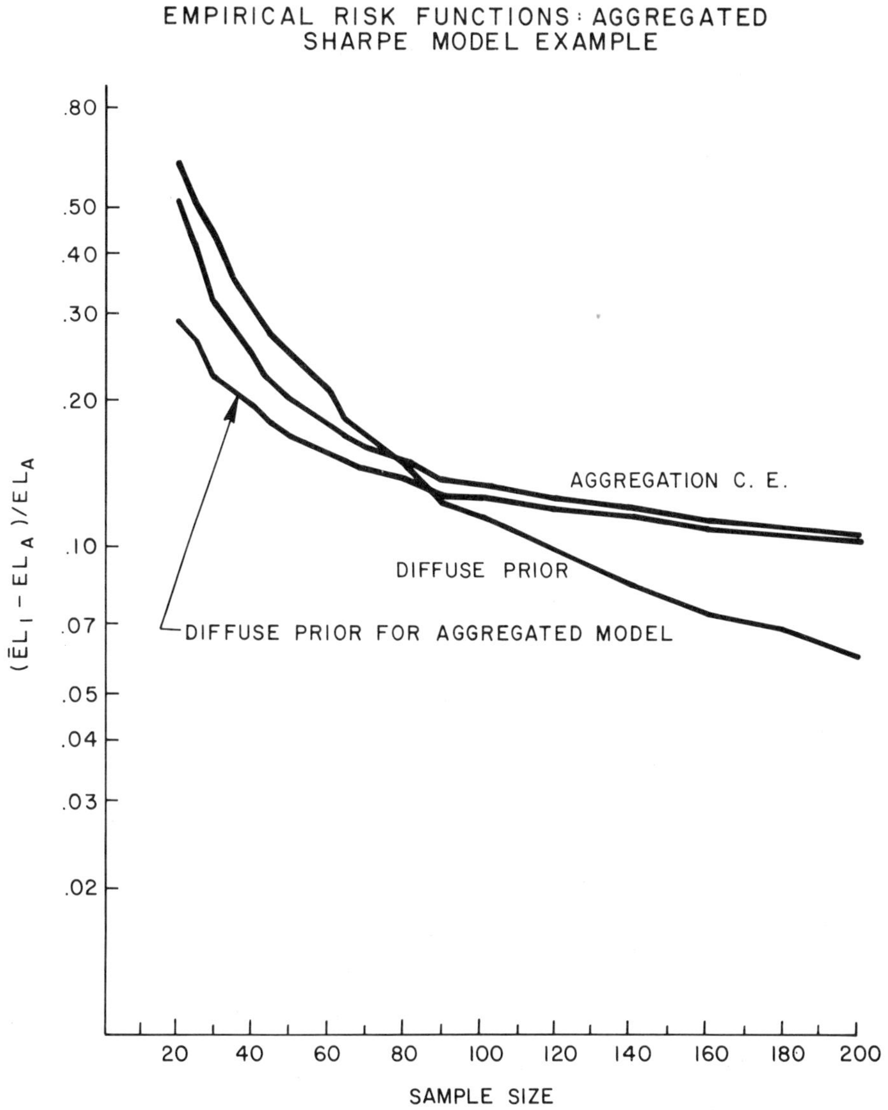
EMPIRICAL RISK FUNCTIONS: AGGREGATED SHARPE MODEL EXAMPLE
$(\bar{E}L_I - EL_A)/EL_A$
.80
.50
.40
.30
.20
.10
.07
.05
.04
.03
.02
AGGREGATION C. E.
DIFFUSE PRIOR
DIFFUSE PRIOR FOR AGGREGATED MODEL
20
40
60
80
100
120
140
160
180
200
SAMPLE SIZE

Figure 8.9

In the two informative prior examples that we study, we shall assume the individual has a normal-Wishart prior for the different parameters of the distribution of returns beginning with observation 18.[19] That is, as of that point of time the investor has a multivariate normal prior for the mean vector, with mean **m** and covariance matrix (1/18) $\boldsymbol{\Sigma}$. His beliefs about $\boldsymbol{\Sigma}^{-1}$ can be captured by a Wishart density with sum of squares parameter **V** and a degree of freedom parameter. Subsequent to the 18th observation, he updates this prior upon receipt of data in accord with Bayes' Theorem.

For the first informative prior example the investor has a *data-based prior*. The vector **m** is given by the sample mean return,

$$\mathbf{m} = (1/18)\sum_{l=1}^{18} \mathbf{R}_l = \overline{\mathbf{R}}$$

and sum of squares parameter,

$$V = \sum_{l=1}^{18} (\mathbf{R}_l - \mathbf{m})(\mathbf{R}_l - \mathbf{m}) = (17)\hat{\boldsymbol{\Sigma}},$$

with 3 (=18−15) degrees of freedom. This model yields the same portfolio solutions as the diffuse prior model of the previous section, where the diffuse prior pertained to the state of knowledge prior to the *first* observation.

In the second example, we took a Sharpe model informative prior. Again the vector **m** was given by the sample mean return. However, the sum of squares parameter is given by

$$\mathbf{V} = (17)\hat{\boldsymbol{\Sigma}}_S,$$

where $\hat{\boldsymbol{\Sigma}}_S$ is the covariance matrix implied by a Sharpe index model estimated on the basis of the first 18 observations. Upon receipt of new data, the prior is updated without further reference to the Sharpe model.[20]

Thus, at each point of time the three models used the *same* data--but each processed those data in different ways.[21] The simulations were repeated using the means and covariance matrix given in Table 8.4. The empirical risk functions were estimated; the results appear in Figure 10. The Sharpe prior model outperforms the Sharpe CE model for all sample sizes considered, and also dominates the data-based prior model.[22]

---

19. For a discussion of this model, see Ando and Kaufman (1965). In the discussion that follows we shall employ their notation. The eighteenth observation is the first observation for which a non-degenerate predictive distribution can be defined.

20. Note that this is not the same as assuming that the Sharpe model restrictions hold at every point of time.

21. The Sharpe CE rule used all available data, while the Bayesian rules required the first 18th observation to form a prior. It is important to have each rule using the same set of information.

22. The standard errors were large relative to the mean differences, and the Hotelling T^2 statistics indicated significant differences at observations 35, 100 and 200.

As can be seen from Figure 8.11 these conclusions are not changed when the underlying parameters are the estimates based on the 1951-58 data, except for a relative deterioration in the performance of the Sharpe CE model.

However, we obtain interesting results in the case where a Sharpe model is indeed responsible for the observed data. In Figure 8.12 the Sharpe prior model dominates the Sharpe CE model. This is not surprising as the Sharpe CE model yields the same portfolio for a given set of sample estimates regardless of the number of observations on which the different estimates are based.

For a small number of observations the Sharpe prior model implies a covariance structure for the predictive distribution of returns that is close to that implied by the restrictions of the Sharpe model. As the number of observations increases, this structure is disturbed to the extent that the data do not yield a predictive covariance matrix exactly meeting the Sharpe restrictions. Hence the performance of the Sharpe CE model improves relative to the Sharpe prior model in repeated samples as the sample size increases. However, as the number of observations increases beyond a certain point, the weight of evidence persuades the Bayesian of the Sharpe model restriction. Thus the performance of the Sharpe prior model improves and converges to that of the Sharpe CE rule.

The improved sampling performance of the Bayes rule undoubtedly arises from the fact that the priors chosen were close to the sample distribution of returns. This sampling performance would deteriorate if the priors were centered far from the true distribution of returns, as can be demonstrated in a simple example (Brown, 1976). This observation is not a prescription for the investor to assess a "correct" prior whatever that might mean. Rather, it questions the relevance of the statistical risk function in this context.

6. Misspecification of the Returns Distribution

Since the Certainty Equivalent rules can be derived without reliance on the restrictive normal distribution assumption; it could be argued that this consideration alone would make the CE rules more robust against possible misspecifications of the process generating security returns. What would happen for example, if the investor assumed that observed returns were being drawn from a normal distribution when the distribution was in fact Student-t with small degrees of freedom?

To answer this question we replicated the previous simulations with drawings from a multivarate Student-t distribution with mean and covariance matrix given in Table 8.4.[23] This distribution was somewhat fat-tailed with 4.79 degrees of freedom, the average degrees of freedom found by Blattberg and Gonedes (1974) in their study of daily returns on individual stocks.

The results of this exercise are somewhat surprising. In the diffuse prior example (Figure 8.13), while the empirical risk has in each case risen, the relative performance of the various strategies remains unchanged. However, it takes a somewhat greater number of observations to perform better than a naive equal weight rule.

23. A full discussion of the simulation procedures used can be found in Brown (1976).

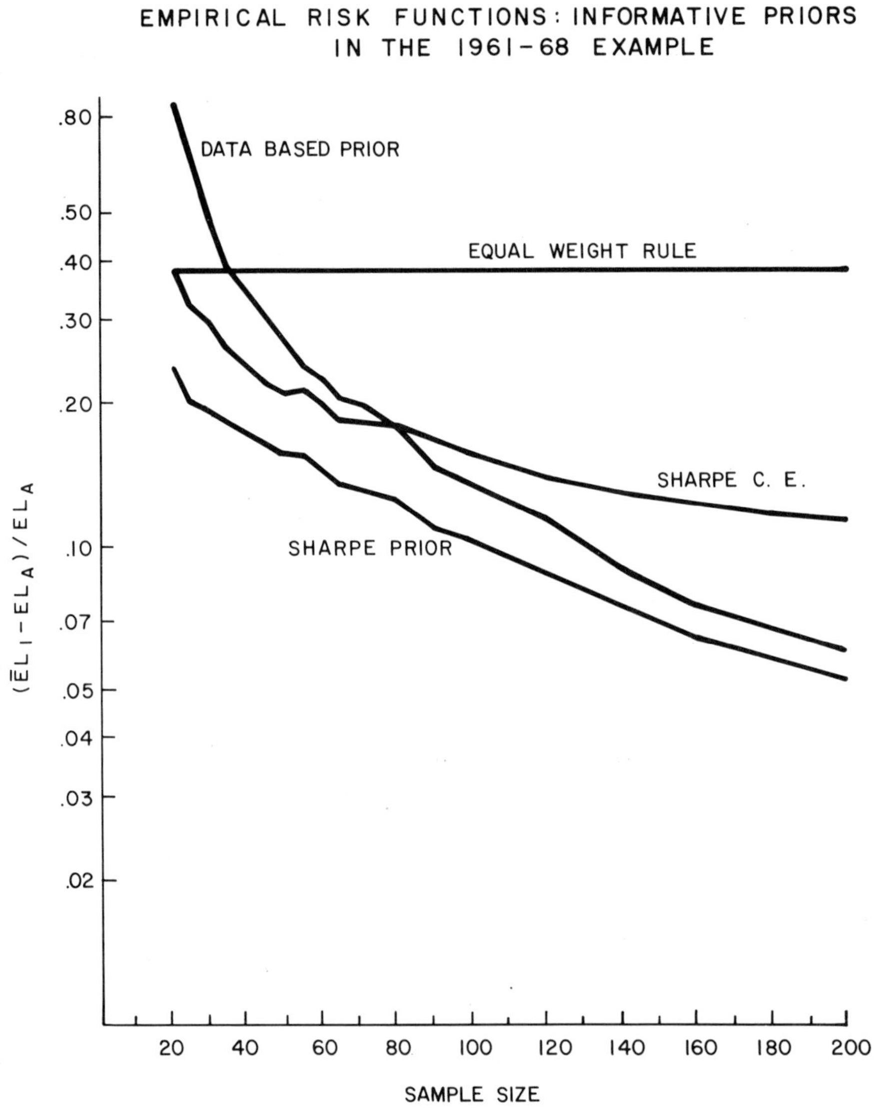
EMPIRICAL RISK FUNCTIONS: INFORMATIVE PRIORS IN THE 1961-68 EXAMPLE
DATA BASED PRIOR
EQUAL WEIGHT RULE
SHARPE C. E.
SHARPE PRIOR
.80
.50
.40
.30
.20
.10
.07
.05
.04
.03
.02
(ĒL I - EL A)/EL A
20
40
60
80
100
120
140
160
180
200
SAMPLE SIZE

Figure 8.10

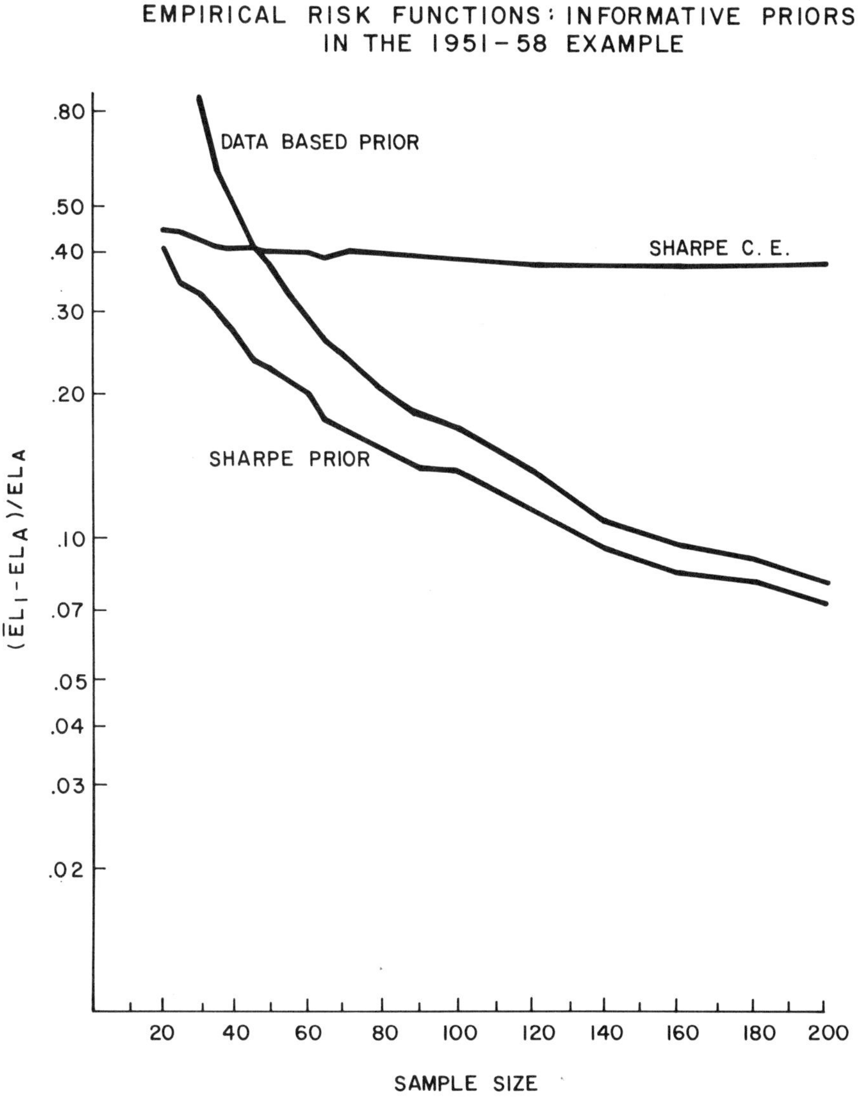
EMPIRICAL RISK FUNCTIONS: INFORMATIVE PRIORS
IN THE 1951-58 EXAMPLE
DATA BASED PRIOR
SHARPE C. E.
SHARPE PRIOR
($\bar{E}L_I$ - ELA)/ELA
.80
.50
.40
.30
.20
.10
.07
.05
.04
.03
.02
20
40
60
80
100
120
140
160
180
200
SAMPLE SIZE

Figure 8.11

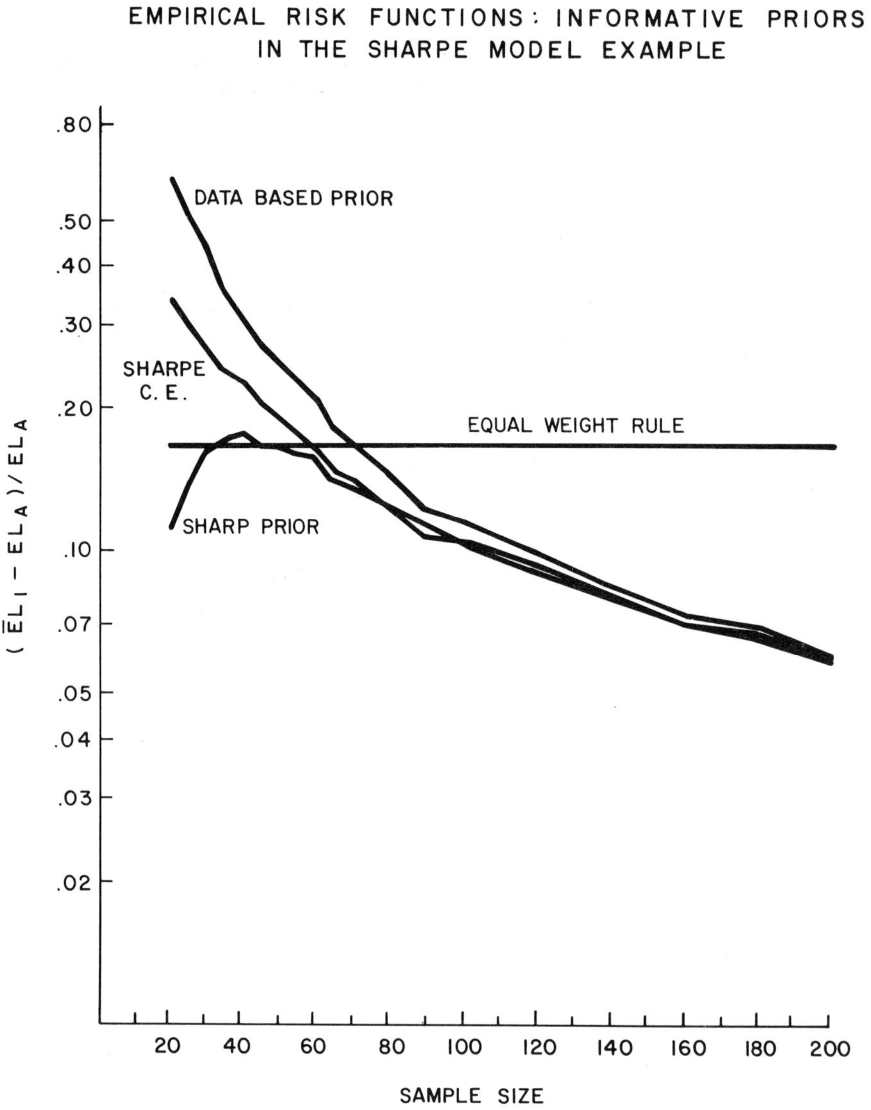
EMPIRICAL RISK FUNCTIONS: INFORMATIVE PRIORS
IN THE SHARPE MODEL EXAMPLE
DATA BASED PRIOR
SHARPE
C. E.
EQUAL WEIGHT RULE
SHARP PRIOR
(ĒL I - EL A)/ EL A
.80
.50
.40
.30
.20
.10
.07
.05
.04
.03
.02
20
40
60
80
100
120
140
160
180
200
SAMPLE SIZE

Figure 8.12

Turning to the informative prior case (Figure 8.14) we find that the Sharpe CE model outperforms the data based prior model for most sample sizes considered. However, the Sharpe prior model dominates both and indeed appears only slightly affected by the relaxation of the normality assumption![24]

It could be argued that these results follow from having assumed that the distribution of returns is symmetric. It is often assumed, particularly in the option pricing literature (e.g., Black and Scholes, 1972, 1973), that the logarithm of security prices is normally distributed. This implies that the logarithm of the price relative, $\tilde{P}_{it}/P_{it-1}$, is normal conditional on P_{it-1}. But, ignoring the complication of dividends,

$$\tilde{P}_{it}/P_{it-1} = (1+\tilde{R}_{it}),$$

and this assumption is then consistent with the vector $(\iota+\mathbf{R})$ having the nonsymmetric multivariate lognormal distribution (see e.g., Press, 1972, pp. 138-140).

We replicated the previous simulations for the multivariate lognormal case, with parameters of this distribution chosen so that the vector of returns would have a mean and covariance matrix as given in Table 8.4. The results as reported in Figures 8.15 and 8.16 are very similar to those reported for the multivariate normal case. It appears that the normality assumption is a good approximation in this case.

Obviously, we have not considered all possible misspecifications of the returns distribution. Officer's (1971) work suggests that the variance of the market can change over time. We have already studied a case in which the market variance can be considered a random variable. Suppose that from period to period the standard deviation of the market behaves like an independent drawing from an inverted gamma density, but that once we know this standard deviation the distribution of returns is multivariate normal. Then we can show (e.g., Zellner, 1971, pp. 388-389) that unconditional on the market variance the distribution of returns will be multivariate Student-t with degrees of freedom given by the process generating the standard deviation of the market. Other processes for the variance are, of course, possible; it would be interesting to compare relative performance if, for example, the variance was generated by a random walk or some autoregressive process.

Thus we have shown not only that the optimal Bayes portfolio is different but also that its relative performance in repeated samples is robust against misspecifications of the process generating security returns.

---

24. In both this and the previous example the mean differences were large relative to their standard errors, and the Hotelling T^2 statistics indicate that the differences were significant for sample sizes of 35, 100, and 200 at the one percent level.

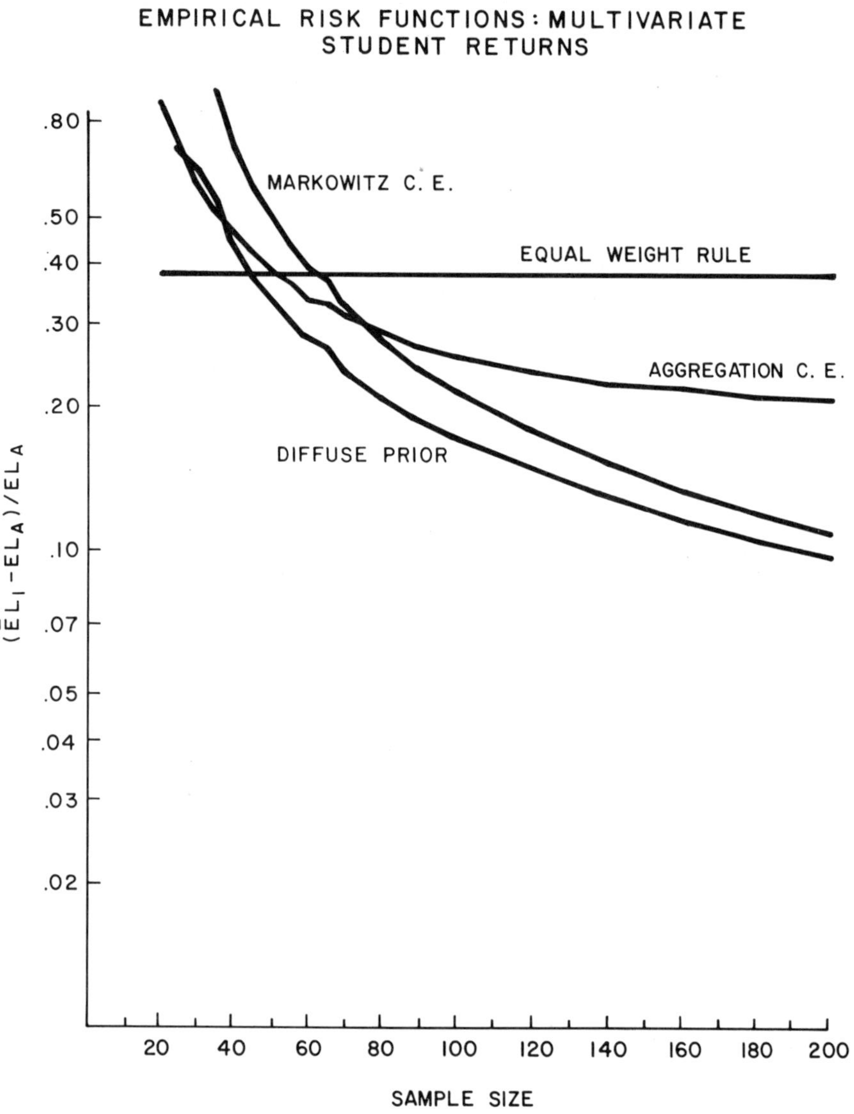
EMPIRICAL RISK FUNCTIONS: MULTIVARIATE STUDENT RETURNS
.80
.50
.40
.30
.20
.10
.07
.05
.04
.03
.02
(ĒL$_I$-EL$_A$)/EL$_A$
MARKOWITZ C. E.
EQUAL WEIGHT RULE
AGGREGATION C. E.
DIFFUSE PRIOR
20
40
60
80
100
120
140
160
180
200
SAMPLE SIZE

Figure 8.13

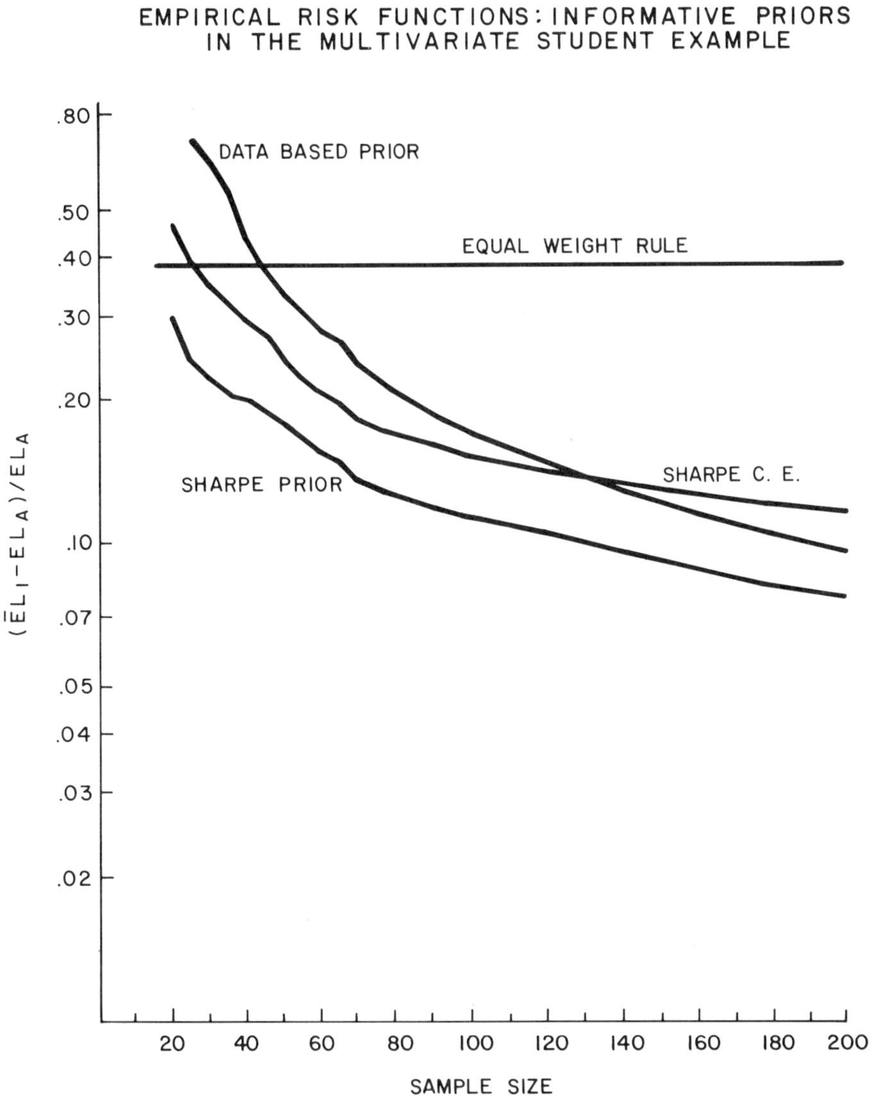
EMPIRICAL RISK FUNCTIONS: INFORMATIVE PRIORS
IN THE MULTIVARIATE STUDENT EXAMPLE
.80
.50
.40
.30
.20
.10
.07
.05
.04
.03
.02
DATA BASED PRIOR
EQUAL WEIGHT RULE
SHARPE C. E.
SHARPE PRIOR
(ĒL_I − EL_A)/EL_A
20
40
60
80
100
120
140
160
180
200
SAMPLE SIZE

Figure 8.14

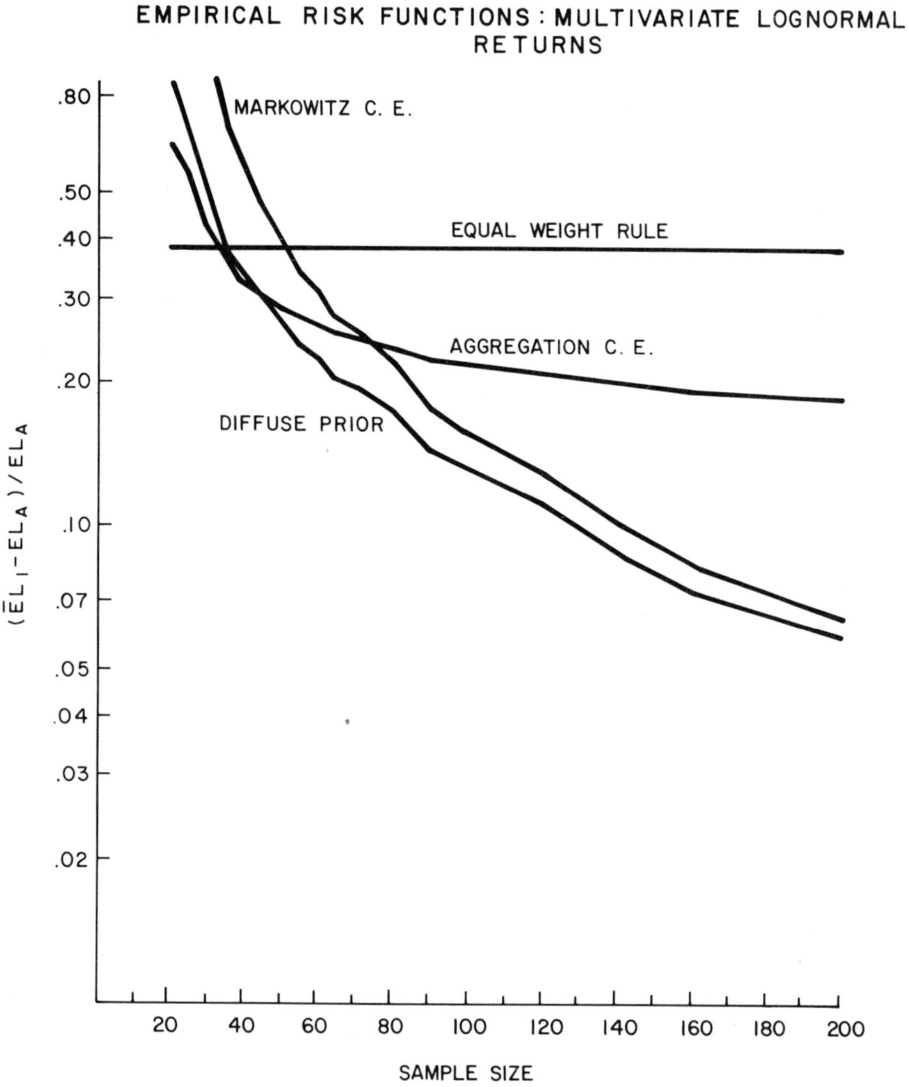
EMPIRICAL RISK FUNCTIONS : MULTIVARIATE LOGNORMAL RETURNS
MARKOWITZ C. E.
EQUAL WEIGHT RULE
AGGREGATION C. E.
DIFFUSE PRIOR
.80
.50
.40
.30
.20
.10
.07
.05
.04
.03
.02
$(\bar{E}L_I - EL_A)/EL_A$
20
40
60
80
100
120
140
160
180
200
SAMPLE SIZE

Figure 8.15

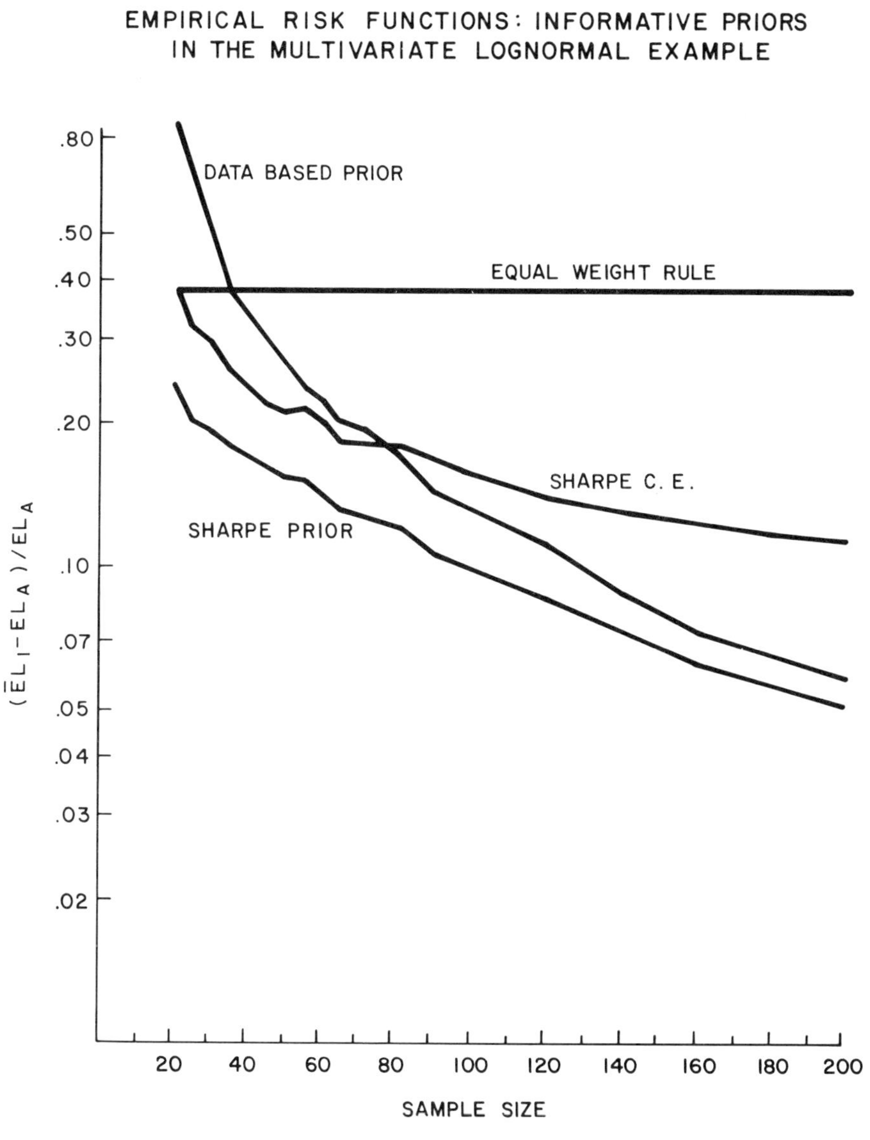
EMPIRICAL RISK FUNCTIONS: INFORMATIVE PRIORS
IN THE MULTIVARIATE LOGNORMAL EXAMPLE
DATA BASED PRIOR
EQUAL WEIGHT RULE
SHARPE C. E.
SHARPE PRIOR
.80
.50
.40
.30
.20
.10
.07
.05
.04
.03
.02
(ĒL I − EL A)/EL A
20
40
60
80
100
120
140
160
180
200
SAMPLE SIZE

Figure 8.16

7. Conclusion

We have considered the problem of optimal portfolio choice where parameter values are unknown and estimation risk is part of the general uncertainty faced by the investor. The optimal Bayes strategy has been compared to the more conventional use of sample estimates as the relevant true parameter values--a Certainty Equivalent rule. The Bayes strategy has also been compared to a series of ad hoc variants to the Certainty Equivalent rule meant to adjust for the factor of estimation risk. We have demonstrated that the Bayes portfolio is measurably different and its sampling performance dominates the Certainty Equivalent alternatives across the range of parameter values we have considered for the different examples we have studied. This superior sampling performance follows even where the probability distribution of returns is severely misspecified.

It is clear that one should consider the Bayesian approach when devising models of capital market equilibrium subject to estimation risk considerations. It is possible to show, though we have not done so here, that there are conditions that guarantee the existence of a market portfolio derived by aggregating individual decisions, that is optimal for utility function parameters and for a set of prior beliefs that are averages over the individuals comprising the market. This being the case, we can devise models of equilibrium asset pricing for a given set of information available to the market. In this context the issue of "measurement error" noted by Miller and Scholes (1972) does not arise.[25] What we have shown is that the Bayes rule "makes a difference" for the individual investor, and that in repeated samples the investor can be hurt by not taking this difference into account. In short, to paraphrase Blume (1970), this study represents a further step towards the practical application of portfolio theory.

25. In fact, for the diffuse prior example it is possible to show that the equilibrium taking full account of estimation risk, is observationally equivalent to a model where the estimates are assumed to represent the relevant true values. In this case one should not adjust sample estimates for 'estimation risk' (Brown 1979).

CHAPTER 9

ESTIMATION RISK AND OPTIMAL PORTFOLIO CHOICE: THE SHARPE INDEX MODEL

Stephen J. BROWN[1]

1. Introduction

In general, an individual has only imperfect knowledge of the values of parameters entering the returns generating process. It is in this context that the issue of estimation risk becomes important in the portfolio choice problem, not only for the individual, but also for the aggregation of individuals representing the market.

Klein and Bawa in Chapter 4 and Brown (1976) have each shown that the consideration of estimation risk will lead to measurably different optimal portfolio choices. However, for their models, this consideration does not affect the definition of an admissible set of portfolios, a result that has some convenient implications for market equilibrium in this context (Brown, 1979).

This result follows from the assumption that the individual can process the available prior information relating to the parameters of the returns distribution as hypothetical samples drawn from that distribution -- that is to say, their information set represents a diffuse or conjugate prior to the returns distribution. For the normal distribution of security returns that these authors consider, the relevant predictive distribution (the distribution of returns averaged over the unknown parameter values) is Student-t with degrees of freedom that represent the amount of information available to the decision maker. This distribution is location-scale (Bawa 1975) for given degrees of freedom, and hence traditional mean-variance analysis applies. Estimation risk simply implies a proportional increase in variance for every level of mean return.

While estimation risk will affect the optimal portfolio choice, it would seem from these results that uncertainty about the distribution of returns can be processed in precisely the same way as other risk faced by the investor. Unfortunately this result is confined to the very special case considered by Klein and Bawa. If we move away from the strict interpretation of information as a conjugate prior to the normal distribution of returns we lose the two parameter characterization of optimal portfolio choices, as this paper shall show. Indeed, if we make a very minor perturbation to the assumptions of Klein and Bawa we would lose this convenient characterization. If the amount of information were to be made a decision variable, we would immediately derive a three parameter rule for portfolio choice. The third parameter, the degrees of freedom could be interpreted as modifying the exposure to estimation risk for a given mean and variance.

The conjugate prior assumption places strong restrictions upon the set of information assumed to be available to the individual investor. Suppose we took a two

---

1. Professor Arnold Zellner suggested this problem, and I am indebted to him for many valuable comments and insights. I acknowledge helpful discussions with Vijay Bawa, Nicholas Gonedes Roger Klein, S. James Press and G. William Schwert but retain responsibility for any remaining errors and omissions.

thousand security example. This model would require that the investor had access to information equivalent to over two thousand observations - eight years of daily data for a period during which the distribution of returns could be considered stationary. The results of Brown (1976) would indicate that information equivalent to a number of observations as many as ten times the number of securities might be required to reduce the level of estimation risk to an acceptable level. The information that the Sharpe model - or one of its variants - actually generates observed security returns will reduce quite substantially the number of observations required to determine an optimal portfolio. As we shall see, though this simplification comes at the cost of inducing a three parameter rule for portfolio choice, the relevant choice rule is only marginally more complex than the more familiar two parameter version. The third parameter, commonly referred to as the 'beta coefficient', is a measure of risk not only because it contributes to variance but also because, given the variance, it determines all the higher order moments as well.

This special interpretation of beta arises as follows. If the parameters of the Sharpe model were known with certainty, the distribution of portfolio returns would be determined up to location and scale by the predictive distribution of the unknown index. When these parameters have unknown values, the predictive distribution is determined up to location and scale only for a *given* level of the estimated portfolio beta. The uncertainty of future returns is due in part to the unknown index and in part to the fact that the parameters of the model have unknown values. The estimate of beta, as a function of portfolio weights, determines the relative contribution of these sources of uncertainty. If we increase beta for a given variance, or equivalently decrease what is termed the contribution of nonsystematic risk, the distribution will converge to one determined up to location and scale by that of the index. As we shall see, changes in beta induce changes in higher order moment measures of spread, directly attributable to the fact that the coefficients of the Sharpe model have unknown values. Therefore beta, the third parameter of the predictive distribution, can be interpreted as determining the degree of exposure to this estimation risk given mean and variance.

In the next section we briefly review the estimation risk problem and introduce the Sharpe index model. We argue that the predictive distribution is the distribution of returns that is relevant in this context, and proceed in Section 3 to derive this distribution for the Sharpe index model case. In Section 4 we demonstrate that this distribution gives rise to a three parameter rule for portfolio choice and show how this rule can be used to define an efficient set of portfolios. We conclude in Section 5 with a summary of our major findings.

2. Estimation Risk and the Sharpe Model

We assume an individual investor maximizes expected utility of wealth W_2, $E[U(W_2)]$.[2] Each investor is small relative to the market and takes the probability distribution of security returns $f(\mathbf{R}|\boldsymbol{\theta})$ as given. The solution to the portfolio

2. Wealth $W_2 \equiv W_1(1+R_p)$ where W_1 represents initial wealth, R_p the rate of return on a portfolio $\mathbf{X}' = \left\{X_1, \ldots, X_m \middle| \sum_{l=1}^{m} X_l=1\right\}$ such that $R_p = \mathbf{X}'\mathbf{R}$ where $\mathbf{R}' = \{R_1, \ldots, R_m\}$ represents a vector of returns on assets held in that portfolio. The vector $\mathbf{R}'$ has a multivariate probability distribution $f(\mathbf{R}|\boldsymbol{\theta})$ for a vector of parameters $\boldsymbol{\theta}$.

problem is well known where the parameters of this distribution $\boldsymbol{\theta}$ are known to the individual. We are concerned with the case where these parameters are not known.

As a practical matter, this problem is usually resolved as follows. The parameters are estimated according to whatever information the individual has at his disposal. These estimates $\hat{\boldsymbol{\theta}}$ are taken to represent the true parameters, $\boldsymbol{\theta}$, for the purpose of portfolio selection. That is, the portfolio choice represents a solution to the problem

$$\underset{\mathbf{X}}{Max}\; E[U(W_2)|\boldsymbol{\theta} = \hat{\boldsymbol{\theta}}\,],\;\; \mathbf{X}\in\mathbf{C} \tag{1}$$

where C represents a portfolio constraint set.

There is a problem that the estimates $\hat{\theta}$ will deviate from the true parameter values, a problem variously referred to as 'estimation risk' or 'measurement error'.[3] Zellner and Chetty (1965) suggest that in this context one should define expected utility with respect to the *predictive* distribution of returns. Such a distribution, $g(\mathbf{R})$ is defined by averaging the returns distribution $f(\mathbf{R}|\boldsymbol{\theta})$ over the posterior distribution $h(\boldsymbol{\theta})$ of the unknown parameter values, $\boldsymbol{\theta}$:

$$g(\mathbf{R}) = \int_{R_\theta} f(\mathbf{R}|\boldsymbol{\theta})h(\boldsymbol{\theta})d\boldsymbol{\theta}$$

As indicated in Chapter 1 of this book, this represents a procedure for taking estimation risk into account that is consistent with the von Neuman Morgenstern axioms. By interchanging the order of integration,[4] we find that the portfolio that maximizes this definition of expected utility also solves the problem[5]

$$\underset{\mathbf{X}}{Max}\underset{\boldsymbol{\theta}}{E}\{E[U(W_2)|\boldsymbol{\theta}]\}\;\; .\;\; \mathbf{X}\in\mathbf{C} \tag{2}$$

If returns have a normal distribution then Klein and Bawa in Chapter 4, and Brown (1976) show that for a diffuse or conjugate prior on the parameters of this normal distribution, the predictive distribution of portfolio returns is Student-*t*. As is the case for the normal distribution, the Student-*t* distribution also falls in the class of two parameter (location and scale) distribution functions, which implies (Bawa 1975) that portfolios with higher (predictive) mean/lower (predictive) variance are preferred. Hence, optimal portfolios can be characterized by simplified mean/variance efficient sets.

However, this result is quite sensitive to the particular assumptions made about the nature of prior information. The conjugate prior for a multivariate normal process with unknown covariance matrix is restrictive to the extent that it implies a

3. Sharpe (1970, p. 181) for example argues that in any sample period a security may perform unusually well, leading to the investor to place too great a weight on that security in his portfolio.

4. Assuming that $h(\boldsymbol{\theta})$ is proper, that is $\int_{R_\theta} h(\boldsymbol{\theta})d\boldsymbol{\theta}$ converges in some finite interval.

5. It is interesting to note that this procedure can be justified in a sampling context as well as from a Bayesian viewpoint. Aitchison (1975) shows that the predictive distribution can be a closer approximation to the true distribution in a Kullback-Liebler information measure sense than the estimative distribution given by replacing the true parameter values by estimates. Brown (1976) shows that the portfolio solutions generated using the predictive distribution are superior in a statistical risk function sense to the portfolios generated using the estimative distribution.

particular dependence in the prior between the mean and covariance matrix (Ando and Kaufman 1965, p. 35) that may or may not correspond to the information available to the investor. In addition, the information requirements are somewhat prodigious. To form an optimal portfolio we need information equivalent to at least two more observations than securities for a period during which the distribution of returns can be considered stationary--or specific information about the $m(m+1)/2$ distinct elements of the covariance matrix. It is relevant to consider simplifications that convey information about the process generating security returns even if these take us outside the class of conjugate priors. Such a simplification has been provided by Sharpe (1963).

Sharpe's model postulates that security returns R_{it}, are related to each other to the extent that they are all related to some index of market activity I_t:

$$\begin{aligned} \tilde{R}_{1t} &= \alpha_1 + \beta_1 \tilde{I}_t + \tilde{\epsilon}_{1t} \\ \tilde{R}_{2t} &= \alpha_2 + \beta_2 \tilde{I}_t + \tilde{\epsilon}_{2t} \\ &\cdot \quad \cdot \quad \cdot\ \cdot \quad \cdot \\ \tilde{R}_{mt} &= \alpha_m + \beta_m \tilde{I}_t + \tilde{\epsilon}_{mt} \\ \tilde{I}_t &= \mu_M + \tilde{\epsilon}_{Mt}, \end{aligned} \tag{3}$$

where $\tilde{\epsilon}_{1t}, \ldots, \tilde{\epsilon}_{mt}, \tilde{\epsilon}_{Mt}$ are zero mean stochastic terms. Sharpe considered these error terms to be independently distributed. It is possible to generalize his model by assuming that the first m errors have a covariance matrix proportional to a positive definite symmetric matrix $\mathbf{\Omega}$, where the $\tilde{\epsilon}_{Mt}$ error term is distributed independently of the others.

Since the set of linear equations (3) is implied by a multivariate normal distribution of returns,[6] for this model to convey information restrictions are imposed on the set of parameters $\boldsymbol{\alpha}$, $\boldsymbol{\beta}$ and $\mathbf{\Omega}$. Sharpe (1963) suggested that $\mathbf{\Omega}$ be considered diagonal, while many cross section regression studies of rates of return implicitly assume that $\mathbf{\Omega}$ is in fact the identity matrix (e.g., Fama and McBeth 1972). Industry effects could be introduced by taking $\mathbf{\Omega}$ to be block diagonal. Press (1972) has suggested that $\mathbf{\Omega}$ take on an intra-class correlation structure. This structure can be generalized by allowing error variances to differ across equations. Asset pricing model (Sharpe 1964, Lintner 1965) considerations suggest that the $\boldsymbol{\alpha}$ and $\boldsymbol{\beta}$ terms are of primary importance in the study of asset pricing behavior. Indeed it is generally assumed that the individual investor knows the values of these parameters with certainty.

Where the parameters of the model take on known values, the analysis of the model is simple. The mean and covariance of returns can be expressed

---

6. This can be demonstrated quite easily using the results in Zellner (1971) p. 620. However, we should be careful to note that this interpretation does not allow $\tilde{I}_t$ to be a linear combination of the $\tilde{\mathbf{R}}_{it}$. This is not as restrictive as it appears since it is sufficient to drop just one security from consideration for this result to follow. In a many security example at least one security will not satisfy data or information requirements.

$$E[\tilde{\mathbf{R}}] = \boldsymbol{\alpha} + \boldsymbol{\beta}\mu_M$$

$$Cov[\tilde{\mathbf{R}}] = \sigma^2\boldsymbol{\Omega} + \sigma_M^2\boldsymbol{\beta}\boldsymbol{\beta}'$$

where $\sigma^2\boldsymbol{\Omega}$ represents the covariance matrix of the error terms $\tilde{\epsilon}_{1t}, \ldots, \tilde{\epsilon}_{mt}$.

This model has some convenient implications. If the vector of stochastic terms $\tilde{\boldsymbol{\epsilon}}$ are distributed as normal, Student-t or stable, the portfolio return

$$\mathbf{R}_{pt} = \mathbf{X}'\tilde{\mathbf{R}}_t$$

will have a two parameter distribution allowing simple location/scale rules for portfolio choice. There is the evident reduction in the number of parameters, and finally, the covariance matrix has a simple structure, allowing simplified algorithms for portfolio choice (Sharpe (1963)).

In the more realistic case where the parameters of the Sharpe model are not known with certainty, the following procedure is adopted. The parameters in (3) are estimated by Ordinary Least-Squares *conditional* on I_t, and the unconditional distribution is derived by taking the estimates to be the true parameter values. This distribution then used to define optimal portfolio choices, will differ from the relevant predictive distribution. To the extent of the difference the estimated distribution will not take account of all available information.

However, the predictive distribution is not easy to derive for this problem. The nature of the information is such that it cannot be represented as a conjugate prior to the multivariate normal distribution assumed to generate security returns. In fact, the predictive distribution does not appear to have a closed form representation. Fortunately, it is still possible to characterize optimal portfolio choices for this distribution of returns.

3. The Predictive Distribution of Returns for the Sharpe Model Case

We shall assume the following:

A. The stochastic terms $\tilde{\epsilon}_{1t}, \ldots, \tilde{\epsilon}_{mt}, \tilde{\epsilon}_{Mt}$ are distributed as multivariate normal with mean zero and covariance matrix $\boldsymbol{\Omega}_\epsilon^* = \begin{bmatrix} \sigma^2\boldsymbol{\Omega} & \mathbf{O} \\ \mathbf{O}' & \sigma_M^2 \end{bmatrix}$ where $\boldsymbol{\Omega}$ is a known, positive definite symmetric matrix.

B. The individual has a diffuse prior for $\boldsymbol{\alpha}$, $\boldsymbol{\beta}$ and σ proportional to the reciprocal of the standard deviation σ.

C. The individual has a diffuse prior for the mean of the market index, which is proportional to a constant. We consider two cases: where the standard deviation is known, and where it is not known. In the latter case we assume a diffuse prior proportional to the reciprocal of the standard deviation, σ_M.

These assumptions can be relaxed quite readily. In particular, the diffuse prior assumptions can be relaxed to incorporate in an obvious way informative conjugate priors for the parameters of the Sharpe model. Thus, the analysis of Vasicek (1973) can be applied in this context.

The most restrictive assumption is that the matrix $\boldsymbol{\Omega}$ is known. Of course, if little were known about $\mathbf{\Omega}$ then the Sharpe formulation would be of little assistance. However, if we know only that $\mathbf{\Omega}$ has a certain structure (e.g., that variances and/or correlations are constant for a given industry group) the fact that the individual elements of $\mathbf{\Omega}$ are not known with certainty will not present a serious difficulty.[7]

In the Appendix we show that for these assumptions T observations on the first (m) equations of the Sharpe model can be expressed as $(T \times m)$ observations on one equation. The problem of determining the predictive distribution of returns is then identical to the problem of determining the predictive distribution of a dependent variable in a regression model where the independent variables for the subsequent period have unknown values - a problem which appears to have no clear resolution in the literature.[8] Conditional on knowledge of the market index for periods 1 through $T+1$ the predictive distribution shall have a Student form. This *conditional* predictive distribution has a mean

$$ER_{pT+1} = \hat{\alpha} + \hat{\beta} I_{T+1}$$

variance

$$Var\ R_{pT+1} = \frac{\nu}{\nu-2}\, \delta_0^2 \left\{ \hat{s}^2 + \hat{s}_{\hat{\alpha}}^2 + 2\hat{s}_{\hat{\alpha}\hat{\beta}} I_{T+1} + \hat{s}_{\hat{\beta}}^2 I_{T+1}^2 \right\}$$

and ν degrees of freedom, where

$$\delta_0^2 = \mathbf{X}'\mathbf{\Omega}\,\mathbf{X} = \sum_{i=1}^{m}\sum_{j=1}^{m} X_i X_j \omega_{ij},$$

$$\hat{\alpha} = \sum_{i=1}^{m} X_i \hat{\alpha}_i \ , \quad \hat{\beta} = \sum_{i=1}^{m} X_i \hat{\beta}_i$$

$$\hat{s}^2 = \sum_{i=1}^{m}\sum_{t=1}^{T} [R_{it} - \hat{\alpha}_i - \hat{\beta}_i]^2/\nu\ , \quad \nu = (T-2)m$$

$$\begin{bmatrix} \hat{s}_{\hat{\alpha}}^2 & \hat{s}_{\hat{\alpha}\hat{\beta}} \\ \hat{s}_{\hat{\alpha}\hat{\beta}} & \hat{s}_{\hat{\beta}}^2 \end{bmatrix} = \hat{s}^2 [\mathbf{W}'\mathbf{W}]^{-1}\ , \quad \mathbf{W} = \begin{bmatrix} 1 & I_1 \\ \cdot & \cdot \\ 1 & I_T \end{bmatrix}$$

and $\hat{\alpha}_i$ and $\hat{\beta}_i$ are Ordinary Least-Squares estimates

7. This follows because in this situation there will be many more observations on the distinct elements of $\mathbf{\Omega}$ than on the other parameters of the model. In this case it is possible to show that a first order expansion of the predictive distribution around the maximum likelihood estimates of the distinct elements of $\mathbf{\Omega}$ will provide a close approximation to the predictive distribution.

8. Gonedes and Roberts (1974) derive the predictive distribution for a special case, the assumptions of which are violated for this example. The mean and covariance matrix of the predictive distribution was derived by Kalymon (1971) for the case where all variances were assumed known.

$$\begin{bmatrix} \hat{\alpha}_i \\ \hat{\beta}_i \end{bmatrix} = [\mathbf{W}'\mathbf{W}]^{-1}\mathbf{W}'\mathbf{R}_i$$

The problem arises that *both* the mean and variance of this Student-t distribution depend on knowledge of I_{T+1}. It is this functional dependence which complicates the process of finding the unconditional predictive distribution defined as the average of the conditional predictive distribution $g[R_{pT+1}|I_{T+1}]$ over the unknown values of the market index, I_{T+1}:

$$g[R_{pT+1}] = \int_{-\infty}^{\infty} f[R_{pT+1}|I_{T+1}]\phi(I_{T+1})\,dI_{T+1}$$

where $\phi(I_{T+1})$ represents the predictive distribution of the market index.[9] Now it does not appear possible to express the predictive distribution of portfolio returns, $g[R_{pT+1}]$ in a closed form expression. However for the assumptions about the process generating the market index I_{T+1}, we can determine the moments of this distribution.

If the individual has a diffuse prior for the mean of the process generating the market index, we can show that the *unconditional* mean is

$$ER_{pT+1} = \hat{\alpha} + \hat{\beta}\bar{I},$$

where $\bar{I}$ is the sample mean of observations on the market index, and a variance that is greater than the portfolio variance one would infer simply by replacing the true parameters by Ordinary Least Squares estimates. This result is not unexpected. We can also show that the odd order central moments of the predictive distribution vanish, which is consistent with the predictive distribution being symmetric. However, this distribution is *not* location and scale in the sense of Bawa (1975). Hence simplified mean and variance or more generalized location and scale portfolio choice rules will not, in general identify optimal portfolio choices. Potentially all the higher order moments will be relevant in choosing optimal portfolios.

9. The density function of this distribution has a kernel given by

$$g[R_{pT+1}]\ \alpha \int_{R_{I_{T+1}}} \frac{1}{\sqrt{\delta_0^2\hat{s}^2\left(k_0+k_1I_{T+1}+k_2I_{T+1}^2\right)}} \cdot \left\{\nu+\frac{[r-\hat{\alpha}-\hat{\beta}I_{T+1}]^2}{\delta_0^2\hat{s}^2\left(k_0+k_1I_{T+1}+k_2I_{T+1}^2\right)}\right\}^{\frac{\nu+1}{2}} \phi(I_{T+1})\,dI_{T+1}$$

where the various parameters are as defined in the Appendix: k_0, k_1, k_2 and $\hat{s}^2$ are functions of the observed sample quantities alone, $\hat{\alpha}$, $\hat{\beta}$, and δ_0^2 are functions of both the sample data and the portfolio chosen. The function ϕ shall represent the kernel of a normal distribution when the individual knows the variance of the market index but has a diffuse prior for the mean; it shall represent the kernel of a Student-t where the individual has a diffuse prior for both parameters.

4. Towards a Three Parameter Rule for Portfolio Choice

The fact that the predictive distribution of returns is not location and scale in the sense of Bawa (1975) is fairly easily demonstrated. As we shall see later, the measure of kurtosis-defined as the fourth central moment (where it exists) divided by the square of the variance -- is a decreasing function of $\hat{\beta}$ for a given variance. The measure $\hat{\beta}$ in turn depends on the portfolio weights - and thus we have the required contradiction.[10]

Yet it is still possible to define an admissible set of portfolios in this context. The predictive distribution depends on alternative portfolio choices through only $\hat{\alpha}$, $\hat{\beta}$ and δ_0^2 and to this extent the distribution can be termed 'three parameter' in the spirit of Bawa (1975).[11] To interpret these parameters we shall consider expansions of the distribution in terms of its moments. While it is true that the sequence of moments derived in the Appendix will not necessarily characterize the predictive distribution (Feller 1966 p. 224),[12] this distribution is liable to be very well approximated by a Gram-Charlier or Edgeworth expansion in terms of the finite number of central moments that exist. In terms of this expansion, the distribution function is seen to depend on alternate portfolio choices through only four parameters: the mean $\mu_{\tilde{R}pT+1}$ and variance $\sigma^2_{\tilde{R}pT+1}$ of the predictive distribution, δ_0^2 and $\hat{\beta}$. However δ_0^2 is redundant once we know $\sigma^2_{\tilde{R}pT+1}$ and $\hat{\beta}$, which suggests that optimal portfolio choice may be characterized through a three parameter rule:

Theorem 1: An optimal portfolio in the Sharpe model case is a member of the class of portfolios that attain a minimum variance given mean and $\hat{\beta}$. This minimized variance is a nondecreasing function of the mean given $\hat{\beta}$.

---

10. From the definition given in Bawa (1975, p. 112) we note that if the distribution of returns is location and scale we can write

$$\tilde{R}_{pT+1} = l_F + s_F\tilde{x}$$

where $\tilde{x}$ has a distribution independent of portfolio choices made. If the first through fourth moments of $\tilde{R}_{pt+1}$ (and hence of $\tilde{x}$) exist then kurtosis, K

$$K = E[\tilde{R}_{pT+1} - E\tilde{R}_{pT+1}]^4 / \left(\sigma^2_{\tilde{R}pT+1}\right)^2$$

$$= E[\tilde{x} - E\tilde{x}]^4 / \left(\sigma^2_{\tilde{x}}\right)^2$$

which is not a function of portfolio choices.

11. For two parameter location and scale distributions, the distribution function of $(\tilde{R}-l_f)/s_f$ is given for location l_f and scale $s_f > 0$. In the present case the distribution function of $\tilde{R}$ is given for $\hat{\alpha}$, $\hat{\beta}$ and δ_0^2. In terms of moment expansions, we shall see later that the distribution is location and scale for a fixed ratio of δ_0^2 to $\hat{\beta}^2$, or (equivalently) for a fixed value of $\sigma^2_{\tilde{R}pT+1}/\hat{\beta}^2$.

12. Both the known counterexamples and the conditions sufficient to avoid this so called 'moment problem' deal with situations where all moments exist. If the number of observations, and hence the number of moments become infinite, then for $\beta > 1$ we can show that the sufficiency condition of Feller (1966, p. 487) will be satisfied. To see this note that for this case, the higher order moments become dominated by the higher order moments of the predictive distribution of the market index which in this limiting case approaches a normal distribution.

The proof proceeds in two stages. First we show that a higher mean is preferred to a lower given the variance and $\hat{\beta}$, and then we demonstrate that this result yields the Theorem.

For the purposes of this Theorem we shall assume that the distribution function of $[\tilde{R}_{pT+1} - \mu_{pT+1}]$ can be represented by a Gram-Charlier or Edgeworth expansion in terms of all the central moments that exist. Then, since given the variance and $\hat{\beta}$ none of the central moments are a function of the mean, the distribution of the difference $[\tilde{R}_{pT+1} - \mu_{pT+1}]$ is invariant to alternative portfolio choices. Hence, the mean of the predictive distribution is a location parameter in the sense of Bawa (1975) and a higher mean is preferred to a lower mean provided that the utility nonsatiation axiom holds (Bawa 1975, p. 100). We have thus completed the first part of the proof.

We shall now show that a portfolio that attains a maximum mean for a given variance and $\hat{\beta}$ will minimize variance for that mean and $\hat{\beta}$, in a region for which the minimized variance is increasing in the mean. In Figure 9.1, consider two portfolios A and B constructed to have the same variance and $\hat{\beta}$, and hence the same higher order moments. Portfolio B, which maximizes mean given variance and $\hat{\beta}$, is always preferred to A by individuals who prefer more to less. At this maximized mean, variance is minimized and we have the Theorem, with the darker line in Figure 9.1 representing the admissible set of portfolios as depicted in mean and standard deviation space for a given $\hat{\beta}$. This argument can readily be made rigorous.[13]

An optimal portfolio is then a member of the class of portfolios that minimize variance for μ_{RpT+1} and $\hat{\beta}$. If we do not place limitations on the potential to sell securities short, this minimum variance frontier can be represented as a parabola in three dimensions, as demonstrated in Appendix B.

For the sake of illustration, fifteen equally weighted portfolios were formed from the set of all New York Stock Exchange listed securities that were continuously traded from July 1953 to June 1968. The rules for selection of these portfolios correspond to those outlined by Fama and McBeth (1973). The returns on each portfolio were computed on a monthly basis from January 1961 to June 1968 inclusive. These data, together with a market index due to Fisher (1966) were used to compute the minimum variance parabola illustrated in Figure 9.2.

Inspection of this figure reveals that there remains a wide range of potentially optimal portfolios depending on the particular choice of mean and $\hat{\beta}$. The objective is to identify a minimal set of portfolios termed 'admissible' or 'efficient' that a rational investor need consider. Since, for a given $\hat{\beta}$, Theorem 1 states that we need only consider that part of the minimum variance parabola that is increasing in the mean, we can immediately reduce the choice set. Figure 9.3 illustrates the restricted range of alternatives in terms of the example of Figure 9.2. A rational investor need only consider combinations of mean, variance and $\hat{\beta}$ represented by

13. Consider minimizing portfolio variance for a given $\hat{\beta}$ and subject to other constraints on portfolio shares including an inequality constraint of the form $\mathbf{X}'\boldsymbol{\mu} \geqslant \mu$. For a positive definite covariance matrix the Kuhn Tucker constraints will provide necessary and sufficient conditions for a global minimum (Hadley 1964 p. 213). Suppose μ is increased to the point where the mean constraint is binding. Since the Lagrange multiplier is now positive, and lies between the left and right derivatives of the minimized variance with respect to μ (Balinsky and Baumol 1968 p. 243), further increasing μ shall trace out a monotonic sequence of minimized variances. Thus a portfolio that maximizes mean will also minimize variance in the feasible range of variances.

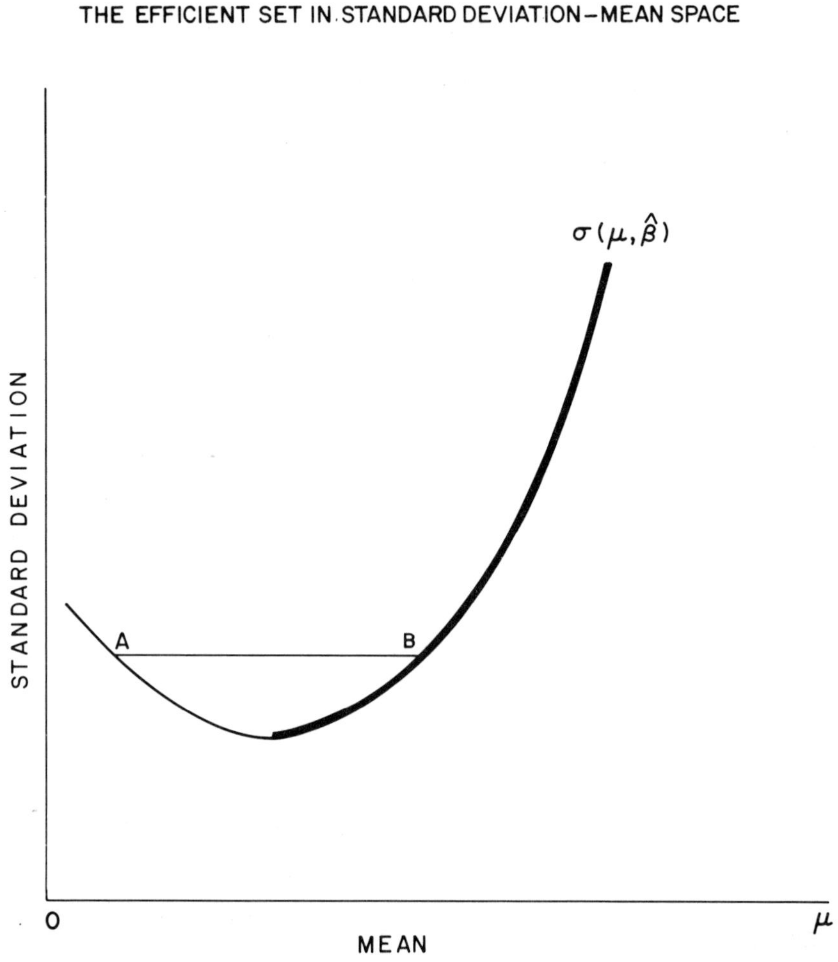
THE EFFICIENT SET IN STANDARD DEVIATION–MEAN SPACE
STANDARD DEVIATION
$\sigma(\mu, \hat{\beta})$
A
B
0
MEAN
μ

Figure 9.1

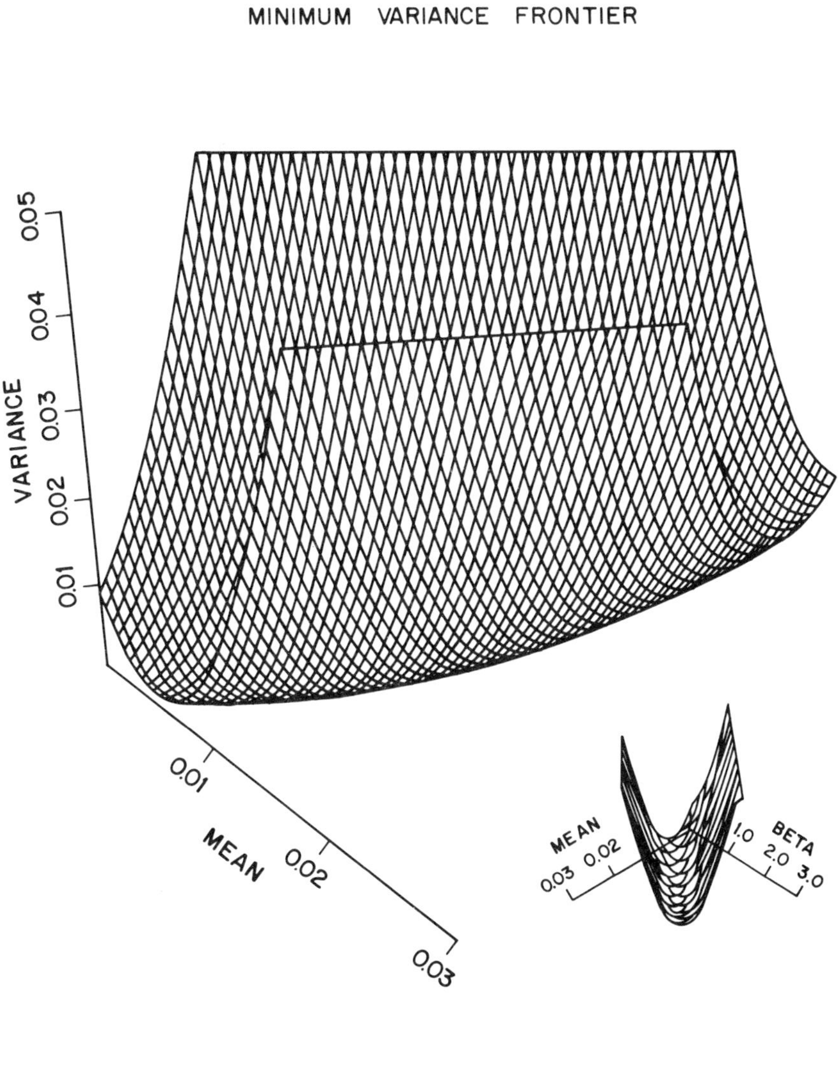
MINIMUM VARIANCE FRONTIER
VARIANCE
0.01
0.02
0.03
0.04
0.05
MEAN
0.01
0.02
0.03
MEAN
0.03 0.02
BETA
1.0
2.0
3.0

Figure 9.2

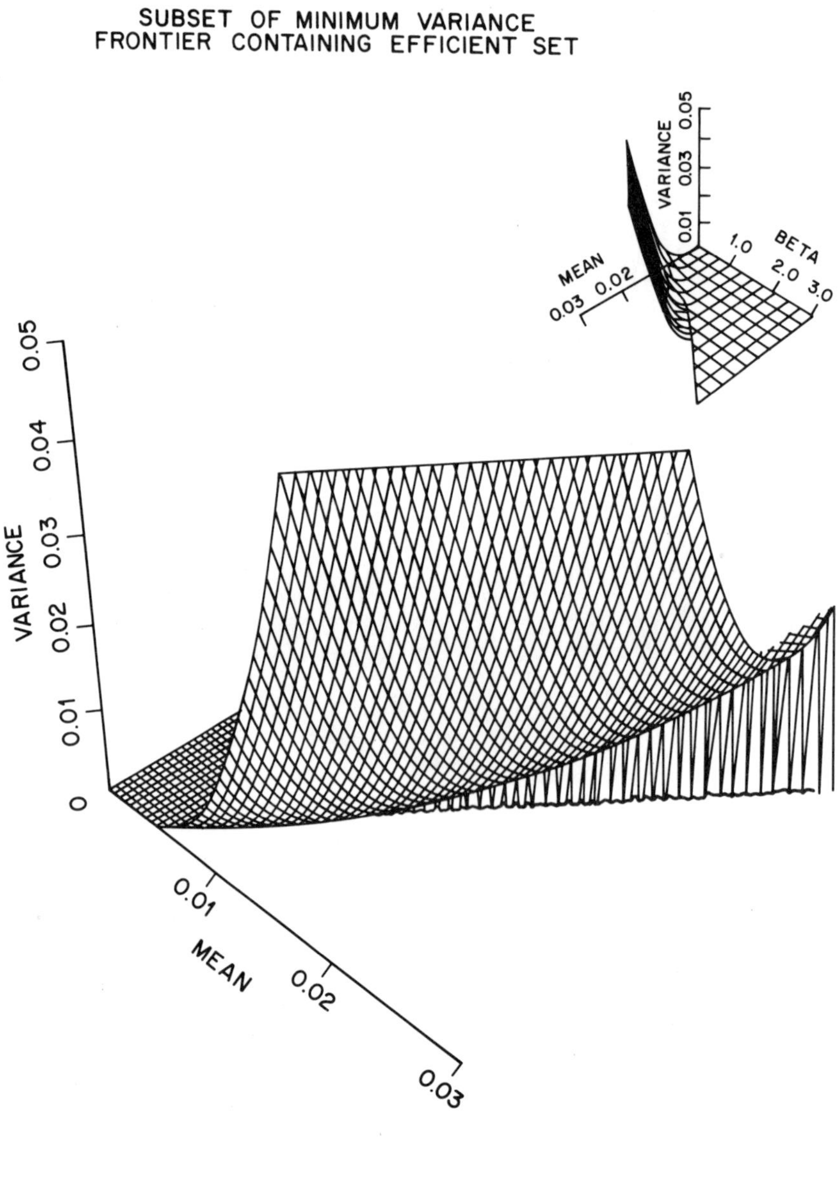
SUBSET OF MINIMUM VARIANCE
FRONTIER CONTAINING EFFICIENT SET
VARIANCE
0.01
0.03
0.05
MEAN
0.02
0.03
1.0
BETA
2.0
3.0
VARIANCE
0
0.01
0.02
0.03
0.04
0.05
MEAN
0.01
0.02
0.03

Figure 9.3

the raised part of the figure.

Theorem 1 allows us to define a set of portfolios that contains, as a subset, the efficient set. To define the efficient set we need to establish a preference ordering for $\hat{\beta}$. Unfortunately, as $\hat{\beta}$ enters into the definition of the higher order moments in a complicated way, in order to establish a convenient preference ordering we require a simplifying assumption. However we conjecture that this result will hold under more general conditions:

Theorem 2: The efficient set of portfolios represent that subset of minimum variance portfolios for which

1. $\dfrac{\partial\sigma(\mu,\hat{\beta})}{\partial\mu} \geqslant 0$

2. $\dfrac{\partial\sigma(\mu,\hat{\beta})}{\partial\hat{\beta}} \leqslant \dfrac{\sigma(\mu,\hat{\beta})}{\hat{\beta}}\ , \ \hat{\beta} > 0$

and, where we approximate the predictive distribution in terms of the first four moments[14]

3. $\dfrac{\partial\sigma(\mu,\hat{\beta})}{\partial\hat{\beta}} > 0\ , \ \hat{\beta} > 0$

where these derivatives exist, for $\sigma(\mu,\hat{\beta})$ *defined to be the standard deviation of the optimal portfolio given* μ *and* $\hat{\beta}$

The first inequality follows directly from Theorem 1. We shall demonstrate the second and third inequalities in terms of Figure 9.4, which depicts the minimum standard deviation as a function of $\hat{\beta}$ given the mean μ. The second and third inequalities rule out all but standard deviation - $\hat{\beta}$ combinations represented by the darker line in Figure 9.4.

Simply by inspection of the expression for the moments given in the Appendix, we find that along any ray from the origin - that is, holding $\sigma/\hat{\beta}$ (and hence $\sigma^2/\hat{\beta}^2$) constant-kurtosis and all higher order normalized moments are constant.[15] Points A and B thus represent portfolios constructed to minimize variance for the same mean, kurtosis and all higher order normalized moments. This being the case, if we write the portfolio returns under A as $\tilde{R}_A = \mu_A + \sigma_A \tilde{x}_A$ and under B as $\tilde{R}_B = \mu_B + \sigma_B \tilde{x}_B$ where $\mu_A = \mu_B$ and $\sigma_B < \sigma_A$, then the sequence of central moments of $\tilde{x}_A$ will be identical to those of $\tilde{x}_B$. Since we assume that the sequence of moments characterizes the distribution of returns, A will differ from B by a scale shift alone and hence will be preferred by risk averse individuals on second order stochastic dominance grounds (Bawa 1975). Thus any point to the

14. Part 3 of the Theorem requires also that kurtosis be a strictly increasing function of $\hat{\beta}$. For this result it suffices that $\sigma^2/\hat{\beta}^2 < \dfrac{T}{T+1}\,\sigma_M^{*2}\left\{k_2\sigma_M^{*2} + (1+\dfrac{1}{T})\right\} + \sigma_M^{*2}$ (Appendix). We should expect this inequality to follow, since for a $\hat{\beta} = 1$, it would be satisfied for a predictive variance σ^2 less than twice the predictive variance of the index σ_M^{*2}.

15. The νth order normalized moment is simply $\mu_\nu/(\sigma^2)^{\nu/2}$ where μ_ν is the νth order central moment, and σ^2 is the variance ($=\mu_2$). Kurtosis is defined as $K = \mu_4/\sigma^4$, and is thus the fourth order normalized moment.

right of C will be dominated leaving us with the second inequality.

To reduce the choice set further, we make the simplifying assumption that the distribution function can be approximated in terms of the first four moments of the distribution.[16] As we noted before, along any ray from the origin, in standard deviation - $\hat{\beta}$ space, kurtosis and all higher order normalized moments are constant. We show in the Appendix that as we decrease the slope of this ray from the origin kurtosis will fall to its limiting value given by the predictive distribution of the market index.

The intuition of this result is as follows. Suppose for simplicity that the variance of the market index is known and hence that the predictive distribution of the market index is normal. Then for a given portfolio variance, if we let $\hat{\beta}$ approach zero, the distribution of returns will approach a distribution with kurtosis somewhat greater than that of the market index. As we increase $\hat{\beta}$, the distribution of returns shall approach a normal with a consequent reduction in kurtosis. That is, as we reduce the contribution to variance of nonsystematic risk we have the intuitive result that the form of the predictive distribution shall approach that of the market index.

In the Appendix we derive sufficient conditions for kurtosis to be a strictly increasing function of the slope of the ray from the origin.[17] If these conditions are met, increasing $\hat{\beta}$ for a given variance - a movement from point B to D in Figure 9.4 - will reduce kurtosis. In terms of the four moment approximation to the distribution of returns, kurtosis is a mean preserving spread (Rothschild and Stiglitz, 1970)[18] and hence B will be dominated for risk averse individuals. Thus, we have the third inequality.

16. For a discussion of the adequacy of such approximations see Johnson and Kotz (1970) 15ff. Actually, in this application all we need for this approximation is that the variation in the higher order moments is negligible as we vary the portfolio compositions.

17. See the footnote to Theorem 2. Since the derivative of kurtosis with respect to $\hat{\beta}^2$ given variance is bounded by a quadratic function in $\hat{\beta}^2$, it suffices that $\hat{\beta}$ be increased over a greater region for which the derivative is positive than for which it is negative for an increase in $\hat{\beta}$ to lead to a reduction in kurtosis.

18. Alternative A is a mean preserving spread if

$$\int_{-\infty}^{x} G_B(t)\,dt \leqslant \int_{-\infty}^{x} G_A(t)\,dt$$

for G_I the c.d.f. associated with alternative I. It is not difficult to show that

$$\frac{d}{dK}\int_{-\infty}^{x} G(t)\,dt \geqslant 0 \qquad \forall x,\ -\infty < x < \infty$$

where we approximate the distribution function in terms of the first four moments. First note that $\int_{-\infty}^{\infty} G(t)\,dt = 0$ for all K, for a given mean. Thus

$$\frac{d}{dK}\int_{-\infty}^{\infty} G(t)\,dt = 0$$

Considering the Gram-Charlier or Edgeworth expansions in terms of the first four moments we find

Theorem 2 establishes a trade-off between variance and $\hat{\beta}$ for an optimal portfolio. A risk averse individual would sacrifice a reduction in portfolio variance in order to make the predictive distribution of returns more closely resemble that of the index. If two parameters of the model were known with certainty, the distribution of returns would be given by the distribution of the index up to location and scale. Hence the increase in variance over and above the minimum variance point for $\hat{\beta}$ reflects the impact of estimation risk upon the optimal portfolio choice.

Figure 9.5 shows the implications of the Theorem for the illustrative example of Figure 9.2. The raised part of the figure reflects the choice of mean, variance and $\hat{\beta}$ available within the efficient set defined in the Theorem. If we were to project points contained in this efficient set onto the mean-variance axis we would have a minimum variance band rather than a minimum variance line. The width of this band would represent the expanded choice set imposed by the presence of estimation risk.

5. Conclusions

We consider the problem of optimal portfolio choice where a generalized stochastic structure initially due to Sharpe generates observed security returns. In the case where the investor does not know the true parameter values, we devise the relevant predictive distribution of returns and show that it is not of a location/scale form. Thus, mean and variance alone will not be sufficient to rank alternative portfolio choices. We derive a new, three parameter rule for portfolio choice in this context. Beta, which is the Ordinary Least-Squares estimate of the regression coefficient obtained by regressing the return of an individual security upon the return on the market, represents the third parameter. It has the interpretation of controlling the degree of exposure to estimation risk. If we establish preference orderings for mean, variance and beta, it is possible to characterize optimal portfolio choices in terms of a three dimensional efficient set, the shape of which tells us the nature of the choice set imposed upon the individual investor by estimation risk.

$$G(t) = -\frac{1}{24}(K-3)(t^3-3t)Z(t) + A(t)$$

where $Z(t)$ is the standard normal c.d.f. $A(t)$ does not depend on kurtosis, and where we assume without loss of generality that the distribution has mean zero and variance one. Consider

$$\frac{d}{dK}\int_{-\infty}^{x} G(t)\,dt = \frac{1}{24}\left\{\int_{-\infty}^{-\sqrt{3}} (3t-t^3)z(t)\,dt + \int_{-\sqrt{3}}^{0} (dt-t^3)Z(t)\,dt\right.$$

$$\left. + \int_{0}^{\sqrt{3}} (3t-t^3)z(t)\,dt + \int_{\sqrt{3}}^{x} (3t-t^3)Z(t)\,dt\right\}, x > \sqrt{3}$$

The term within the first integral is always positive, and that within the second always negative. However the sum of the first and second integrals is .08303. Hence, for all values of x between $-\infty$ and 0, the derivative is positive. The third integral is positive greater than the negative of the second. Hence the sum of the integrals is bounded between zero and a number which is greater

We have not described the effects of these results upon the statement of conditions defining market equilibrium in this context, although it is possible to derive those results for the case where the investor has access to an asset yielding a known rate of return. With this risk-free asset, it is possible to devise market equilibrium conditions that explicitly recognize the estimation risk faced by individuals within the market.

than zero. Thus for all x, $-\infty < x < \infty$, the derivative is positive.

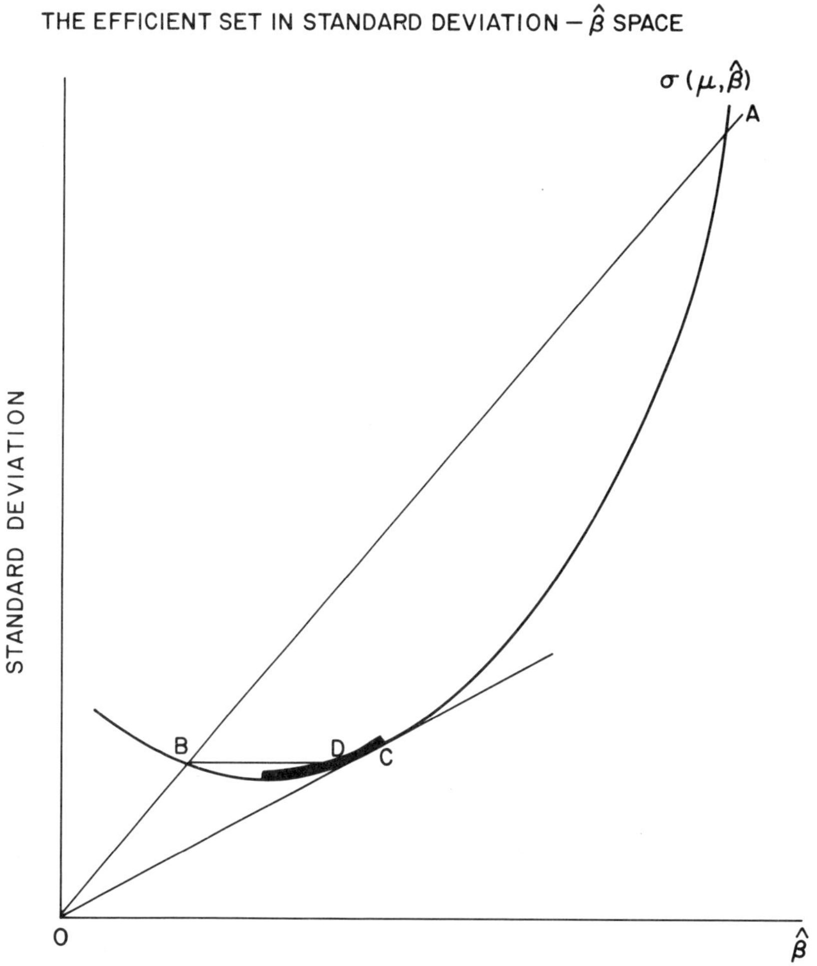
THE EFFICIENT SET IN STANDARD DEVIATION — $\hat{\beta}$ SPACE
$\sigma(\mu,\hat{\beta})$
A
STANDARD DEVIATION
B
D
C
O
$\hat{\beta}$

Figure 9.4

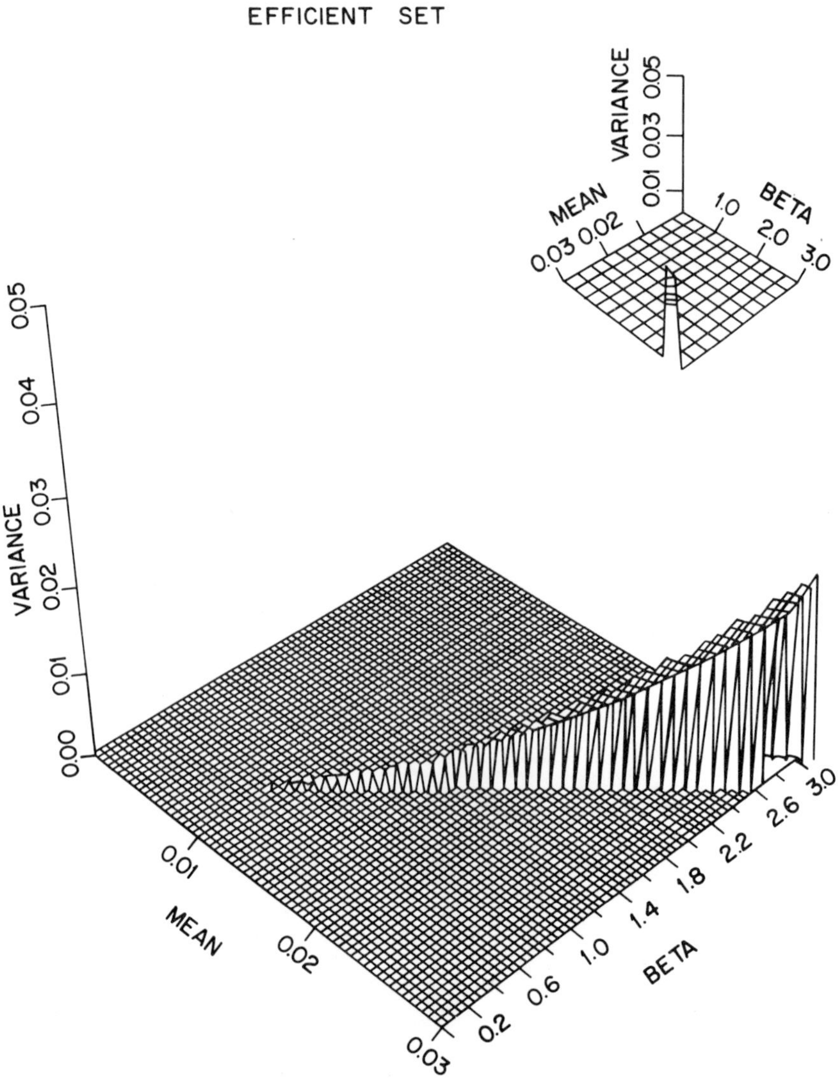
EFFICIENT SET
VARIANCE
0.01 0.03 0.05
MEAN
0.03 0.02
1.0
2.0
3.0
BETA
VARIANCE
0.00
0.01
0.02
0.03
0.04
0.05
0.01
MEAN
0.02
0.03
0.2
0.6
1.0
1.4
1.8
2.2
2.6
3.0
BETA

Figure 9.5

Appendix A: The Derivation of the Predictive Distribution of Returns

Suppose the individual has T observations on the process described by (3)

$$\left.\begin{aligned} R_{1t} &= \alpha_1 + \beta_1 I_t + \epsilon_{1t} \\ R_{2t} &= \alpha_2 + \beta_2 I_t + \epsilon_{2t} \\ &\cdot \quad \cdot \quad \cdot\ \cdot \quad \cdot \\ R_{mt} &= \alpha_m + \beta_m I_t + \epsilon_{mt} \\ \\ I_t &= \mu_M + \epsilon_{Mt} \end{aligned}\right\} \quad t = 1,\ldots,T$$

The first m equations can be written

$$\mathbf{R}_l = \mathbf{W}\boldsymbol{\gamma}_l + \boldsymbol{\epsilon}_l \qquad l = 1,\ldots,m \tag{A1}$$

where

$$\mathbf{R}_l' = \{\mathbf{R}_{l1}, \ldots, \mathbf{R}_{lT}\}, \ \boldsymbol{\epsilon}_l' = \{\epsilon_{l1}, \ldots, \epsilon_{lT}\}$$

and

$$\mathbf{W} = \begin{bmatrix} 1 & I_1 \\ \vdots & \vdots \\ 1 & I_T \end{bmatrix}$$

If we premultiply each side of (A1) by the inverse of $\boldsymbol{\Omega}$, we can express the Sharpe model equations as

$$\mathbf{y} = \mathbf{Z}\boldsymbol{\gamma} + \boldsymbol{\zeta} \tag{A2}$$

where

$$\mathbf{y} = \{\boldsymbol{\Omega}^{-1} \otimes \mathbf{I}\}\mathbf{R}$$

$$\mathbf{Z} = \boldsymbol{\Omega}^{-1} \otimes \mathbf{W}$$

and

$$\boldsymbol{\zeta} = \{\boldsymbol{\Omega}^{-1} \otimes \mathbf{I}\}\boldsymbol{\epsilon}$$

where $\otimes$ represents the Kronecker product operator (e.g., Theil, 1971, p. 303), and $\mathbf{I}$ is the identity matrix.

Note that

$$E\boldsymbol{\zeta} = \mathbf{O}$$

and

$$E\boldsymbol{\zeta}\boldsymbol{\zeta}' = \sigma^2\mathbf{I}$$

Now, the objective is to derive the predictive distribution of a portfolio **X** of the securities the returns on which are generated by the Sharpe model (3). The strategy will be to derive the predictive distribution of returns conditional on $I_1, \ldots I_T$, I_{T+1}; and then to derive the distribution of returns unconditional on I_{T+1}, the market index for the subsequent period.

If we assume that the individual has diffuse prior for the parameters of the form

$$p[\boldsymbol{\gamma}, \sigma] \alpha\ 1/\sigma \quad \begin{cases} -\infty < \alpha_l, \beta_l < \infty \\ 0 < \sigma < \infty \end{cases}$$

then we have precisely the model described by Zellner (1971, pp. 72-74) and we can write down that

$$p[\mathbf{y}_{T+1} | \mathbf{y}, \mathbf{Z}, \mathbf{Z}_{T+1}]\ \alpha \left\{ \nu + (\mathbf{y}_{T+1} - \mathbf{Z}_{T+1}\hat{\boldsymbol{\gamma}})' H (\mathbf{y}_{T+1} - \mathbf{Z}_{T+1}\hat{\boldsymbol{\gamma}}) \right\}^{-(\nu+m)/2}$$

where

$$\mathbf{Z}_{T+1} = \boldsymbol{\Omega}^{-1} \otimes [1, I_{T+1}]$$

$$H = \left(I + \mathbf{Z}_{T+1}(\mathbf{Z}'\mathbf{Z})^{-1}\mathbf{Z}'_{T+1} \right)^{-1} / s_0^2$$

for

$$s_0^2 = (\mathbf{y} - \mathbf{Z}\hat{\boldsymbol{\gamma}})'(\mathbf{y} - \mathbf{Z}\hat{\boldsymbol{\gamma}})/\nu$$

and

$$\hat{\boldsymbol{\gamma}} = (\mathbf{Z}'\mathbf{Z})^{-1}\mathbf{Z}'\mathbf{y}\ , \quad \nu = m(T-2)$$

from this we see that

$$\mathbf{R}_{T+1} = \{\boldsymbol{\Omega} \otimes I\} \mathbf{y}_{T+1}$$

will be distributed as multivariate Student-t with ν degrees of freedom. After some simplification we find that the mean of $\mathbf{R}_{T+1}$ will be given by

$$E[\mathbf{R}_{T+1} | I_{T+1}] = \hat{\boldsymbol{\alpha}} + \hat{\boldsymbol{\beta}} I_{T+1}$$

with covariance matrix

$$Cov\ [\mathbf{R}_{T+1} | I_{T+1}] = \boldsymbol{\Omega}\, s^2 \frac{\nu}{\nu - 2}$$

where

$$s^2 = \hat{s}^2 + \hat{s}_{\hat{\alpha}}^2 + 2\hat{s}_{\hat{\alpha}\hat{\beta}} I_{T+1} + \hat{s}_{\hat{\beta}}^2 I_{T+1}^2$$

for

$$\hat{s}^2 = \sum_{i=1}^{m} \sum_{t=1}^{T} \left[R_{it} - \hat{\alpha}_i - \hat{\beta}_i I_t\right]^2 / \nu,$$

$$\begin{bmatrix} \hat{s}^2_{\hat{\alpha}} & \hat{s}_{\hat{\alpha}\hat{\beta}} \\ \hat{s}_{\hat{\alpha}\hat{\beta}} & \hat{s}^2_{\hat{\beta}} \end{bmatrix} = \hat{s}^2[\mathbf{W}'\mathbf{W}]^{-1}$$

where $\hat{\alpha}_i$ and $\hat{\beta}_i$ are Ordinary Least-Squares estimates,

$$\begin{bmatrix} \hat{\alpha}_i \\ \hat{\beta}_i \end{bmatrix} = [\mathbf{W}'\mathbf{W}]^{-1}\mathbf{W}'\mathbf{R}_i$$

Given this result it is clear that the return on a portfolio **X**

$$\mathbf{R}_{pT+1} = \mathbf{X}'\mathbf{R}_{T+1}$$

shall have a conditional distribution that is Student-t with ν degrees of freedom, with mean

$$E[R_{pT+1} | I_{T+1}] = \hat{\alpha} + \hat{\beta} I_{T+1}$$

and variance

$$Var\ [R_{pT+1} | I_{T+1}] = \delta_0^2 s^2 \frac{\nu}{\nu - 2}$$

where

$$\hat{\alpha} = \sum_{l=1}^{m} X_l \hat{\alpha}_l\ ,\ \hat{\beta} = \sum_{l=1}^{m} X_l \hat{\beta}_l \text{ and } \delta_0^2 = \mathbf{X}'\mathbf{\Omega}\,\mathbf{X} = \sum_{l=1}^{m} \sum_{k=1}^{m} X_l X_k \omega_{lk}$$

As noted in the text, it does not appear possible to express the unconditional distribution in a closed form representation. The form of the distribution will clearly depend on the distribution of I_{T+1}. If the process generating the observed I_t and I_{T+1} is normal with mean μ_M and variance σ_M^2 and if the individual has a diffuse prior for the mean proportional to a constant, the predictive distribution shall be normal[19] with mean $\mu_M^* = D[I_{T+1}] = \bar{I}$, the sample mean, and variance

$$\sigma_M^{*2} = Var\ [I_{T+1}] = \left\{1 + \frac{1}{T}\right\} \sigma_M^2$$

If the individual has a diffuse prior for both parameters proportional to $1/\sigma_M$ then the predictive distribution for I_{T+1} shall be Student-t[20] with mean $\mu_M^* = \bar{I}$ and variance

19. Zellner (1971) pp. 29-30.

20. Use Zellner (1971), p. 22 to show that the posterior distribution is of a normal - inverted gamma form, and apply result in Raiffa and Schlaifer (1961), p. 304.

$$\sigma_M^{*2} = \left[\frac{T-1}{T-3}\right]\left(1 + \frac{1}{T}\right)\hat{\sigma}_M^2$$

where $\hat{\sigma}_M^2$ is the sample variance,

$$\hat{\sigma}_M^2 = \sum_{t=1}^{T}\{I_t-\bar{I}\}^2/(T-1) .$$

We can express the higher order moments of the predictive distribution of R_{pT+1} in terms of the moments of this distribution. Note that the unconditional mean of R_{pT+1} will be given by

$$ER_{pT+1} = \underset{I_{T+1}}{E}\{E[R_{pT+1}|I_{T+1}]\} = \hat{\alpha} + \hat{\beta}EI_{T+1} = \hat{\alpha} + \hat{\beta}\bar{I}$$

The rth order central moment, where it exists will be given by

$$E\left[R_{pT+1}-ER_{pT+1}\right]^r = \sum_{j=1}^{r}\binom{r}{j}E\left[R_{pT+1}-\hat{R}_{pT+1}\right]^{r-j}\left[I_{T+1}-\bar{I}\right]^j\hat{\beta}^j$$

where $\hat{R}_{pt+1} = \hat{\alpha} + \beta I_{t+1}$. This can be written as

$$E\left[R_{pT+1}-ER_{pT+1}\right]^r = \sum_{j=1}^{r}\binom{r}{j}\underset{I_{T+1}}{E}\,\delta_0^{r-j}s^{r-j}\left[I_{T+1}-\bar{I}\right]^j\hat{\beta}^j \tag{A5}$$

for

$$s^l = \underset{R_{pT+1}|I_{T+1}}{E}\left[R_{pT+1}-\hat{R}_{pT+1}\right]^l$$

$$= f_s[\nu,l]\,(\hat{s}^2)^{l/2}\left(k_0+k_1I_{T+1}+k_2I_{T+1}^2\right)^{l/2}$$

The function $f_s[\nu,l]$, a function defining the central moments of the Student-t distribution, is defined for l , ν and is given by

$$f_s[\nu,l] = 0, \quad l \text{ odd}$$

$$= \frac{\Gamma[(l+1)/2]\Gamma[(\nu-l)/2]\nu^{l/2}}{\Gamma[1/2]\Gamma[\nu/2]}$$

$$l \text{ even}, \ l < \nu .$$

where Γ denotes the gamma function.

In particular

$$f_s[\nu,2] = \nu/(\nu-2)$$

and

$$f_s[\nu, 4] = 3\nu^2/(\nu-2)(\nu-4)$$

The constants k_0, k_1 and k_2 are given by $\left(1 + s_{\hat{\alpha}}^2/\hat{s}^2\right)$, $-2\hat{s}_{\hat{\alpha}\hat{\beta}}/\hat{s}^2$, and $\hat{s}_{\hat{\beta}}^2/\hat{s}^2$ respectively.

Noting that

$$k_1 = -2\bar{I}k_2$$

and

$$k_0 - \bar{I}^2 k_2 = (1+1/T)$$

We can simplify (5) to find

$$E[R_{pT+1} - ER_{pT+1}]^r$$

$$= \sum_{\begin{bmatrix} j=r \\ even \\ r-j \end{bmatrix}}^{r} \binom{r}{j} \delta_0^{2f} (\hat{s}^2)^f f_s(\nu, 2f) \sum_{i=0}^{f} \binom{f}{i} E\left[I_{T+1} - \bar{I}\right]^{r-2i} k_2^{f-1} \left\{ i + \frac{1}{t} \right\}^i \hat{\beta}_j$$

for

$$f = (r-j)/2 \tag{A6}$$

which represents an expansion of the moments of the predictive distribution in terms of the moments of the predictive distribution of I_{t+1}. If this distribution is Student then all odd order moments, where they exists, will vanish. Hence by inspection of (A6) we find that all odd order moments of the predictive distribution of R_{pt+1} *also* vanish.

In particular, the variance of the predictive distribution is given by

$$\sigma_{R_{pT+1}^2} = E\left[R_{pT+1} - ER_{pT+1}\right]^2 = \hat{s}^2 \delta_0^2 \frac{\nu}{\nu-2} \left[\sigma_M^{*2} k_2 + \left(1 + \frac{1}{T}\right)\right] + \sigma_M^{*2} \hat{\beta}^2$$

and the fourth moment is given by

$$E\left[R_{pT+1} - ER_{pT+1}\right]^4$$

$$= \delta_0^4 (\hat{s}^2)^2 \frac{3\nu^2}{(\nu-2)(\nu-4)} \left[\mu_4 k_2^2 + 2\sigma_M^{*2} k_2 \left(1 + \frac{1}{T}\right) + \left(1 + \frac{1}{T}\right)^2\right]$$

$$+ 6\delta_0^2 \hat{s}^2 \hat{\beta}^2 \frac{\nu}{\nu-2} \left[\mu_4 k_2 + \sigma_M^{*2} \left(1 + \frac{1}{T}\right)\right] + \hat{\beta}^4 \mu_4$$

where

$$\mu_4 = E\left[I_{T+1} - EI_{T+1}\right]^4.$$

Kurtosis, $K = E\left[R_{pT+1} - ER_{pT+1}\right]^4 / (\sigma_{R^2_{pT+1}})^2$ will clearly depend on both δ_0^2 and $\hat{\beta}$. To examine the nature of this relationship it will prove convenient to consider kurtosis as a function of the ratio of δ_0^2 to $\hat{\beta}^2$, $x = \delta_0^2/\hat{\beta}^2$. Then we can write

$$K = \frac{x^2\gamma_1 + x\gamma_2 + \gamma_3}{x^2\lambda_1 + x\lambda_2 + \lambda_3}$$

where the coefficients $\gamma_1 > \lambda_1 > 0$, $\gamma_2 > \lambda_2 > 0$, and $\gamma_3 > \lambda_3 > 0$ are defined in terms of the coefficients defining the central moments and do not depend on alternative portfolio choices.

If we decrease the ratio x and hence decrease the ratio of variance to $\hat{\beta}^2$, kurtosis shall approach $\gamma_3/\lambda_s = \mu_t/(\sigma_M^{*2})^2$ the kurtosis of the predictive distribution of the market index. On the other hand, if we increase x, kurtosis shall approach

$$\gamma_1/\lambda_1 = \frac{3(\nu-2)}{(\nu-4)}\left\{\frac{\mu_4 k_2^2 + 2\sigma_M^{*2} k_2(1+\frac{1}{T}) + (1+\frac{1}{T})^2}{(\sigma_M^{*2})^2 k_2^2 + 2\sigma_M^{*2} k_2(1+\frac{1}{t}) + (1+\frac{1}{T})^2}\right\} \tag{A7}$$

which is greater than the kurtosis of the index, in the case where the variance of the index is known.[21] With a diffuse prior for the variance, kurtosis is greater than kurtosis of returns conditional on the index, $3(\nu-2)/(\nu-4)$, but will be *less* than the kurtosis of the index.

It is possible to derive conditions under which kurtosis is a strictly increasing function of x. In the case where the variance of the market index is known, we can simplify the expression for the derivative of kurtosis with respect to x to find:

$$\frac{dK}{dx} > \left\{\frac{12x^2\nu^3}{(\nu-2)^2(\nu-4)}\left[-(\sigma_M^{*2})^3[1+\frac{1}{T}]k_2^2(\hat{s}^2)^3 - (\sigma_M^{*2})^3[1+\frac{1}{T}]^2 k_2(\hat{s}^2)^3\right]\right.$$
$$+ \frac{12x\nu^2}{(\nu-2)(\nu-4)}\left[+(\sigma_M^{*2})^4 k_2^2(\hat{s}^2)^2\right]$$
$$\left. + \frac{12\nu}{(\nu-2)}\left[+(\sigma_M^{*2})^4 k_2 \hat{s}^2\right]\right\}/D \tag{A8}$$

for $D = \{x^2\lambda_1 + x\lambda_2 + \lambda_3\}^2 > 0$. For small x the derivative is positive, while for large x it may be negative. However, it will be positive for $\hat{s}^2 < (\nu-4)/\nu$ and $x < \dfrac{T(\nu-2)\sigma_M^{*2}}{(T+1)\nu\hat{s}^2}$. We can ensure the first inequality by an appropriate normalization of the $\mathbf{\Omega}$ matrix. The second inequality implies that the ratio of predictive variance to the square of $\hat{\beta}$ given by

$$\frac{\sigma^2_{R_{pT+1}}}{\hat{\beta}^2} = x\hat{s}^2\frac{\nu}{\nu-2}\left[k_2\sigma_M^{*2} + (1+\frac{1}{T})\right] + \sigma_M^{*2}$$

21. Divide numerator and denominator by $(\sigma_M^{*2})^2 k_2^2$. In the case where the variance of the index is known, the result follows directly, since $\mu_4/(\sigma_M^{*2})^2 = 3$.

will satisfy the following inequality

$$\frac{\sigma^2_{\tilde{R}_{pt+1}}}{\hat{\beta}^2} < \frac{T}{T+1}\,\sigma^{*2}_{M}\left[k_2\sigma^{*2}_{M}+(1+\frac{1}{T})\right] + \sigma^{*2}_{M} \qquad \text{(A9)}$$

where kurtosis is an increasing function of x. In particular, if $\hat{\beta} = 1$ it suffices that predictive variance is less than twice the predictive variance of the market index for this result to follow. Where there is a diffuse prior for the variance, the result will follow for moderate to large sample sizes.[22]

Since the variable x is linearly related to the ratio of portfolio predictive variance to $\hat{\beta}^2$ it follows that (A9) will suffice for kurtosis to be a strictly increasing function of this ratio as well.

22. An alternative derivation of these results for both cases can be found in Brown (1977).

Appendix B: The Minimum Variance Frontier

If we denote by $\boldsymbol{\mu}$ and Σ the mean and covariance matrix of the unconditional predictive distribution of returns, and by $\hat{\boldsymbol{\beta}}$ the vector of OLS estimates of $\boldsymbol{\beta}$, the portfolio $\mathbf{X}$ that attains a minimum variance for given mean and $\hat{\beta}$ shall be a solution to the problem

$$\underset{\mathbf{X}}{Min}\ \mathbf{X}'\Sigma\mathbf{X}$$

$$\text{Subject to } \mathbf{X}'\boldsymbol{\mu} = \mu$$

$$\mathbf{X}'\hat{\boldsymbol{\beta}} = \hat{\beta}$$

$$\mathbf{X}'\boldsymbol{\iota} = 1$$

for $\boldsymbol{\iota}' = \{1,\dots 1\}$ and where we assume no limits to potential short sales.

Forming the Lagrangean

$$L = \mathbf{X}'\Sigma\mathbf{X} + 2\phi(\mathbf{X}'\hat{\boldsymbol{\beta}}-\hat{\beta}) + 2\lambda(X'\boldsymbol{\mu}-\mu) + 2\zeta(\mathbf{X}'\boldsymbol{\iota}-1)$$

we can write down the necessary conditions for a constrained minimum variance

$$\begin{bmatrix} \Sigma & \hat{\boldsymbol{\beta}} & \boldsymbol{\mu} & \boldsymbol{\iota} \\ \hat{\boldsymbol{\beta}}' & 0 & 0 & 0 \\ \boldsymbol{\mu}' & 0 & 0 & 0 \\ \boldsymbol{\iota}' & 0 & 0 & 0 \end{bmatrix} \begin{bmatrix} \mathbf{X} \\ \phi \\ \lambda \\ \zeta \end{bmatrix} = \begin{bmatrix} \mathbf{O} \\ \hat{\beta} \\ \mu \\ 1 \end{bmatrix}$$

or

$$\mathbf{Mz} = \mathbf{y}$$

where

$$\mathbf{M} = \begin{bmatrix} \Sigma & \mathbf{B} \\ \mathbf{B}' & \mathbf{O} \end{bmatrix} \quad \text{for } \mathbf{B} = [\hat{\boldsymbol{\beta}}, \boldsymbol{\mu}, \boldsymbol{\iota}]$$

$$\mathbf{z} = \mathbf{M}^{-1}\mathbf{y}.$$

provided $\mathbf{M}$ is nonsingular. The matrix $\mathbf{M}^{-1}$ can be evaluated using the rule for partitioned inverses

$$\mathbf{M}^{-1} = \begin{bmatrix} \Sigma^{-1}(\mathbf{I}-\mathbf{B}(\mathbf{B}'\Sigma^{-1}\mathbf{B})^{-1}\mathbf{B}'\Sigma^{-1}) & \Sigma^{-1}\mathbf{B}(\mathbf{B}'\Sigma^{-1}\mathbf{B})^{-1} \\ (\mathbf{B}'\Sigma^{-1}\mathbf{B})^{-1}\mathbf{B}'\Sigma^{-1} & -(\mathbf{B}'\Sigma^{-1}\mathbf{B})^{-1} \end{bmatrix}$$

Thus

$$\mathbf{X}_e = \left[\Sigma^{-1}(\mathbf{I}-\mathbf{B}(\mathbf{B}'\Sigma^{-1}\mathbf{B})^{-1}\mathbf{B}'\Sigma^{-1}),\ \ \Sigma^{-1}\mathbf{B}(\mathbf{B}'\Sigma^{-1}\mathbf{B})^{-1}\right]\begin{bmatrix}\mathbf{O}\\ \hat{\beta}\\ \mu\\ 1\end{bmatrix}$$

or

$$\mathbf{X}_e = \Sigma^{-1}\mathbf{B}(\mathbf{B}'\Sigma^{-1}\mathbf{B})^{-1}\begin{bmatrix}\hat{\beta}\\ \mu\\ 1\end{bmatrix}$$

Note that the variance of the optimal portfolio is given by

$$\sigma_e^2 = \mathbf{X}_e'\Sigma\mathbf{X}_e = [\hat{\beta}\ \mu\ 1](\mathbf{B}'\Sigma^{-1}\mathbf{B})^{-1}\begin{bmatrix}\hat{\beta}\\ \mu\\ 1\end{bmatrix}$$

Therefore, the minimum variance frontier can be represented as a quadratic surface in three dimensions.

If we write

$$\Sigma = \frac{\nu}{\nu-2}\ Es^2\boldsymbol{\Omega} + \sigma_M^{*2}\hat{\boldsymbol{\beta}}\hat{\boldsymbol{\beta}}'$$

where $Es^2 = \hat{s}^2\left[\sigma_M^{*2}k_2 + \left(1 + \frac{1}{T}\right)\right]$, then, after some simplification we find

$$\sigma_e^2 = \frac{\nu}{\nu-2}\ Es^2(\mathbf{B}'\boldsymbol{\Omega}^{-1}\mathbf{B})^{-1} + \hat{\beta}^2\sigma_M^{*2}$$

which can be evaluated upon the finding the inverse of only the 3×3 matrix, $\mathbf{B}'\boldsymbol{\Omega}^{-1}\mathbf{B}$.

CHAPTER 10

CONCLUSIONS

In this book, we have examined a realistic decision problem in which the decision-maker's utility function depends on random variables whose joint probability distribution is not completely known. We have termed this distributional uncertainty as estimation risk, and have employed the Bayesian approach to directly incorporate this risk in the determination of optimal portfolio choice. We now summarize briefly the salient points raised in the preceding chapters.

1. We have argued, both explicitly and implicitly, that the Bayesian approach should be employed to analyze choice problems involving estimation risk. In the Bayesian approach, decisions are based on the predictive distribution for the random variables over which the utility is defined. This distribution is conditional only on the information that is available to the decision-maker. We have contrasted this approach with the parameter certainty equivalent (CE) approach that is frequently proposed in this context. In the CE approach, decisions are based on a returns distribution that is obtained by replacing the unknown parameter values with their point estimates.

We have discussed and illustrated several advantages of the Bayesian approach over the CE approach. First, the Bayesian approach, unlike the CE approach, has an axiomatic foundation. These axioms provide a systematic and consistent framework, within which data and prior information can be combined to obtain the predictive distribution required for decision-making. Moreover, as new information becomes available, these axioms also provide for an updating mechanism to reflect the new information. Second, the Bayesian method has the appealing property of maximizing (minimizing) average value (risk) when these measures exist. As a result, and as is stated more fully below, this approach can be justified in terms of its performance in repeated data samples. Third, the Bayesian approach, as demonstrated in this book, properly reflects estimation risk. We have seen that estimation risk arises in many diverse applications, and that its effects can be very pronounced. Indeed, in one application that we surveyed, the expected loss incurred by ignoring estimation risk was shown to be infinite.

2. Throughout this book, we have emphasized the Bayesian approach within a parametric context. In so doing, we have argued that there is information on the parametric form of the probability distribution facing decision-makers. However, since in some cases, such information may not be available, we have also dealt with decision-making in a nonparametric context. We have found and

demonstrated that there is a major difference between these two cases. In the parametric case, we have seen that it is seldom valid to employ the CE approach; an adjustment for estimation risk must usually be made. In the nonparametric case, with minimal prior information, we have seen that the predictive distribution function is the empirical distribution function that is often advocated in the CE approach. Accordingly, unlike the parametric case, it is not necessary to make an adjustment for estimation risk.

3. This book concentrates on the special case of the portfolio choice problem. We have shown, in several different contexts, that the Bayesian investor will tend to invest relatively more in those securities about which the most information is available. First, to reduce estimation risk, a risk-averse investor would tend to invest more in a riskless security than he or she would were there no estimation risk. Indeed, as an investor's total information (prior and data) about the risky securities decreases, investment in the risky securities approaches zero. Second, we have examined the case in which an investor has abundant information in some sense about one subset of securities and minimal total information about the other. In this case, diversification into this low information subset approaches zero as the information on this subset decreases. In other words, estimation risk can reduce or even eliminate (asymptotically) diversification into those securities which are characterized by low degrees of information.

4. We have examined how various types of prior information can interact with estimation risk to affect an individual's optimal portfolio choice. Indeed, as previously stated, one of the advantages of the Bayesian approaches is that it provides an internally consistent framework for incorporating such information. As an illustration, we examined the case in which the investor has prior beliefs that the portfolio mean is positively correlated with the variance. In other words, in the prior, the investor believes that a higher mean could be obtained only at the expense of a greater variance. This relationship can be incorporated into the prior distribution. In taking this prior information into account, a risk-averse investor might, in comparing two portfolios with identical mean estimates, prefer the one with the larger variance. Intuitively, because the mean is positively correlated with the variance in the prior, the investor acts as if the estimated mean of the high variance security were relatively too low, and adjusts it upwards.

5. We have also examined capital market equilibrium in parametric and nonparametric contexts. In the parametric context, we have examined the frequently employed normal distribution model under several different specifications of prior information. We have shown that capital market equilibrium, with estimation risk considered, is observationally equivalent to such equilibrium when this risk is ignored (i.e., when the CE approach is employed). In a nonparametric context, with minimal prior information, the empirical distribution function is the relevant distribution for decision-making. However, in this case it is extremely difficult for an investor to compare portfolios. It has been argued that a two parameter mean-lower partial moment (MLPM) rule can serve as an approximation for this case, and that this rule is computationally feasible. Within the MLPM framework, capital market equilibrium is no longer given by the traditional mean-variance Capital Asset Pricing Model (CAPM), but by an alternative model which contains the traditional CAPM as a special case. The new model yields the intuitively reasonable result that only downside deviation contributes to risk.

6. To quantify the advantage to the Bayes approach, in a repeated sampling framework we have compared Bayes rules (for different prior specifications) with CE rules on the basis of the statistical risk function. We first examined a single risky asset case with a normal distribution of asset returns and a diffuse prior for the parameters of this distribution. The Bayes approach, at each sample size, dominated the CE approach for every parameter value. In other words, the CE approach was statistically inadmissible. For the many risky asset cases, returns were generated from several different distributions, with parameter values fixed at sample estimates. Under the different prior specifications, the Bayes' rule was compared with the CE rules computed on the basis of the same information. With returns correctly assumed to be multivariate normal, for most sample sizes the Bayes' rule had lower risk than the corresponding CE rules. We also examined the case in which returns were actually Student-t with small degrees of freedom. With returns now incorrectly assumed to be multivariate normal, the superior performance of the Bayes' rules persisted.

7. We have shown how the Bayesian approach can be employed to incorporate the estimation risk relating to the unknown parameter values of the returns distribution. We have argued that this approach is very flexible in that it can process all relevant information. We have further demonstrated this flexibility in analyzing the well known Sharpe index model. Here, returns are generated from a very informative structure that relates individual security returns to the returns on a market index and we want to take this information into account. However, unlike previous cases, not only are the parameter values in this model unknown, but so also is the value of the market index at the time the investment decision is made. In other words, we have a problem analogous to the typical prediction problem, where we must make a prediction from a model with unknown values of parameters and future exogenous variables. Therefore, we now require the Bayesian approach to account for two sources of estimation risk: the unknown values of the parameters and the unknown value of a future exogenous variable (the market index). We have shown that the Bayesian approach can be applied to analyze these two sources of estimation risk. Despite the fact that the predictive distribution does not have a closed form representation, we have obtained a simplified three parameter rule for portfolio choice and have illustrated its use with New York Stock Exchange data.

We have argued that the problem of portfolio choice is very important in itself, and that it is a canonical representation of many problems of choice under uncertainty. Accordingly, we have analyzed many aspects of estimation risk that we believe are important to the problem of portfolio choice. As is evident from the summary above and the preceding chapters, estimation risk has many important and practical implications for portfolio theory. Furthermore, we have argued that the Bayesian approach is one that appropriately processes all relevant information to take this risk into account. There are many important areas, such as multiperiod analysis and nonstationarity, that we have not addressed in this book. In addition, it is crucial to examine in some greater detail the problem of elicitating prior information relevant to making portfolio choices. Some work has begun on the above areas. We hope that this book will stimulate further research into these and related topics.

REFERENCES

Abowd, J. and A. Zellner (1977) Bayesian regression analysis package: BRAP users manual, Version 1.0 9/8/77 (University of Chicago, Chicago, IL).

Aitchison, J. (1975) Goodness of prediction fit, *Biometrika* 62, 547-554.

Albright, S. C. (1977) A Bayesian approach to a generalized house selling problem, *Management Science* 24,432-440.

Ando, A. and G. M. Kaufman (1965) Bayesian analysis of the independent multinomial process--neither mean nor precision known, *Journal of the American Statistical Association* 60, 347-353.

Ang, S. L. (1975) A note on the *E, SL* portfolio selection model, *Journal of Financial and Quantitative Analysis* 10,849-857.

Apostol, T. M. (1975) *Mathematical analysis* (Addison-Wesley, Reading, MA).

Arrow, K. J (1965) *Aspects of the theory of risk bearing* (Yrjö Jahnsson Säätö, Helsinki).

(1974a) *Essays in the theory of risk bearing* (North-Holland, Amsterdam).

(1974b) The use of unbounded utility functions in expected-utility maximization: Response, *Quarterly Journal of Economics* 88, 136-138.

Balinsky, M. and W. J. Baumol (1968) The dual in nonlinear programming and its economic interpretation, *The Review of Economic Studies* 35, 237-256.

Barry, C. B. (1973) A Bayesian approach to portfolio analysis, unpublished D.B.A. dissertation, Graduate School of Business, Indiana University, Bloomington, Indiana.

(1974) Portfolio analysis under uncertain means, variances, and covariances, *Journal of Finance* 29, 515-522.

(1976) Stochastic parameter variation in economic analysis, *Journal of Economics and Business* 29, 139-144.

(1978) Effects of uncertain and nonstationary parameters upon capital market equilibrium conditions, *Journal of Financial and Quantitative Analysis* 13, forthcoming.

Barry, C. B. and R. L. Winkler (1976) Nonstationarity and portfolio choice, *Journal of Financial and Quantitative Analysis* 11, 217-235.

Barry, C. B. and A. R. Wildt (1977) Statistical model comparison in marketing research, *Management Science* 24, 387-392.

Bawa, V. S. (1975) Optimal rules for ordering uncertain prospects, *Journal of Financial Economics* 2, 95-121.

(1976) Admissible portfolios for all individuals, *Journal of Finance* 31, 1169-1183.

(1977a) A nonparametric theory of choice under uncertainty, *Bell Laboratories Economic Discussion Paper* 87 (Bell Laboratories, Holmdel, N.J.).

(1977b) Capital market equilibrium: Robustness of the linear risk-return relationship, unpublished manuscript, presented at the 4th Annual Meeting of the European Finance Association, Bad Homburg, W. Germany.

(1978a) Safety first, stochastic dominance and optimal portfolio selection, *Journal of Financial and Quantitative Analysis* 13, 255-271.

(1978b) On optimal portfolio selection rules, unpublished notes.

(1979a) On stochastic dominance and estimation risk, in: H. Levy, ed., *Research in Finance, Volume II* (Jai Press), forthcoming.

(1979b) Portfolio choice and capital market equilibrium with unknown distributions; this book, Chapter 7.

Bawa, V. S. and S. J. Brown (1979) Capital market equilibrium: Does estimation risk matter?, this book, Chapter 6.

Bawa, V. S. and L. M. Chakrin (1977) Optimal portfolio choice and equilibrium in lognormal security markets, *Bell Laboratories Economic Discussion Paper* 86; forthcoming in *Management Science.*

Bawa, V. S., E. J. Elton, and M. J. Gruber (1978) Simple rules for optimal portfolio selection in stable paretian markets, *Bell Laboratories Economic Discussion Paper* 133 (Bell Laboratories, Murray Hill, New Jersey); *Journal of Finance,* forthcoming.

Bawa, V. S., D. Goroff, and W. Whitt (1978) On the fundamental approximation theorem of portfolio analysis in terms of mean and lower partial moment, unpublished manuscript.

Bawa, V. S. and E. B. Lindenberg (1977) Capital market equilibrium in a mean/lower partial moment framework, *Journal of Financial Economics* 5, 189-200.

Beaver, W., P. Kettler and M. Scholes (1970) The association between market determined and accounting determined risk measures, *The Accounting Review* 45, 654-682.

Black, F. (1972) Capital market equilibrium with restricted borrowing, *Journal of Business* 45, 444-455.

Black, F., M. C. Jensen and M. Scholes (1972) The capital asset pricing model: Some empirical tests, in: M. C. Jensen, ed., *Studies in the theory of capital markets* (Praeger, New York) 77-121.

Black, F. and M. Scholes (1972) The valuation of option contracts and a test of market efficiency, *Journal of Finance* 27, 399-417.

(1973) The pricing of options and corporate liabilities, *Journal of Political Economy* 81, 637-654.

(1974) From theory to a new financial product, *Journal of Finance* 29, 399-412.

Black, F. and J. L. Treynor (1973) How to use security analysis to improve portfolio selection, *Journal of Business* 46, 66-86.

Blackwell, D. (1973) Discreteness of Ferguson selections, *Annals of Statistics* 1, 356-358.

Blattberg, R., and N. Gonedes (1974) A comparison of the stable and student distributions as statistical models for stock prices, *Journal of Business* 47, 244-280.

Blume, M. (1968) The assessment of portfolio performance, unpublished Ph.D. dissertation, University of Chicago, Chicago IL.

(1970) Portfolio theory: A step towards its practical application, *Journal of Business* 43, 152-173.

(1971) On the assessment of risk, *Journal of Finance* 26, 1-10.

Bowman, H. W. and A. M. Laporte (1972) Stochastic optimization in recursive equation systems with random parameters with an application to control of the money supply, *Annals of Economic and Social Measurement* 1, 419-435.

Box, G. E. P. and G. Tiao (1973) *Bayesian inference in statistical analysis* (Addison-Wesley, Reading, Mass).

Brainard, W. (1967) Uncertainty and the effectiveness of policy, *American Economic Review* 57, 411-425.

Brown, S. J. (1976) Optimal portfolio choice under uncertainty: A Bayesian approach, unpublished Ph.D. dissertation, University of Chicago, Chicago IL.

(1977) Estimation risk and optimal portfolio choice: The Sharpe index model *Bell Laboratories Discussion Paper* 103 (Bell Laboratories, Holmdel, N.J.).

(1978) The portfolio choice problem: Comparison of certainty equivalence and optimal Bayes portfolios, *Communications in Statistics B* 7, 321-334.

(1979) The effect of estimation risk on capital market equilibrium, *Journal of Financial and Quantitative Analysis* 14, forthcoming.

Center for Research in Security Prices--CRSP (1974) *Proceedings of seminar on security prices* (Graduate School of Business, University of Chicago, Chicago IL).

Chow, G. C. (1973) Effect of uncertainty on optimal control policies, *International Economic Review* 14, 632-645.

(1973) Multiperiod predictions from stochastic difference equations by Bayesian methods, *Econometrica* 41, 109-118.

(1976) The control of nonlinear econometric systems with unknown parameters, *Econometrica* 44, 685-695.

de Finetti, B. (1974) *Theory of probability* 1 (John Wiley & Sons, New York)

Dickenson, J. (1974) The reliability of estimation procedures in portfolio analysis, *Journal of Financial and Quantitative Analysis* 9, 447-462.

Elton, E. J., and M. J. Gruber (1973) Estimating the dependence structure of share prices: Implications for portfolio selection, *Journal of Finance* 28, 1203-1232.

Fama, E. F. (1965a) Portfolio analysis in a stable paretian market, *Management Science* 11, 404-419

(1965b) The behavior of stock market prices, *Journal of Business* 38, 34-105.

(1968) Risk, return, and equilibrium: Some clarifying comments, *Journal of Finance* 23, 29-40.

(1970) Multiperiod consumption-investment decisions, *American Economic Review* 60, 163-174.

(1971) Risk, return, and equilibrium, *Journal of Political Economy* 79, 30-55.

(1972) Components of investment performance, *Journal of Finance* 27, 551-567.

(1973) A note on the market model and the two-parameter model, *Journal of Finance* 28, 1181-1185.

Fama, E. F. and J. MacBeth (1973) Risk, return, and equilibrium: Empirical tests, *Journal of Political Economy* 81, 607-635.

Fama, E. F., and M. Miller (1972) *The theory of finance* (Hold, Rinehart & Winston, New York).

Feldstein, M. (1969) Mean variance analysis in the theory of liquidity preference and portfolio selection, *Review of Economic Studies* 36, 5-12.

Feller, W (1966) *An introduction to probability theory and its applications* 2 (John Wiley & Sons, New York).

Ferguson, T. S. (1973) A Bayesian analysis of some nonparametric problems, *Annals of Statistics* 1, 209-230.

(1974) Prior distributions on spaces of probability measures, *Annals of Statistics* 2, 615-629.

Fisher, L. (1966) Some new stock market indices, *Journal of Business* 39, 221-240.

Fisher, W. D. (1962) Estimation in the linear decision model, *International Economic Review* 3, 1-29.

Frankfurter, G., H. Phillips, and J. Seagle, (1971) Portfolio selection: The effects of uncertain means, variances, and covariances, *Journal of Financial and Quantitative Analysis* 6, 1251-1262.

Geisser, S. (1965) A Bayes approach for comparing correlated estimates, *Journal of the American Statistical Society* 60, 602-607.

Goldberger, A., (1964) *Econometric theory* (Wiley, New York).

Graybill, F. A. (1961) *An introduction to linear statistical models* 1 (McGraw-Hill, New York).

Gonedes, N. and H. Roberts (1974) Bayesian assessment of the unconditional mean square error of repeated predictions from a regression equation, *Journal of Econometrics* 2, 221-240.

Hadley, G. (1964) *Nonlinear and dynamic programming,* (Addison-Wesley, Reading Mass.).

Hakansson, N. H. (1970) Optimal investment and consumption strategies under risk for a class of utility functions, *Econometrica* 38, 587-607.

(1972) Mean variance analysis in a finite world, *Journal of Financial and Quantitative Analysis* 5, 1873-1880.

Harkema, R. (1975) An analytical comparison of certainty equivalence and sequential updating, *Journal of the American Statistical Association* 70, 348-350.

Hogan, W. W. and J. M. Warren (1972) Computation of the efficient boundary in the $E-S$ portfolio selection model, *Journal of Financial and Quantitative Analyses* 7, 1881-1896.

Howard, R. J., J. Matheson, and D. North (1972) The decision to seed hurricanes, *Science* 176, 1191-1202.

Jeffreys, H. (1961) *Theory of probability,* 3rd ed. (Oxford University Press, London).

Jensen, M. C. (1972a) Capital markets: Theory and evidence, *Bell Journal of Economics and Management Science* 3, 357-398.

(1972b) ed., *Studies of the theory of capital markets* (Praeger, New York).

Johnson, N., and S. Kotz (1970) *Continuous univariate distributions -1* (Houghton Mifflin Company, Boston).

Joyce, J. M., and R. Vogel (1970) The uncertainty in risk: Is variance unambiguous?, *Journal of Finance* 25, 127-134.

Kadane, J. B., J. M. Dickey, R. M. Winkler, W. S. Smith and S. C. Peters (1977) Interactive elicitation of opinion, *Technical Report* 150 (Dept. Statistics, Carnegie-Mellon University, Pittsburg PA).

Kalymon, B. A. (1971) Estimation risk in the portfolio selection model, *Journal of Financial and Quantitative Analysis* 6, 554-582.

Katzner, D. W., (1970) *Static demand theory* (Macmillan, London).

King, B., (1966) Market and industry factors in stock price behavior, *Journal of Business* 39, 139-190.

Klein, R. W. (1978) Generalized least-squares with autocorrelated errors, unpublished manuscript.

Klein, R. W. and V. S. Bawa (1976) The effect of estimation risk on optimal portfolio choice, *Journal of Financial Economics* 3, 215-231.

(1977) The effect of limited information and estimation risk on optimal portfolio diversification, *Journal of Financial Economics* 5, 89-111.

Klein, R. W., L. C. Rafsky, D. S. Sibley, and R. D. Willig (1978) Decisions with estimation uncertainty, *Econometrica* 46, 1363-1387.

Langbein, J., and R. Posner (1976) Market funds and trust investment law,

American Bar Foundation Research Journal 1, 1-34.

Lehmann, E. (1959) *Testing statistical hypotheses* (John Wiley & Sons, 1959).

Lindley, D. V. (1972) Bayesian statistics, a review, *Regional Conference Series in Applied Mathematics,* S.I.A.M.

Lintner, J. (1965) Security prices, risk, and maximal gain from diversification, *Journal of Finance* 30, 587-615.

(1972) Equilibrium as a random walk and lognormal securities markets, *Discussion Paper* 235 (Harvard Institute of Economic Research, Harvard University, Cambridge, Mass.)

Mao, J., and C. Särndal (1966) A decision theory approach to portfolio selection, *Management Science* 12, 323-339.

Markowitz, H. (1952) Portfolio selection, *Journal of Finance* 7, 77-91.

(1959) *Portfolio selection: Efficient diversification of investments* (Wiley, New York).

Merton, R. C. (1971) Optimum consumption and portfolio rules in a continuous-time model, *Journal of Economic Theory* 3, 373-413.

(1972) An analytic derivation of the efficient portfolio frontier, *Journal of Financial and Quantitative Analysis* 7, 1851-1872.

Merton, R. C., M. Scholes, and M. Gladstein (1978) The returns and risk of alternative call option portfolio investment strategies, *Journal of Business* 51, 183-242.

Miller, M. and M. Scholes (1972) Rates of return in relation to risk: A re-examination of some recent findings, in: M. C. Jensen, ed., *Studies in the theory of capital markets* (Praeger, New York) 47-77.

Mood, A., F. Graybill, and D. Boes (1974) *Introduction to the theory of statistics* (McGraw-Hill, New York).

Mossin, J. (1966) Equilibrium in a capital market, *Econometrica* 34, 768-783.

Officer, R. (1971) An examination of the time series behavior of the New York Stock Exchange, unpublished Ph.D. dissertation, University of Chicago, Chicago IL.

Praetz, P. D. (1972) The distribution of share price changes, *Journal of Business* 45, 49-55.

Pratt, J. (1964) Risk aversion in the small and in the large, *Econometrica* 32, 122-

136.

Pratt, J. W., H. Raiffa, and R. Schlaifer (1964) The foundations of decision under uncertainty: an elementary exposition, *Journal of the American Statistical Association* 59, 353-375.

Prescott, E. C. (1971) Adaptive decision rules for macroeconomic planning, *Western Economic Journal* 9, 369-378.

(1972) The multiperiod control problem under uncertainty, *Econometrica* 40, 1043-1058.

Press, S. J. (1972) *Applied multivariate analysis* (Holt, Rinehart and Winston, New York).

Raiffa, H. and R. Schlaifer (1961) *Applied statistical decision theory (M.I.T.* Press, Cambridge).

Rosenberg, B., and J. Guy (1975) The prediction of systematic risk, *Working Paper* 33 (University of California, Berkeley, CA).

Rosenberg, B., and W. McKibben (1973) The prediction of systematic and specific risk in common stocks, *Journal of Financial and Quantitative Analysis* 8, 317-333.

Ross, S. A (1978) Mutual fund separation in financial theory--The separating distributions, *Journal of Economic Theory* 17, 254-286.

Rothschild, M., and J. E. Stiglitz (1970) Increasing risk I: A definition, *Journal of Economic Theory* 2, 225-243.

(1971) Increasing risk II: Its economic consequences, *Journal of Economic Theory* 3, 66-84.

Samuelson, P. A (1967) Efficient portfolio selection for Pareto-Levy investments, *Journal of Financial and Quantitative Analysis* 2, 107-122.

(1969) Lifetime portfolio selection by dynamic stochastic programming, *Review of Economics and Statistics* 51, 239-246.

Savage, L. J. (1954) *The Foundations of statistics* (Wiley, New York) and (1972), (Dover, New York).

Sharpe, W. F. (1963) A simplified model for portfolio analysis, *Management Science* 9, 277-293.

(1964) Capital asset prices: A theory of market equilibrium under conditions of risk, *Journal of Finance* 29, 425-442.

(1970) *Portfolio theory and capital markets,* (McGraw-Hill, New York).

Simon, H. (1956) Dynamic programming under uncertainty with a quadratic criterion function, *Econometrica* 24, 74-81.

Theil, H. (1964) *Optimal decision rules for government and industry* (North Holland, Amsterdam).

(1971) *Principles of econometrics* (John Wiley & Sons, New York).

Tiao, G. C. and A. Zellner (1964) On the Bayesian estimation of multivariate regression. *Journal of the Royal Statistical Society* Series B, 26, 277-285.

Tobin, J. (1958) Liquidity preference as behavior towards risk, *Review of Economic Studies* 25, 68-86.

(1965) The theory of portfolio selection, in : F. H. Hahn and F. P. R. Brechling, eds., *The theory of interest rates* (Macmillian, London).

Varian, H. R. (1975) A Bayesian approach to real estate assessment, in: S. E. Fienberg and A. Zellner, eds., *Studies in Bayesian econometrics and statistics* (North Holland, New York) 195-208.

Vasicek, O. (1973) A note on using cross sectional information in Bayesian estimation of security betas, *Journal of Finance* 28, 1233-1239.

Von Neumann, J. and O. Morgenstern (1944) *Theory of games and economic behavior* (Princeton University Press, Princeton) and, (1967), (Wiley, New York).

Voranger, J. (1976) Formulations Bayesiennes de modeles economiques classiques d'affectation, *Econometrica* 44, 697-712.

Williams, J. T. (1977) Capital asset prices with heterogenous beliefs, *Journal of Financial Economics* 5, 219-239.

Winkler, R. L. (1972) The assessment of probability distributions for future security prices, in: J. L. Bicksler, ed., *Methodology in finance - Investments* (Heath, Lexington, Mass.)

Winkler, R. L. (1973) Bayesian models for forcasting future security prices, *Journal of Financial and Quantitative Analysis* 8, 387-406.

Winkler, R. L., and C. B. Barry (1975) A Bayesian model for portfolio selection and revision, *Journal of Finance* 30, 179-192.

Zellner, A. (1971) *An introduction to Bayesian inference in econometrics* (John Wiley & Sons, New York).

Zellner, A. and V. Chetty (1965) Prediction and decision problems in regression models from the Bayesian point of view, *Journal of the American Statistical Association* 60, 608-616.

Zellner, A. and M. Geisel (1968) Sensitivity of control to uncertainty and form of the criterion function, in: D. C. Watts, ed., *The future of statistics* (Academia press, Oshkosh, Wisc.)

Zellner, A. and G. C. Tiao (1964) Bayesian analysis of the regression model with autocorrelated errors, *Journal of the American Statistical Association* 59, 763-778.

AUTHOR INDEX*

* The notation *m*(*n*) refers to page *m*, footnote *n*.

SUBJECT INDEX*

* The notation *m*(*n*) refers to page *m*, footnote *n*.